# Theology of Priestly Celibacy

# By the same author

*Les tendances nouvelles de l'ecclésiologie*

*The Relevance of Physics*

*Brain, Mind and Computers*
(Lecomte du Nouy Prize, 1970)

*The Paradox of Olbers' Paradox*

*The Milky Way: An Elusive Road for Science*

*Science and Creation: From Eternal Cycles
to an Oscillating Universe*

*Planets and Planetarians: A History of Theories
of the Origin of Planetary Systems*

*The Road of Science and the Ways to God*
(Gifford Lectures: University of Edinburgh, 1975 and 1976)

*The Origin of Science and the Science of its Origin*
(Fremantle Lectures, Oxford, 1977)

*And on This Rock: The Witness of One Land
and Two Covenants*

*Cosmos and Creator*

*Angels, Apes and Men*

*Uneasy Genius: The Life and Work of Pierre Duhem*

*Chesterton: A Seer of Science*

*The Keys of the Kingdom: A Tool's Witness to Truth*

*Lord Gifford and His Lectures: A Centenary Retrospect*

*Chance or Reality and Other Essays*

*The Physicist as Artist: The Landscapes of Pierre Duhem*

*The Absolute beneath the Relative and Other Essays*

(continued on p. [224])

# THEOLOGY OF
# PRIESTLY
# CELIBACY

Stanley L. Jaki

Christendom Press

Published by

Christendom Press
Front Royal, Va 22630

1997

© Stanley L. Jaki

Jaki, Stanley L. (1924– )
Theology of priestly celibacy

1. Biblical and patristic theology. 2. Oriental churches. 3. Theology of the legislation on celibacy. 4. New theological trends.

ISBN 0-931888-69-7

Printed in the United States of America

# Contents

To the philosophic eye
the vices of the clergy are far less dangerous
than their virtues

Edward Gibbon
*Decline and Fall of the Roman Empire*

# Introduction

Ten years ago I went on record with my plan to write a book-length essay on the theology of priestly celibacy.[1] The urge to implement it has since seized me repeatedly, but other projects kept barging in. They have a way of piling up and keeping out of focus anything else. On occasion, though, I almost felt as if caught by my mop, like Habakkuk of old, to be carried into action.

One such moment came five years ago when there appeared on the front page of the Tuesday, July 10, 1991 issue of *The New York Times* an article with the headline: "Growing Pressures for a Married Priesthood," followed by words running across the top of another page: "Married Priesthood: an Issue that Refuses to Die." The issue will not die as long as there will be men and women of flesh and blood, and in particular such who earn their living by reporting to a media all too eager to publicize Catholic scandals but not Catholic virtues. More importantly, the issue will not die as long as the Gospel will be preached by those whom Christ sent with the power of binding and loosing. This, however, also means that priestly celibacy will never become an overriding issue, that is,

---

[1] The context was an article of mine, "Man of One Wife or Celibacy," in the January 1986 issue of *Homiletic and Pastoral Review*.

1

an issue ultimately undermining those with that kind of power. This is, of course, a point that will be appreciated only as long as priestly celibacy is seen in its proper theological light.

It was not, however, headlines with less than praiseworthy motivations that finally made me feel an overwhelming sense of urgency to start writing this book, whose material has been growing for some years in my files. Nor was anything particularly prompting in the photograph displayed on the front page of that omniscient daily that hands down more infallible judgments every day than the papacy does in a century. The photo showed a former priest and his wife (a former nun) as they held their bicycles and smiled at their two children standing on the steps of their home. It is not wise to be fazed on seeing at regular intervals in *The New York Times,* a zealous champion of certain human rights for some, though not for all humans, a report which advocates, directly or indirectly, the right of Catholic priests to marry. This undying solicitousness for Catholic priests on the part of that illustrious daily may seem puzzling. After all, its editors do not care for the priesthood taken in a theological sense that alone justifies priestly celibacy. They never tire of celebrating "liberalized" views on sexual rapport between men and women, men and men, women and women, and have covert praises for "theoretical" pedophilia as well. Only those unmindful of logic would be surprised if those praises were to be followed in the not-too-distant future by accolades of "theoretical" bestiality. They are logical in their crusade against the defenders of "species-ism," that is, those who assign a very special place to the human species in the great biosphere.

Only the notoriously unwary would have difficulty in fathoming why *The New York Times* is so eager to let priests acquire the right to marry. For one should be almost blind not to see the increasingly tendentious anti-Catholicism of that daily, and much of the secular media, for that matter. The makers of publicity have a mind-set that makes them rebroadcast any alleged proof of the undesirability of priestly celibacy with the alacrity of a cuckoo-clock gone berserk. Their real aim in pushing for the marriage of Catholic priests is not their desire to see the range of human rights further extended. Their objective is something far more visceral. For here too, as all too often in other contexts as well, the antagonists of the Catholic Church seem to know much better than many Catholics, the area where a most damaging blow can be inflicted on the Church.

The report in *The New York Times* provides in this connection an evidence as brief as it is inexhaustible in its instructiveness. It comes, hardly unintentionally (editors of *The New York Times* are too accomplished anti-Catholic strategists to let this happen by chance), as a subtle finale to a story aimed at playing on the readers' emotions. The scene of the story is the campus of the Jesuit University of Santa Clara in California, where the three hundred or so American bishops gathered for a particularly private semi-annual meeting. It was then that hundreds of former priests (forming the association CORPUS, or Corps of Reserve Priests United for Service) expressed with a candlelight vigil their wish to be re-admitted to priestly functions.

Such a story obviously lends itself to loud dramatization, especially when it fails to repeat a claim, reported a few days earlier, of the president of CORPUS. He claimed nothing less than that the candlelight vigil had been planned to take place at the Santa Clara campus with no knowledge that the bishops would have their meeting there. Some things happen through a very intentional chance, although this goes largely unnoticed because of the pro-verbial shortness of human memory on which modern news-papers heavily rely in order to flourish from week to week.

But back to that far more and, indeed, supremely instructive part of our story and its quietly dramatic conclusion. It begins with a reference that some bishops (their number was not estimated, possibly because they were but a few) joined the former priests in their prayer vigil. According to the report, Bishop Francis Quinn of Sacramento was "one of the few bishops willing to go on record saying that he would like to see the married priests return." He was quoted as having said: "As a bishop, I am still obedient to the Holy Father and the church's teaching. But humanly speaking, it looks like that is the way the church should go."

This statement, especially the words, "humanly speaking," represent a strange miscomprehension of the way the Church has been going for almost two thousand years now. For the Church, so different from individual churchmen and from their various groups, did not, even in most troubled times, show readiness to let her priests go the way indicated by Bishop Quinn. To be sure, at the very start the Church took some of her priests from among married men, who had already proved themselves as faithful husbands and worthy fathers. However, among those men were not those who had been widowed and then remarried. Whatever their natural right to remarry, Saint Paul, in his first letter to Timothy (of which more later), declared them ineligible for the priesthood. For the priesthood is about something very supernatural, namely, about the dispensing of gifts of God, absolutely above what mere nature can dream of. Therefore the logic of priesthood may be expected to be far superior to the logic even of nature's legitimate urges.

There have since been several other moments when I felt prompted to start writing this book immediately. For instance, when the news broke that an Irish bishop was sued in Court for not paying enough alimony for an 18-year-old son of his, or when the Archbishop of Atlanta had to resign after his paramour found insufficient the money she could extort from him. Then came the word that a young German priest, with a promising career in the Vatican, mockingly declared that he found the wedding ring to be a far greater prize than a bishop's ring. Relief accompanied pain when the young Bishop of Basel disclosed on television that his woman companion was expecting a baby, but that he nonetheless had the highest regard for priestly celibacy. The urge to get on with this project was not enhanced by the news, in mid-September 1996, that the Roman Catholic Bishop of Argyle and the Isles had resurfaced after a ten-day's disappearance, with a woman on his arm, a divorcee of thirty-nine with three children of her own, and was selling his story to newspapers feverishly interested in the unbeatable combination of scandal and titillation.

Scandals, however painful, did not prompt me to write. So many evidences of man's chronic weakness, such scandals have always been around and will be forever. Nothing is more natural than human weakness, especially in an area, sexual urges, where human nature is so powerfully driven and is so deeply wounded. Any student of modern marriage who still views marriage as an institution basic for the survival of the human race, knows this all too well. Those priests, who became further instances of that weakness, deserve, together with their unfortunate partners, the utmost compassion. Even when their missteps never become public, such priests carry to the grave a deep remorse about incalculable spiritual and psychological damage done, which no sacramental absolution can undo.

The Scottish Bishop's tragedy was followed by headlines that revealed a symptom in a sense more painful than all those sad moral derailments. Time and again some bishops were found who urged that priestly celibacy be optional. They, of course, should have known better. The authoritative rulings were all too clear even in times marked by heavy inroads of worldly preoccupations into the Church. Even clearer are those rulings today. During the three decades that have followed Vatican II, popes and synods of bishops repeatedly and emphatically reaffirmed the discipline of priestly celibacy and expounded the theological reasons underlying it. Clearly, then, it is most painful to read on the front page of *The Times* (London) that according to the Roman Catholic Bishop of Arundel and Brighton, described there as a "senior bishop,"[2] it was "only a matter of time before the question of ordination of married men came up in Rome." Shortly afterwards the bishop was quoted as having said that the ordination of married men was likely to be considered in future "by the bishops in communion with the Pope. This is a discipline and the church could change it." Then the reporter added that just as the Cardinal Archbishop of Westminster, the Bishop of Arundel and Brighton too "spoke strongly in favor of celibacy."[3]

Obviously, what interested a big secular daily, still relatively dignified, was a word, a phrase that could be used as a signal,

[2] A rank invented and used by the media whenever a dissenting priest or a bishop is made to appear far more important than he actually is.

[3] September 18, 1996.

however indirect, that the celibacy of the Catholic clergy was on its way out. The reasons why the secular media are looking eagerly for any straw in the wind along these lines, will be discussed later. Against their twisting and bending of any statement from popes and bishops there is no defense. But one wonders whether they would have found food for thought in the statements of those two dignitaries, if both of them had avoided offering a loophole, however narrow. Such a loophole, and very doubtful, is the reference to the Church's apparent readiness to ordain married men. For, as will be seen from this book, the celibacy rule is much deeper than just not being married. That rule is basically a rule of sexual continence, the very point which secular mentality, uninterested in the permanence of marriage, finds utterly repugnant. Perhaps because of this, in this age of "good feeling," many theologians and some bishops find it repugnant to be utterly outspoken on the subject.

This is the really painful aspect of the turmoil about priestly celibacy: not that the world would ever appreciate it, but that those, whose sacred duty it would be in these troubled times to uphold it with no if's, and's and but's, mix subtle-looking though really transparent qualifications into their reaffirmations of the rule. They do this in these very times, that is, in decades during which popes and synods of bishops most emphatically set forth in document after document not only the rule but also a great deal of the theological rationale of priestly celibacy. Unfortunately, during that period no action has been taken against those theological writers, who keep promoting optional celibacy by obfuscating the theology of priestly celibacy with heavy doses of psychology and sociology. Nor can one say that bishops have uniformly and firmly echoed the tone of those documents.

The documents of Vatican II spoke clearly and unequivocally on the matter of priestly celibacy. Those statements represent its true spirit, which is to set the tone of episcopal discourse, and all the more so as Vatican II in particular was a bishops' council. Subsequently its passages on priestly celibacy were further articulated by a special encyclical of Paul VI, who in turn presided, in 1971, over a Synod of Bishops that categorically reaffirmed the rule of priestly celibacy. The present pope emphatically and repeatedly stated that the age-old rule of priestly celibacy would remain unchanged. In other words, that rule and the theological ethos it embodies is not supposed to be subject to a review, a process very different from reflection. Furthermore, it would not be theological to overlook the immense array of papal, conciliar and better-grade episcopal statements that never, in almost two thousand years, as much as hinted about a possible revision. Any reference to the eventual policy of ordaining married men is merely throwing a red-herring, as anyone should see who knows something about the real situation of married clergy in the Eastern Orthodox Church. Only the half-blind would look in that direction, misled by the glitter of the motto: "ex oriente lux."

Or should one bank on the eventual death of the present pope? Would his death give the long-awaited opportunity to champions of priestly marriage? Has not the unrelenting uphill struggle of so many popes over so many centuries provided a solid lesson? The lesson is about the steadiness of those, who, for all their shortcomings, are charged to steady the Church, and above all her priests. Was not Peter charged with the never ending task of strengthening, that is, steadying his brethren? Was not Vatican II meant to foster precisely that long view and a deeper perception of the lessons of the Church's history? Or perhaps once more, as so often in the past, the "spirit" identified with a Council, or with any notable event in the Church, is not so much the Lord's very Spirit, but the spirit of the times?

Against the spirit of all times, which was always a downward pull, the Church kept pulling upward and did so relentlessly. Did she do so solely through human considerations, however worthy? Yet even in occasions that seem to suggest precisely this, the opposite reasserts itself with an elemental force. Here an utterance of John XXIII remains particularly illuminating. It came during a personal audience he granted during the Fall of 1963 to Etienne Gilson. Earlier that year Pierre Hermand, the former Dominican Prior of Marseille, stirred up a huge storm by his book, *Condition du prêtre, Mariage ou célibat?,* in which he, mostly on psychological grounds, urged a change in the law of celibacy and all the more so because, according to him, the majority of priests in France wanted to be freed from an unbearable restriction.[4]

It was almost inevitable that the Pope, who served several years as a Nuncio in Paris and always kept a lively contact with French intellectuals, should touch on that storm. "Would you like to know," he told Gilson, "what distresses me most? I do not mean as a man, but as a Pope. The thought of those young priests who bear so bravely the burden of ecclesiastical celibacy causes me constant suffering." Then the Pope, according to Gilson, continued with a sort of a violent outcry: "For some of them it is a martyrdom. It often seems to me as if I was hearing a kind of plea—oh, I do not mean right here but from a great distance—as if voices were demanding that the Church free them from this burden." Next the Pope raised a question and gave it also an answer, which casts a unique light on a point of utter importance for grasping the real issue connected with a theology of priestly celibacy: "Can I do it? ... It is not impossible in itself. Ecclesiastical celibacy is not a dogma. The Scriptures do not impose it. It is even easy to effect the change. I take up a pen, I sign a decree, and, the next day, priests who wish to may get married. But I cannot. Celibacy is a sacrifice which the Church has imposed freely, generously, heroically. I recently said to the Cardinals: 'Can we face the prospect that the Church can no longer be called one, holy and chaste?' We cannot. No, we cannot do that."[5]

---

[4] An English translation, *The Priestly State — Marriage or Celibacy?* quickly followed (Baltimore: Helicon, 1965). In the report on Father Hermand in E. Schillebeeckx's *Celibacy*, tr. C. A. L. Jarrott (New York: Sheed and Ward, 1968), pp. 49–50, nothing is suggested about the fact that many truly apostolic and compassionate priests, past and present, never approved of the remedy suggested by Father Hermand. They would profoundly disagree with Schillebeeckx, who saw something heroic in Hermand's zeal for optional celibacy, although it went hand in hand with his inability to see something permanently good and valid in a policy from which the Apostolic See has never departed.

[5] Gilson made public these words of the Pope, following the publication of a splashy article in the Paris *Match* on November 23, 1963, in which it was claimed that Vatican II was seriously considering a change in the rule. An English translation of Gilson's disclosures appeared in *The Commonweal*, May 15, 1964, pp. 223–24, which in turn is based on the French text in *Documentations catholiques*, Dec. 1, 1963. In the latter the official spokesman of the French Hierarchy was also quoted: "Among the hundreds of interventions in the Council not one looked

The Pope's words cast all the more light on the issue, because they may, contrary to the Pope's intention, convey the idea that the Scriptures have little to do with priestly celibacy, and that, being therefore a purely disciplinary matter, it can be changed at a stroke of the papal pen. But as the Pope himself admitted, he could not consider changing a policy for which the Church had struggled so much and which is so much at the heart of the idea of a Church which is one, holy and chaste. For the issue is precisely this: why has the Church engaged itself in an unrelenting and an obviously always uphill struggle? It could not be unknown to the Pope that in France and Italy there were several thousand former priests, al-most all of them married.[6] In 1963 the Pope could not, of course, know that soon a scholarly re-examination would be under way with a most surprising result. For whatever one may think of the origin of the relentless support given by the Apostolic See to the law of priestly celibacy, a thorough re-examination of the patristic record forces one to connect that rule with the apostles them-selves.[7] The documents of that record breathe a dedication to a dif-ficult ideal which had to be bequeathed by those very apostles whom Jesus Christ himself trained to live up, at even the greatest cost, to his incomparably high ideals.

Good Pope John XXIII's answer to his own question reveals indeed his deep awareness that the Church always took priesthood and celibacy for a seamless garment which Christ wore when he acted out his very priesthood at the Last Supper and the Cross. This is why the Church never allowed that garment to fall prey to the divisive forces of topsy-turvy theological moods, let alone to the always downward pull of human nature, which, let us not for-get, is ready to destroy genuine married love and the institution of marriage itself. The struggle of the Church for priestly celibacy has always been an uphill struggle; always an arduous way upward and never a gentle sliding down on a grassy hillside, let alone a precipi-

toward the possibility of a modification of the law of celibacy in force in the Latin Church."

[6] The figures, 4,000 and 15,000 respectively, given in *Time* were patently in-flated.

[7] I have in mind C. Cochini's book, to be discussed in detail in Chapter 3.

tous headlong fall, such as the one engineered by Luther, whose agitation against priestly celibacy went hand in hand with his denial of the priesthood. One can see this even if one reads hastily Luther's *Babylonian Captivity of the Church*. More than any single factor, priestly celibacy saved the Church from being turned into a docile slave to cesaropapism and, what is even worse, into a hapless advocate of various "virtues" which are plain sins, though perhaps not in the light of a "deeper" theological reflection. Only a Church with a celibate priesthood was able to keep up an always uphill struggle against the ever fresh downward pull of fallen human nature.

The tenaciousness of that struggle cannot be explained by conspiracy on the part of those in power, eager to safeguard their position. Such a conspiracy cannot be maintained through more than a couple of generations. At any rate, had not something superhuman been at work in the Church, both during its "iron age" as well as during soft Renaissance times, the law of celibacy would have been swept away. It would have been humanly most logical for Pius V to heed the emperor Maximilian's plea and restore priests who had taken wives to their status by validating their marriage.[8] Only the blind could ignore the obvious: forty years after Luther's rise priests were few and far between even in those parts of Germany that were not controlled by Lutheran princes. But Pius V was both a pope and a saint and nothing more was heard of the emperor's plea.

Time proved right the Pope who must have thought of the dictum of his fellow Dominican, Thomas Aquinas, that even though a strict screening of candidates to the priesthood reduces

---

[8] Pius V was all the more right in ignoring that demand because already during the reign of Pius IV, his immediate predecessor, it became clear that the emperor's demand had much to do with the arbitrary ideas of the Nuncio (Delfino) in Vienna, which contradicted the instructions given to the papal legates, Marini and Guicciardini. See L. Pastor's *History of the Popes*, Vol. XVI (London: Kegan Paul, Trench, Trubner, 1928), pp. 137–38. This is invariably ignored in the recent propaganda campaign on behalf of optional celibacy and even in its apparently scholarly kind, such as J. E. Lynch, "Marriage and Celibacy of the Clergy: The Discipline of the Western Church: An Historico-Canonical Synopsis," *The Jurist* 32 (1972), pp. 14–38 and 189–212. See especially, p. 209, and the reference there to pp. 112–137 of Pastor's work, which makes Lynch's procedure even more deplorable.

the number of ordinations, God will always provide enough priests for his Church.[9] Pius V had not been dead for thirty years, when priests were again everywhere in a Germany devastated by the Reformation in so many ways. History once more showed, to recall a phrase of Newman that cannot be recalled often enough: "All who take part with Peter are on the winning side."[10] Luther proved this, when in old age he mused that had he suspected what his movement would lead to, he would not have started it. By then he could see that time was running out on his predictions about the quick demise of the papacy. Unfortunately, such and similar hard facts of history are not the guideposts of an ecumenical discourse for which optional celibacy (devoid of a theology of priestly celibacy, but chock-full of psychology) has become a shibboleth of covert naturalism.

A saint like Pius V must have seen some specially supernatural force channelled to priests through their vow of celibacy. John XXIII intimated this forcefully when he said to Gilson that celibacy is the foremost gift which the Church can bestow on her priests. Just before his death, the same Pope turned to his secretary, Mgr Capovilla, with words which he intended to be his last message: "You will be speaking to priests and seminarians. You must tell them that one of the reasons for my untroubled serenity now, on the point of appearing before God in unaltered peace, is the certainty of having preserved chastity, loved it, done honor to it, and of having nothing to reproach myself with in that respect." Mgr Capovilla introduced John XXIII's last message by stating that the Pope "always bravely asserted and cheerfully sang the praises of the law of celibacy."[11]

This aspect of the question of priestly celibacy was sorely missing in hints that the rule of priestly celibacy would be reconsidered at the earliest opportunity. For behind that rule

[9] See *Summa theologica*, Supplement, Part III, qu. 36, art. 4, ad 1am. The passage is quoted in full in Chapter 7.

[10] From a statement Newman made as the Rector of the Catholic University of Dublin. First published in 1896; reprinted in S. L. Jaki (ed.), *Newman Today* (San Francisco: Ignatius Press, 1989), pp. 221-23.

[11] Quoted from the Turin daily, *La Stampa*, February 6, 1970, p. 2, in J. Coppens (ed.), *Priesthood and Celibacy* (Milano: Editrice Ancora, 1972), p. 962.

there lies a spirited dynamism, which a theology of priestly celibacy must exude if it claims to be a theology and not a branch of religious studies, or something even less. Without that dynamism the entire topic of priestly celibacy sinks into the flatland of sociology and psychology, and from there to the morasses of psychoanalysis and rude statistics à *la* Kinsey on the frequency and intensity of climax. Therefore it is far from enough to restate, as a British Archbishop did in connection with that mid-September tragedy, that the question of celibacy should not be reopened. Far more appropriate would it have been not so much to refer to the resolve of the Church to hold on to the celibacy of priests as to restate unambiguously—and with total disregard for the incomprehension of typical reporters—the supernatural parameters of celibacy.

Those parameters are strictly theological; indeed, they alone make possible a theology of priestly celibacy. They also make it absolutely imperative. Yet, even in better-grade seminaries (and their numbers have steadily dropped during the last 30-40 years) only that all-important bulwark of celibacy has been emphasized which is a no-nonsense spiritual life and not an ecology-coated dreaming about it. During these years all sorts of new courses have been introduced, such as theology of the environment, theology of culture, and theology of leisure, to boot, at the detriment of the essentials. The results were at times truly pathetic. I met young priests, who spent precious minutes in adjusting their hairdo before Sunday Mass, so that they might appear "relevant" to their congregation. Other young priests came out from seminaries prepared to act out their priesthood as ordained game co-ordinators. Still others thought that their priesthood's aim was to serve as presiding officers at "eucharistic" banquets where the words of consecration were pronounced not over genuine altar bread but over cupcakes. It was totally alien for them to think that instead of presiding, they had to act out in a most real sense the sacrifice which constituted Christ's priesthood.

This is not to blame them. How many are the seminaries where at least one conference has been given about the theology of priestly celibacy? Yet in this age, which madly pursues and glorifies sexual pleasure, could one think of any form of theology that would have been as vitally important for future priests as a theology of priestly celibacy? One might argue that a theology of priestly celibacy would have merely reproduced topics dealt with in the main theological courses on christology and sacramental theology. Indeed, christology is the logical place to set forth the infinite value of the redeeming act of the sacrifice of the cross, of its being anticipated by the last Supper, and the latter's re-enactment in each and every mass. Sacramental theology is a logical place for setting forth the awesome spiritual reality of the priesthood as the exclusive means whereby Christ's body is made present on the altar. The daily reception of the Eucharist during seminary years (with weekly confession) can indeed teach immensely more about the theology of priestly celibacy than a specific course on it.

In a sense nothing can be added to the theological truths set forth in Cardinal Manning's *Eternal Priesthood,* although even such a classic work can become dated. There the appreciation by priests of their celibacy and their observance of it is taken for granted. Indeed Manning's book contains only a brief and indirect reference to celibacy. It comes in connection with rules regulating the presence of women in the priest's residence. The chapter dealing with the dangers to the priest lists four: on leaving the seminary he finds himself deprived of an appropriate ambience; as the years go by his keen sense of the sacred may get dulled; too much work may diminish the time he spends on prayer; too little work may not provide enough challenge to his apostolic zeal.[12] One can envy an age when basic duties did not need to be spelled out and reargued again and again. But times change and we change with them, often without noticing that the word of the Lord remains forever.

The basic truths that constitute the theology of the priesthood certainly contain an aspect, a thrust, which needs to be articulated above all so that they may convey a timely theology of priestly

[12] Manning's *The Eternal Priesthood* was first published in 1883, and since then reprinted many times. See reprint by The Newman Press (Westminster MD., n.d.), ch. vii.

celibacy. The thrust in question is existential or dynamic in a far more vivid sense than is the case with a number of other timely points in theology, including the ones on papal primacy and infallibility. The theology of priestly celibacy goes against the grain in a far more existential sense than do other branches of theology, that is, against the always rebellious human flesh. It is that rebellion, and the unrelenting divine pedagogy to counter it, that should form a major aspect of the theology of priestly celibacy. This applies especially to our times, when that rebellion is set up as a sacred right of human nature, a right "sacralized" through the studiedly foggy phraseology of a new theology.

The last three decades have served many instances of this sad procedure, which took not only the form of books and articles, but also of institutional frameworks, such as national associations of priests, a curious product of post-Vatican II times. Those associations have all too often become the platforms for the touting of sheer naturalism dressed up in "biblically in-depth reflections." A very recent and pathetic example of this is the declaration (full of protestations of loyalty, of course) of one such association. The document contains not a word of explicit support for the repeated post-Vatican II papal utterances on priestly celibacy. While there celibacy is a God-given calling and duty, in the declaration the emphasis is put on purely psychological points. Thus it is stated that "many priests live out their commitment as celibates in a happy and life-giving way," as if "happiness" were more important than one's good conscience of having done one's God-imposed obligation in the spirit of our Lord's words: "We are useless servants; we have done no more than our duty" (Lk 17:10). One can safely bet that focusing on this idea brings more lasting joy to the priest than endless self-evaluations about the measure in which his life is self-fulfilling.

No wonder that this introspective concern translates itself into dubious concern for fellow priests who left the "active ministry," and for "talented" friends who do not want to join the priesthood because of the celibacy inseparable from it. One may indeed wonder about some hidden agenda beneath words that give themselves away by their trendiness: "We want to see much deeper reflection on the cost of mandatory celibacy in recruitment to the priesthood and on the loss of talent and experience when priests leave active ministry."[13] One wonders whether plain shallowness is the true character of "a much deeper reflection" in which there is no place for the theological lessons available from the Church's unrelenting struggle on behalf of priestly celibacy. One wonders what a Saint John Vianney would have said, or rather not said, about that "much deeper reflection" set forward in the name of compassion. Instead of saying anything, that official patron saint of priests would have scourged himself in expiation for such searches for greater depths in priestly spirituality done in the name of "Christian compassion."

In his plain wisdom the Saint might note something akin to the point of the Bulgarian proverb: "Those who want to drown should not torture themselves in shallow waters." He might repeat the elementary wisdom of Pascal's remark about the fickleness of human nature, nowhere so fickle than in respect to steadiness in marriage: "He no longer loves the woman he loved ten years ago. I can believe it; she is not the same person, neither is he. He was young, and so was she; now she is quite different. Perhaps he would still love her if she were as she was then."[14] And in an age that finds young men increasingly unable to make up their minds and decide on a career, the Saint would put his finger at the word, "perhaps," so innocent-looking, yet so damning, in Pascal's remark. The Saint might also point out that what motivates that "Christian compassion" is a kind of sentimentalism that parades as if it were the compassion of Christ, although flagrantly unrealistic about a human flesh forever rebellious even within marriage.

To bring some cure to that flesh God provided a most efficacious means in the celibate priesthood as part of the overall divine pedagogy. The dynamics of that pedagogy is forever an uphill

---

[13] I am quoting from a two-page, mimeographed "Conference Report 1996" of the National Conference of Priests of England and Wales, shown to me while I was participating in the Plenary Session of the Pontifical Academy of Sciences in the Vatican in late October 1996.

[14] Pascal, *The Pensées*, #112, tr. J. M. Cohen (Penguin Classics, 1961), p. 65. Pascal has another bit of food for thought for youngsters whom the media hoodwinked into thinking that they should expect continual excitement: "The condition of man: inconstancy, weariness, unrest."

struggle, which is also the perpetual lot of the Church. Whatever form a theology of priestly celibacy would take, it should keep this uphill dynamics in its focus. The reflections here offered have only the modest aim of promoting this perspective.

# 1

# The Fullness of a Celibate

Theology is a reasoned, that is, consistent discourse about what God revealed concerning human destiny. Briefly, this revelation means that man is called to share in the life of the triune God, the highest conceivable fullness of life. Every branch of theology, every particular topic in any branch of it, must show a connection with this calling of man. Otherwise the theologian's diction may run the risk of degenerating into learned fantasies as to what he thinks that God should have revealed, if he cares at all about revelation properly so-called.

This is why a genuine theology of priestly celibacy should not turn into a theologically coated exercise in psychology and sociology about what brings fullness to man and therefore to the priest. Of course, that theology ought to be about fullness, although not because this age of ours, tortured by emptiness, tolerates no propositions unless they promise ready-made, quick-order fulfillment. The theology of priestly celibacy is about fullness inasmuch as it is riveted in considerations about the One through whom the fullness of the triune God is given to man, or that Jesus of whom Saint Paul categorically stated that "it pleased God to make absolute fullness reside in him" (Col 1:19). And lest his reader should miss the overriding importance of this point, Saint Paul repeated the same in the same letter: "In Christ the fullness of deity resides in bodily form" (Col 2:9). The priest is called to let others benefit from that fullness as much as possible. The priest's celibacy is an integral part of this function of his, which in turn derives from his special share in the effects of Christ's fullness.

The idea of this sharing is conveyed whenever emphasis is put on "the specific ontological bond which unites the priesthood [of the New Testament] to Christ, the High Priest and Good Shepherd." This phrase is from the Apostolic Exhortation which John Paul II issued following the Eighth Synod of Bishops that dealt with the nature, purpose and obligation of priests. Again, the idea of that fullness is conveyed in the same Exhortation with a reference to the priest as "a living and transparent image of Christ the Priest." The same papal Exhortation qualifies such a reference as "the absolutely necessary key for understanding the reality of priesthood." In a more biblical phrasing the celibacy of the priest will, according to the same Exhortation, logically appear as a condition and consequence of the love which he has to bear towards the Church in the same way in which Christ loved the Church as His own bride.[1]

It should therefore be all too clear that the fullness of the priesthood, taken in a theological sense, is of decisive importance for an equally theological understanding of priestly celibacy. Any oversight of this connection would invite psychology and sociology to play a theological role, to the discredit of both. Certainly, as happens all too often, theology is bartered away in the process.[2] The fullness which priestly celibacy is and ought to be has to be anchored in the foremost theological truth of the theandric fullness of Jesus, or else it will be replete with pleasing, though purely natural phraseology. Most importantly, talk of priestly celibacy might miss its all important task, which is to inculcate that the fullness of priestly celibacy, though ontologically given, is also a goal to achieve, indeed an arduous, life-long objective to implement. But, let it not be forgotten, so is marriage, a fact that should be

---

[1] John Paul II, Apostolic Exhortation, *Pastores dabo vobis*, March 25, 1992.

[2] For instance, J. H. Fichter, *Wives of Catholic Clergy* (Kansas City, MO: Sheed and Ward, 1992).

particularly obvious nowadays, especially to anyone who claims to discourse meaningfully about priestly celibacy.

At any rate, it is not easier to talk nowadays about the theandric fullness of Jesus than about a celibate priest's fullness. Ever since the Enlightenment Western man has prided himself on being his own master and proposed various ways to divinize himself. All this, of course, amounted to mere boasting, such as when the ageing Kant drew the ultimate implications of his critical philosophy and jotted down repeatedly the astonishing phrase: "Ich bin Gott."[3] Ten or so years earlier Kant showed his true antitheological color when he discoursed on a theology confined within the limits of reason alone, that is, his own very uncritical kind of reason.[4] By the time Hegel raised his version of the Kantian flag, there was no reason for him to fear reprisals from the Prussian government that had almost removed Kant from his chair for having meddled in theology in a way that could only displease the still orthodox Lutheran establishment. Using a style that went one better on Kant's verbal obfuscations, Hegel succeeded to a remarkable degree with the "critical" project of abolishing the difference between man and God. Towards the end of the 19th century Nietzsche announced that God was dead,[5] while celebrating the divinity of Superman.

It has indeed become a cultural *faux-pas* to accord divinity to Jesus. Biographers of Jesus who want to obtain a hearing must cut him to a purely human size, however exalted. They accordingly present him as just another religious genius. The first major step in this direction was taken by Samuel Reimarus, who became the revered model for those who try to make names for themselves as critical students of the life of Jesus.[6] On the more literary level

[3] For details, see ch. 8. in my Gifford Lectures, *The Road of Science and the Ways to God* (Chicago: University of Chicago Press, 1978).

[4] I. Kant, *Religion within the Limits of Reason* (New York: Harper and Row, 1960).

[5] F. Nietzsche, *Thus Spake Zarathustra* (sec. 2), where Zarathustra wonders why the old saint in the forest has not heard yet that "God is dead." It is often overlooked that in *The Joyous Wisdom* (aph. 125) Nietzsche lets a madman declare God's death.

[6] Very revealing are the accolades heaped on Reimarus by Albert Schweitzer in his *The Quest of the Historical Jesus: A Critical Survey of its Progress from Reimarus to*

many have tried, though in vain, to match the artistic standards set by Ernest Renan's comments on Jesus' last words on the cross. They are, however, at one with him in the tactic whereby everything is granted to the man Jesus, so that all the more effective may become their sneaky art of mocking, with Renan, at belief in Jesus' divinity: "Rest now in thy glory, noble initiator. Thy work is completed; thy divinity is established. Fear no more the edifice of thy efforts crumble through a flaw. . . . Between thee and God, men will no longer distinguish. Complete conqueror of death, take possession of thy kingdom, whither, by the royal road thou has traced, ages of adorers will follow thee."[7]

The essence of that sneaky art was largely to use words familiar to the faithful, but to give them a meaning totally at variance with their fondest beliefs. Already in the Preface of his book, however, Renan made it absolutely clear where he stood with respect to Jesus. There Renan dismissed all miracles of Jesus on the ground that up "to this [Renan's] time, a miracle has never been proved."[8] Renan's Jesus was indeed a god who did not and could not work miracles. Nor are miracles worked by Jesus as portrayed by Renan's latter-day imitators. They fuel a cultural propaganda aimed at debunking belief in Jesus as the one in whom resides the fullness of divinity in a bodily form. Within this kind of "best-selling" atmosphere it is doubly difficult to find a hearing for a presentation of priestly celibacy which predicates the celibate priest's fullness on the fullness of Jesus the celibate.

It is of no real help that on occasion somebody with skillful journalistic pen exposes the inanity of Jesus biographies in which Jesus is deprived not only of his divinity, taken in the fullest possible sense, but all too often also of his full humanity. A. N. Wilson's *Jesus* was not yet in the shopwindows when Bernard Levin, an agnostic Jew, took Wilson to task for not seeing the obvious fullness of Jesus' character: "Suppose, . . . that Mr Wilson, rather than Chris-

*Werde*, tr. by W. Montgomery from the first German edition, 1906 (London: A. & C. Black, 1910), p. 26, where he praises Reimarus' work "as the magnificent overture in which are announced all the motifs of the future historical treatment of the life of Jesus."

[7] E. Renan, *The Life of Jesus* (New York: Modern Library, 1927), p. 368.

[8] Ibid., p. 59.

tian religion, is right about virgin births and resurrections; will those tremendous metaphors—is there anything in all history to touch them?—wither and die? Is not the nature of Christ, in the words of the New Testament, enough to pierce to the soul anyone with a soul to be pierced? . . . Whether he rose from the grave or whether he was playing possum, he still looms over the world, his message still clear, his pity still infinite, his words still full of glory, wisdom and love."[9] Wonderful as all that fullness of Jesus may sound, it does not constitute the solid ground on which to base a theology of priestly celibacy, especially at a time when leading newspapers and magazines do not miss a Christmas or an Easter to trumpet the latest achievements of "critical" scholarship on Jesus.[10] They also take for a martyr of universal compassion any priest who is disciplined by the Church for his refusal to endorse the divine fullness in Jesus.[11]

The media never report on the progress of "critical" scholarship on Moses. Does this mean that Freud's *Moses and Monotheism* failed to inspire further scholarship? Of course, Moses made no claims about himself even remotely similar to the ones made by Jesus. Moreover, Moses explicitly referred to a prophet to come who would complete the great work he had initiated at God's command. In view of Moses' enormous stature, his utterance, "A prophet like me will the Lord, your God, raise from among your own kinsmen; to him you shall listen" (Dt 18:15), could not mean just anyone speaking in God's name. Jewish tradition took that utterance to mean the Messiah, the Anointed, the Christ to come. This is also clear both from the reaction of the crowds to Jesus, as the Prophet who is to come, the Messiah indeed (Jn 6:14 and 7:40) and from the declaration of Peter (Acts 3:22) and Stephen (Acts 7:37). The latter also cited the sequel to Moses' utterance, namely, that refusal to listen to that prophet entails extirpation

[9] *The Times* (London), June 6, 1991.

[10] *The New York Times* and *Time*.

[11] See the lengthy report in *The New York Times* (Jan. 7, 1997, pp. A1 and A8) about the excommunication of Father Tissa Balasurya of Sri Lanka, a member of the Oblates of Mary Immaculate, who is set up as the hero of an ecumenism within which there can no be unique role for Christ as the Redeemer. Tellingly, *The New York Times* found only one theologian to interview, Hans Küng.

from the people. Clearly, Stephen meant an approval of that Prophet, Jesus, that should infinitely transcend the noncommittal approach that cultivates mere opinions about him.

Just as Moses and the Apostles did not suggest that it was up to man to leave undecided the status of the Prophet, Jesus, Christian apologists and theologians were just as uncompromising. Only during the last four or so decades has it become a mark of theological "profundity" to recast christology into a process of cultural evaluation. Tellingly, much was made of a new fad in the interpretation of science as a chain of paradigm shifts of man's perception about it.[12] A typical procedure on the part of theologians who did not know what really went on in science. By borrowing trendy phrases relating to science, they hoped secure indisputable respectability to their christology. It should have been obvious that the emphasis they put on the different conceptual or cultural moulds within which one would think about Christ, could have but one main effect: to draw attention away from what remains the same about Him in the midst of sundry thoughts about Him. It was therefore inevitable that this process (by partly aligning itself with process theology) would generate scepticism about the perennial truths of christological dogmas.

Further impetus to that development came from the respect accorded to interpreters of the New Testament who, while roundly distancing themselves from the camp of "Higher Criticism," denied that Christ was inerrant in the measure demanded by the fullness of divinity residing in him. New twists and turns were added to the fact that being truly human, his human knowledge was subject to development—as if this had any bearing on the clarity with which he had always perceived his unique mission. No outcry follows when, under the pretext of stressing the eschatological perspective of his message, Jesus is held to be right about his eventual coming again, but very much mistaken about its timing.[13] That

[12] Thus E. Schillebeeckx, *Christ: The Experience of Jesus the Lord,* tr. J. Bowden (New York: Crossroad, 1981), pp. 31 and 853, where his uncritical acceptance of such debatable contentions gives itself away.

[13] A good illustration of this is the accolade given to two books of O. Cullmann, *Peter: Disciple, Apostle, Martyr* (Philadelphia: Westminster Press, 1953) and *Jesus and*

concurrently with this relativization of christological truths there
should arise a wholesale uncertainty about the merits of priestly
celibacy should surprise only those who cannot put two and two
together.

The root of the difficulty for a Catholic priest today lies in this
"Christian" relativization of christology and not so much in the
secularist crusade aiming at Christ and the Church. This crusade,
which goes hand in hand with a continual exposure of scandals of
celibate priests and with a sedulous sympathy for priests who plug
for the abolition of priestly celibacy, may pain the priest, but it has
also something unintentionally positive for him. It should help lib-
erate him from the illusion that he can count in any sense on the
culture in which he lives. A brief appraisal of that crusade and sympathy should be enough to help him perceive his cultural and societal isolation. Unlike even a generation or two ago, he can count
only on part of the faithful not yet infected by culturally correct
theological fads. What is truly threatening to him is that he can no
longer count on a theological consensus within the Church itself.
He therefore has to fall back on former times, and especially on
the company of those upon whose shoulders fell the culturally
most difficult task: to work out and defend the christological dogmas that stand for the fullness of divinity given to man in Jesus. A
priest then may take great comfort from the fact that, as will be
seen, the first explicit and thematic articulations of priestly celibacy coincided with that historic fight aimed at formulating and
defending the christological dogmas.

It was a fight, in line with Christ's words that no disciple can
be greater than his Master, or find greater comfort in this world
than he did. After all he clearly said that if he was contradicted, his
disciples too would also be contradicted. In saying to them, "Woe
to you when all speak well of you" (Lk 6:26), he in fact forewarned
them about the deadly threat of conforming as so many false
prophets do to the culture in which they live. Today, nothing
would make them more a part of their culture than suggesting that

the Revolutionaries (New York: Harper & Row, 1970), in both of which Jesus is
presented as expecting to come again within a few decades. See pp. 192-97 and
pp. 20-21 in the two books respectively.

Jesus was just one of the religious geniuses but not the One in whom alone resided the fullness of divinity, and bodily at that. They should take some comfort from the fact that even Christ found no task more difficult than putting across to his own disciples, let alone to his people or culture, that anyone who saw him really saw the Father, because he was truly the Son of God the Father.

About this too it remains supremely true that all that happened about him, did so "for our instruction and admonition" (1 Cor 10:11). There is a perennial lesson in the fact that even the bodily presence of Christ had a great difficulty in breaking down resistance to his being accepted as the one who had the fullness of God in him. This should help explain why it remains difficult for us to keep alive our faith in his fullness despite the momentum of two millennia of faith behind us. That faith in him means much more than that perspective which Nathanael conjured up in exclaiming, right at the start of Jesus' public mission: "Rabbi, you are the Son of God, the King of Israel!" (Jn 1:49). By blithely equating the two expressions—one with a heavenly thrust, the other with a very earthly one—Nathanael could not perceive what Jesus meant by assuring them with a prophecy about himself: "You will see much greater things . . . . You shall see the sky opened and the angels of God ascending and descending on the Son of Man" (Jn 1:50-51). The fullness of Jesus was hardly grasped when at the same time Andrew brought the news to his brother Simon: "We have found the Messiah." Upon being introduced to Jesus, Simon must have certainly looked at Jesus as the Messiah, otherwise Jesus would not have told him that his name would be Peter. Peter, however, had still to be seized by a far superior view about Jesus the Messiah. Only then was he told by Jesus that he was indeed the Rock or Peter, upon whom a Church would be built against which even the powers of hell would not prevail, a Church which, revealingly enough, has not ceased upholding the standard of priestly celibacy.

The first group of disciples were far from having that superior view of Jesus as they witnessed his first miracle in Cana and "believed in him" (Jn 2:11). Nor could they suspect at that time that the Master would demand that they should renounce for themselves the joy of marital life. Even in the wake of the miraculous multiplication of bread and of Jesus' interpretation of it, Peter merely reasserted his and the Twelve's faith in Jesus the Messiah by declaring that their Master had the words of everlasting life. They must have been struck by the possibility of much higher perspectives about Jesus on having heard him declare that the Son of Man was even the Lord of the Sabbath, that the Son of Man has the power to forgive sin, that in the Son of Man they saw someone greater than Solomon. It is difficult to specify what they meant in worshipping him with the words, "truly you are the Son of God" (Mt 14:33), after they saw him walk on the water. For only under the impulse of an enlightenment from above did Simon Peter realize at Caesarea Philippi that Jesus was much more than Jeremiah, or Elijah, or one of the prophets.

Yet even then it remained partly hidden to Simon Peter what really was meant by being "the Son of the living God" (Mt 16:16). He failed to grasp how such a status could be reconciled with suffering, although it was to be followed by resurrection. Moreover, the Lord said not a word more on the subject of his being the Son of the living God. In fact he forbade them to tell anything about it to anybody. This did not mean at all a hesitation or doubt on his part about his true identity. He asserted it, without blinking an eye and in full awareness of the death sentence in store for him, before the High Priest who adjured him "by the living God" to answer plainly: "Art thou the Christ, the Son of God?" (Mt 26:63) "the Son of the Blessed One?" (Mk 14:61). Jesus' answer made it clear that he was leaving no room for the view that he did not consider himself to be that very Son. Indeed he was so firm on this point as to underline, with a reference to his Second Coming, the eternal responsibility of any human reaction to him. He did not suggest that it was permissible to have a mere opinion about him.[14]

---

[14] Or as C. S. Lewis emphasized with an eye on the psychological miracle that underlies Jesus' moral teaching: "You must make a choice. Either this man was, and is, the Son of God: or else a madman or something worse. You can shut Him up for a fool, you can spit at Him and kill Him as a demon; or you can fall at His feet and call Him Lord and God. But don't let us come with any patronising nonsense about His being a great human teacher. He hasn't left that

In all this he did not reveal any character flaw in himself. He was no megalomaniac in whom unbalanced and inconsistent reasoning are the rule. On the contrary, his statements about his infinitely superhuman status are marked by stunning lucidity. While the thrust of most of his phrases whereby he had intimated and stated the fullness of his Sonship can only be appreciated against the Jewish theological background, there is a metaphysical universality in his claim, whatever its Jewish coloration: "Before Abraham came to be, I am" (Jn 9:58). On hearing this, the Jews, though hardly experts in metaphysics, wanted to stone him to death. They accurately realized that, in saying this, Jesus made himself equal to God. They all sensed that one who claimed to exist in the remote past as if it were present, put himself above time, and thereby exempted himself from the law of universal transitoriness and decay. Those Jews, ready to stone him, needed no philosophy to know what the concluding stanza of Psalm 102 taught them. It taught them the absolute rule of universal change, or a beginning and an end for everything and everybody, and gave them the phrase appropriate for praising God alone: "But you neither change, nor have an end," or in philosophical terms: you always exist. By clearly understanding this, those Jews took Jesus' words to be a blasphemy, a crime punishable by death.

That encounter of his with the Jews followed by a year that momentous event at Caesarea Philippi, at the mid-point of his training of his apostles. From that point on their education about the true status of their Master consisted in watching him as he gave brief but powerful glimpses of that status to the Jews, without giving them further elaborations on it. Time and again Jesus declined to satisfy the Jews, who could not tolerate being left in suspense about him. He left them baffled with his suggestion that David called him his master. Nothing is reported in the Gospels of what the Twelve thought on hearing Jesus declare to the Jews that before Abraham was he had already been. What in fact Jesus said at that moment about himself, "I am," had a striking resemblance to the most sacred name, Yahweh, the fullness of life and of existence. Yet the difference between their understanding of what Jesus had just

open to us. He didn't intend to." *The Case for Christianity* (New York: Macmillan 1948), p. 45.

revealed about his fullness and that of the Jews may have simply amounted to the fact that unlike the Jews they loved him and would not have thought even for a moment of stoning him. They sensed something divine in Jesus, without daring to admit it even to themselves.

For the time being they saw in Jesus a prophet, so much unlike all the previous prophets. They saw him fully engaged in most varied human activities, yet never constrained by any of them. They found him to be fully a Jew of his times; yet time and again something timeless and universal transpired through his views. He never compromised the independence of his poverty, while he accepted the occasional hospitality of the well-to-do. Uncompromising as he was on the wholehearted service of God, he was not a dour ascetic. He took part in sumptuous meals, while retaining even then his superior sense of mission. Though one who firmly rejected the suspicion that he would be guilty of any sin (Jn 8:46),[15] he had an unbounded compassion for sinners, provided they showed some awareness of their wretchedness and displayed a readiness to repent. His stern lecturing of the Pharisees and Sadducees did not undermine the credibility of his call that all should come to him because he was meek and humble of heart.

Although filled with the utmost zeal to fulfill a mission, he kept a striking pace of moderation and calm, so different from the thundering of the prophets of old. Though capable of performing the most astounding miracles, he never let himself be drawn into the role of a miracle monger. They saw him flee into the mountain when the crowd wanted to make him a king. Though not exposed to rabbinical training, he proved himself a superior rabbi: he mastered, with superior ease, all the traps that rabbis, scribes, Pharisees,

---

[15] This claim of Christ of his absolute sinlessness is best appreciated against the admission by many a noble pagan of man's inability to remain free of sin. Libanius' phrase, "Not to sin is divine, and proper to God alone," adds a crowning touch to statements of Epictetus, Seneca, and others that man shall be committing faults to the end of time. See H. Felder, *Jesus of Nazareth*, tr. B. Bittle (Milwaukee: Bruce Publishing Co., 1953), p. 99. Nietzsche, who as a classicist must have known all such statements, could not have portrayed better modern men than in stating in their name: "We are most unfair to God: we do not allow Him to sin." *Beyond Good and Evil*, aph. 65A.

Sadducees, and earthly potentates set for him. On two occasions he used trite objects, mere coins, to illustrate profound lessons: first, to set forth a basic perspective between homage due to God and to man; second, to show his submission to the Law, while displaying his plain superiority over it. He did so by letting Peter catch a fish with a coin in its mouth, so that he could pay the Temple tax for both of them. Time and again he displayed a mastery of the finesses of the Law, which he could readily turn on those claiming supreme expertise in it. The apostles heard him teach as no one did before or after him, yet his words were within the comprehension of any and all. He was not reluctant to set forth—his list of beatitudes are the proof—the most otherworldly precepts for happiness, while he could be most solicitous about the comfort of others. No sooner had he raised the ten-year-old daughter of Jairus, than he told her parents to give her some food. On seeing the apostles tired, he took them to an out-of-the-way place to rest. Unlike some prophets of old, he could be charmingly communicative with little children.

The Twelve did not need to be familiar with the categories of modern psychology to see in Jesus a startling measure of fullness. His human fullness had to it also something superhuman, a fact which some turn-of-the-century psychiatrists in vain tried to gloss over as evidence of dementia.[16] Equally fatuous was A. Schweitzer's attempt to counter such efforts by setting up Jesus as a normal Jew of his time, subject to their error of expecting an imminent onset of the Messianic Kingdom.[17] For all that, Jesus' personality did not fail to provoke the admiration of some Freudian explorers of the labyrinths of the human psyche and character.[18] Compared with their analytical depth, rationalist theologians

[16] For details, see H. Felder, *Christ and the Critics,* tr. J. L. Stoddard (New York: Benziger, 1924), vol. 2, pp. 18-72, ch. 1, "The Psychic Soundness of Christ."

[17] A. Schweitzer, *The Psychiatric Study of Jesus. Exposition and Criticism,* tr. C. R. Joy (Boston: Beacon Press, 1948).

[18] An early case for this is in *Jesus the Christ in the Light of Psychology,* by the American psychologist G. Stanley Hall, who entered the history of psychology by making Freud, Jung, Ferenczi, and other pioneering psychoanalysts appear in the United States in 1909. According to Hall, "Jesus incorporates all the good tendencies in man. He is the embodiment of all his resistances to evil through the ages. In the contemplation of his character, achievements, and teachings man remem-

could offer only rhetoric in singing Jesus' unique greatness. Their finest performance is still Wilhelm Bousset's now century-old accolade of Jesus' sanctity, tenderness, dignity, and, last but not least, of his "superprophetic consciousness." Jesus felt, according to Bousset, "that he stood in such closeness of communion with God the Father as belonged to none before or after him. He was conscious of speaking the last and decisive word; he felt that what he did was final and that no one would come after him. . . . We cannot eliminate from his personality without destroying it the trait of superprophetic consciousness, the consciousness of the accomplisher to whose person the flight of the ages and the whole destiny of his followers is linked."[19]

These soaring words removed from focus the real question about Jesus: not so much whether he *felt* that closeness to God the Father, but whether he said that he *was* one with the Father and wanted all his hearers to confront it as a *fact* and not as a sentiment, however exalted. In the former case it was not utterly beyond the power of any other human being to achieve the same consciousness. This is precisely what Bousset had in mind: "In his heroic stature and his absolute self-devotion, in his exclusive insistence upon the highest and the best and scorning of anything less, he stands *perhaps* at an unattainable distance from us."[20] Had Bousset himself emphasized the word *perhaps,* he would have conveyed with one word all that his rationalism, however biblically coated, allowed him to say about Jesus. Bousset should have realized

bers his better, unfallen self, and by seeing the true ideal of his race incarnated even the most formal recognition of this enfleshed ideal does some thing to evoke power to resist evil within and without, and gives some incentive to reapproximate his unfallen self, and indeed may start subliminal agencies that will issue in a regenerate life, bring a new sense of duty, a new passion of service, and give man self-reverence, self-knowledge and self-control" (Definitive edition, New York and London, 1923, p. 244). Such a statement, coming as it does from genuinely Freudian circles, gives the lie to the Freudian dogmas that without sexual experience no one, either man or woman, can mature; that without sexual experience it is almost impossible to escape the grip of neurosis; that only sexual experience, whether in marriage or apart form it, can prevent the mutilation of one's personality.

[19] W. Bousset, *Jesus,* tr. J. P. Trevelyan (New York: G. P. Putnam's Sons 1906), p. 179.

[20] Ibid., p. 157.

that he merely echoed Arius of old, without wanting to emulate his not too hidden agenda. For Arius meant nothing less than to help man to achieve his own fullness by claiming that Jesus is far, though not infinitely above us. But if Jesus, while fully human, had not had been genuinely divine at the same time, there remained no logical explanation of his teaching about himself as well as about us.

Modern psychiatrists are at one with rationalist exegetes in having no use for the divine aspects of the long instructions of Jesus, although they were within the reach of any and all. This double aspect characterized the list of his beatitudes; the list of the qualities that anyone aiming to be his disciple had to possess; the list of the signs that would announce the destruction of Jerusalem and his second coming. The last detailed instruction which the Twelve received from their Master was plainly about the divine fullness in him. He wanted them to believe in God and believe also in him (Jn 14:1), a startling juxtaposition indeed. He wanted their understanding of him to blossom in full as he insisted that they in fact knew where he would go. A most generous, indeed overly generous appraisal, one would be prompted to note, because Philip interjected: "Lord we do not know where you are going, and how can we know the way?" In reply Jesus not only declared himself to be the way to the Father, but also that "henceforth you do know him, and you have seen him." And as if to make all this even more concrete, Jesus claimed that he who sees him, sees the Father. Furthermore, as if to drive home even more the idea of his equality with the Father, he addressed first to Philip, and then the Twelve the question, "Do you not believe that I am in the Father and the Father in me?" (Jn 14:10-11), that called for only one answer.

Jesus also made it clear, right there and then, that the fullness of his equality with the Father aimed at bringing the Twelve too, and through them all men, into sharing in that fullness, a fullness of life: "Yet a little while and the world no longer sees me. But you see me, for I live and I shall live. In that day you will know that I am in my Father, and you in me, and I in you" (Jn 14: 19-20). All this inconceivable process of union was a matter of love: "As the

Father has loved me, I also have loved you. Abide in my love" (Jn 15:9). Further, it was a process that demanded the guidance of a very special Spirit, the Advocate, the Spirit of heavenly encouragement, the Spirit of Truth, a further link in that union between the Son and Father: "For he will not speak on his own authority, but whatever he will hear he will speak . . . He will glorify me, because he will receive of what is mine and declare it to you" (Jn 16:13-15). They still did not understand. They were bogged down in the "little while" and "said to one another: We do not know what he is saying" (Jn 16:18). They missed the point, the fullness of Jesus and the fullness it was meant to impart to them and through them to all.

Yet once that Spirit descended on them, they knew that in substance there was nothing else to preach and that compared with that fullness all else counted as nothing. Now they understood that those eight beatitudes were to be taken literally, but only because the fullness of reward was also literally true. They had to despise riches, because in return they could expect a hundredfold, though not in the form of goods that moth and rust could devour. They had to give up house and land (Mk 10:29), these basics of ordinary, safe, and sufficient human life. Last but not least, they were to give up family life: father and mother, brothers and sisters, wife and children (Mt 19:29, Mk 10:29, Lk 18:29).[21] Again, this total self-emptying of one's humanness was to be rewarded by a fullness, denoted by the word hundredfold, which, however, included persecutions as well.

A strange fullness to be had from the one who claimed to be the fullness of life. After all, this was his most emphatic claim: he came to bring life so that we may have it more abundantly; he said he was life itself; he said he was the bread of life; eternal life was to be had only through eating his very body and drinking his very blood; he was everything to everybody, and yet he eschewed marriage, the source of life on earth. In this too, he was very much unlike all the other prophets, beginning with Moses, with the sole

---

[21] Possibly this is the only occasion when in all three synoptics the same is asserted in a verse denoted by the same number.

exception of Jeremiah, who, partly because of his chosen celibacy, is hardly a favorite with Jews, old or new.[22]

He had very un-Jewish views on marriage and married life, so un-Jewish indeed that he made at one point the Twelve exclaim: "If the case of a man with his wife is so, it is not expedient to marry" (Mt 19:10). Yet, they never saw any trace in him that today would be classed as misogynistic. They saw from day to day, what is hardly noted nowadays, that Jesus and they were followed by a group of women, who assisted them from their means (Lk 8:1-3). He must have talked to those dedicated women again and again, if he was willing, and to the consternation of his disciples, to converse with the woman who was not only a Samaritan but, as they learned, had gone through five husbands. The quiet compassion with which he turned in Naim to the widow accompanying the body of her only son is hardly the trait of a misogynist. His attitude towards women revealed not a trace of that implicit contempt for them that could be inspired by the standard morning prayer for Jews in which men give thanks to "the Lord our God, King of the universe, who hast not made me a woman."[23] Had he agreed with the Rabbis that women should not be exposed to religious teaching,[24] he would not have insisted

---

[22] In dismissing Jeremiah's celibacy as un-Jewish, H. and H. A. Frankfurt, editors and co-authors of *The Intellectual Adventure of Ancient Man* (Chicago: University of Chicago Press, 1946), tellingly take a stab at the Catholic doctrine of the Immaculate Conception as well: "Celibacy and a special 'immaculate conception' are ideas that have come into our religious tradition from sources other than the Old Testament" (p. 260). Franz Werfel in his biography of Jeremiah, *Hearken to the Word*, describes him as tempted to marry the daughter of an Egyptian high priest and kept chaste only because the high priest lets his daughter die. This is, however, hardly the reason why this extraordinary book, containing an epic-sized portrayal of the nationalistic fanaticism of Jews as the cause that brought about the destruction of Jerusalem in 587 B.C., gained no popularity.

[23] See the Morning Service in *The Authorized Daily Prayer Book*, rev. ed., Hebrew Text. English translation with commentary and notes by Dr. Joseph Hertz (1945; New York: Bloch Publishing Co., 1985), pp. 20-21. A particular irony of this prayer is that it immediately precedes the invocation to be made by women, who bless the Lord for having created them according to His will and for having opened the eyes of the blind.

[24] Rabbi Eliezer went in fact so far as to claim: "Whoever teaches his daughter Torah teaches her lasciviousness." See the article, "Women," in L. Jacobs, *The Jewish Religion: A Companion* (Oxford University Press, 1995), pp. 592-96.

to Martha that Mary's listening to his teaching must not be interrupted.

A deep compassion for women transpires from the manner in which he cured the one with an issue of blood (Lk 8:42–48). The same is to be said about his strictures of the Pharisees who "devour the houses of widows" (Mk 12:40 and Lk 20:47). There is more than what meets the eye in his noticing that poor widow who put two small coins, her entire livelihood, into the Temple treasury (Mk 12:43 and Lk 13:3). He clearly wanted to extol the act of total commitment to God, often much more palpably evident in women than in men. And if one does not take it for a mere invention of the first Christian community that nothing happened to him or about him unless he wanted it, his approval of the same commitment transpires in more than one detail about his life. Such is the fact that apart from one man, John, women alone stood by his cross. Another such fact is that he let a woman, Mary Magdalene, be the first announcer of his resurrection.

The manner in which he handled the adulteress shows, however, that his compassion, whether for women or men, served his overriding concern to be a redeemer of them all from their sins and wretchedness. He said not a word that would have hurt her feelings in the presence of her accusers—all men. Rather he made them blush in her full view, as they had to depart from the scene, one after another. And when he stood there alone with that poor creature, he first comforted her by pointing out that no one remained there to condemn her. Nor was he to condemn her. But he added: "Go your way, and from now on sin no more" (Jn 8:11). About that sin of hers, adultery, he did not let anyone imagine that it may perhaps be allowed, if it is done in deep love and with full commitment, to recall the modern jargon of some wayward divines.[25] They are supremely oblivious to the fact that Jesus categorically restricted the use of sex to marriage when he said that any man "who so much as looks with lust at a woman has already committed adultery with her in his heart" (Mt 5:28). He

---

[25] Even the writers of the cover story, "Adultery," of *Newsweek*'s September 30, 1996, issue seemed to know better.

returned to this point in a more general way when he warned the Pharisees that real impurity comes from the heart, and he specified thoughts of adultery and immorality (Mt 15:19). Clearly, he could not exclude purity with respect to the use of sex, when he praised the blessedness of those who were pure of heart, because they would see God.

By holding high purity as an ideal for all, he did not suggest that all should remain celibate. Still, it cannot be emphasized enough that Jesus was a celibate and that this was part and parcel of the superhuman fullness of his character. He chose a country wedding (rather boisterous occasions) for the scene of his first miracle, though not in order to support further merrymaking. In view of the utter unity and consistency of his character, one must say that he performed his first miracle for no other purpose than the purpose served by all his miracles: the rescuing of man from the bondage of sin which more than anything throws man into deprivation. Therefore the purpose of the miracle at Cana had to further the point that married life too was to be rescued from that bondage so that it may attain to the fullness of its ideal. Such an inference should not appear preposterous at a time, such as ours, when in formerly Christian countries the average duration of marriage is but a few years, with adultery and divorce being spoken of less and less as a sin even by those who should know better.

These "enlightened" Christians should recall that redemption from sin stood always in the focus of Jesus' consciousness. By redemption he meant a fullness for human life, or a life with immortality. Eternal life was not, however, to be taken for a replica of earthly happiness. Jesus' most telling illustration of this came precisely from a reference to marriage: "When people rise from the dead, they neither marry nor are given in marriage but live like angels in heaven" (Mt 22:30, Mk 12:25, Lk 20:35-36). His reason was that eternal life was a sharing in the life of the living God, a life incomparably superior to the life which is given and propagated through marriage.

It is noteworthy that all three synoptics report this encomium of eternal life as contrasted to married life, a contrast that hardly makes it popular for latter-day theologians who try to extol the married state as the sole avenue to fullness. Moreover, Matthew adds that on hearing those words of his, the crowds were spellbound. Clearly, even ordinary Jews of the time, for whom celibacy was at best an oddity and the having of offspring a foremost blessing, could understand his teaching that married life was not necessarily the supreme good in human existence. Noteworthy is Mark's reporting that Jesus had some special words of rebuttal for the Sadducees, who tried to discredit eternal life through reference to marriage: "You are therefore entirely wrong." As to some divines, they should emulate the insight and docility of the scribe who, as Luke reports it, said: "Master, you have said well" (Lk 20:39).

More than such an insight and docility were needed when the celibate Jesus held up celibate life as the highest model of the fullness of life he was preaching and ready to impart. He went far beyond putting on the spot all modern legislation with its quick divorces. He claimed that remarriage was not permitted even in the case of adultery, nor on any of the lesser grounds permitted by Mosaic legislation, let alone on the latter's extension by rabbinical casuistry to flimsy reasons. He did not qualify his statement, even though he must have known its shock effect on his very apostles. They indeed reacted in a way that does not fail to keep its ring of modernity: "If the case of a man with his wife is so, it is not expedient to marry" (Mt 19:10). He went on to shock them even more with words which humanistic Christianity, let alone its secular counterpart, cannot stomach. Indeed what he said was nothing less than that the understanding of his idea of marriage can be grasped in full and adhered to uncompromisingly only by those who espouse total, life-long celibacy: "Not all can accept this teaching; but those to whom it has been given. For there are eunuchs who were born so from their mother's womb; and there are eunuchs who were made so by men. And there are eunuchs who have made themselves so for the sake of the Kingdom of Heaven. Let him accept it who can" (Mt 19:11-12).

All the apostles had to accept it, and this made a memorable impact on the manner in which they preached the fullness of life to be had in Christ. This comes through with particular force in

the writings of John and Paul. John, of course, was a direct
beneficiary of the effusion of the Spirit on Pentecost who,
according to Christ's promise, would enlighten them about
everything he had taught them. Nothing qualified better to be
included in that "everything" than the absolute fullness residing in
Christ. The Prologue of John's Gospel starts indeed with a
statement about the divine fullness of the Word who became
incarnate and comes to a close with an assertion of man's sharing
in that fullness: "Of his fullness we all had a share, love following
upon love" (Jn 1:16). No different was the logic of the prologue of
John's First Letter, which began with stating the supreme topic of
Christian kerygma and the supreme message entrusted to the
apostles and all those delegated by them: "This is what we
proclaim to you: what was from the beginning, . . . what we have
seen and heard we proclaim in turn to you so that you may share
life with us" (1 Jn 1:1–3). The life in question had, of course, to be
its fullness, otherwise the letter could not have ended with the
declaration: "I have written this to you to make you realize that
you possess eternal life—you who believe in the name of the Son
of God" (1 Jn 5:13).

This fullness is the theme which Paul emphasized as he approached, in his letters to the Ephesians and to the Colossians, the
theological heights of the fourth Gospel. In the former he states as
his fondest wish that the Ephesians may "attain to the fullness of
God himself" (Eph 3:19). Such a wish is, however, not a wishful
thinking, for "it pleased God to make absolute fullness reside in
Christ" and therefore in Christ "the fullness of deity resides in
bodily form" (Col 1:19 and 2:9). Consequently, the God-given
destiny of all men was to "come to the stature of the fullness of
Christ" (Eph 4:13). Therefore Paul could speak of the community
of those men, the Church, as Christ's body, or "the fullness of him
who fills the universe in all its parts" (Eph 1:23).

It was in this sense that Paul claimed to carry the Gospel in
its fullness (Rom 15:29) about the one who was "born of a woman" (Gal 4:4) and was similar to us in that he "was tempted in every way that we are, yet never sinned" (Heb 4:15). Clearly, if a
single one of those temptations of Jesus had come from his own

self, divinity (or the infinitely sacred and holy) would not have dwelt bodily within him. Fully aware of the fact that Elias was not married and that with John the Baptist (himself not married) Elias himself had returned, the apostles could not have found it strange that Jesus was not married and showed not the slightest indication of planning to marry. They might have wondered on seeing Jesus rebuff his mother, his brethren and sisters, but they must have found him very consistent in claiming that those who heard and kept the word of God were his mother, and sisters and brothers. It was only after they received the Holy Spirit that they became privy to the fact that the one who, above all, kept the word of God was Mary, the handmaid of Nazareth. Then they also learned about the utter fidelity which Joseph showed to the words God's angel had spoken to him; about Mary having been greeted by Elizabeth; about the telltale ease with which, nine months later, she took her newborn son, "wrapped him in swaddling clothes and laid him in a manger" (Lk 2:7); about her peaceful acceptance of the prophecy that a sword would pierce that heart of hers which had just leapt for joy on hearing Simeon sing the *Nunc dimittis*. The Prologue of John's Gospel indirectly said the same in stating that Jesus was to benefit those who were born anew in him, after they had been begotten by blood and by carnal desire (Jn 1:13).

From the start the virginity of Christ was an essential part of the Christian kerygma. His virginal conception, his birth that left intact his mother, and his virginal status were seen as the very pledge of his divine fullness, that is absolute holiness, which alone could give full satisfaction to God for man's sins and bring about man's redemption. Thus already Saint Ignatius of Antioch wrote in his letter to the Ephesians: "For our God, Jesus Christ, was conceived by Mary in accord with God's plan: of the seed of David, it is true, but also of the Holy Spirit . . . The virginity of Mary, her giving birth, and also the death of the Lord, were hidden from the prince of this world:—three mysteries loudly proclaimed, but wrought in the silence of God."[26]

[26] Quoted from W. A. Jurgens, *The Faith of the Early Fathers* (Collegeville MN: Liturgical Press, 1970), vol. 1, p. 18.

What is implied in this somewhat cryptic statement soon was spelled out in proof that the great martyr bishop did not speak cryptically as if he merely guessed something. A generation after him Aristides of Athens stated that Christians trace their origin to Christ, confessing him "to be the Son of the Most High God. He was born of a holy Virgin without the seed of man, and took flesh without defilement."[27] Here was another partly cryptic phrase that soon received its explicit formulation. Within a decade or so Justin Martyr, voicing the virginal conception of Christ, added that this happened so that the salvation of man from sin might be brought about. Justin Martyr was the first to draw the parallel between two virgins, Eve and Mary: the former's disobedience making necessary the latter's obedience.[28] Then towards the end of the century Irenaeus dispelled any doubt as to what was the full meaning of that defilement mentioned by Aristides of Athens and of the disobedience of Eve mentioned by Justin Martyr. Irenaeus did more than strengthen the parallel between Eve and Mary: "The knot of Eve's disobedience was loosed by the obedience of Mary. What the virgin Eve had bound in unbelief, the Virgin Mary loosed through faith."[29] Irenaeus specified that disobedience of the first parents as he reflected on their realization that they were naked and thereby incurred God's wrath: "Resisting the wanton impulse of the flesh, for he had lost his natural disposition and child-like mind, and had come to a knowledge of evil, [Adam] girded himself and his wife with a bridle of continence, fearing God and expecting his coming, and indicating something such as this: 'Inasmuch,' he said, 'as I had lost by disobedience the mantle of holiness which I had from the Spirit, I do acknowledge that I am worthy of such a covering, which provides no comfort, but stings and irritates the body'."[30]

Half a century later Saint Cyprian almost explicitly named generation the very act whereby original sin was transmitted. He did so in arguing that if the greatest sinner is not held back from

---

[27] *Apology*, ibid., p. 49.
[28] *First Apology,* 1, 127; ibid., p. 55.
[29] *Adversus haereses*, 3, 22, 4; ibid., p. 93.
[30] Ibid.

baptism, "how much more should an infant not to be held back, who, having but recently been born, has done no sin, except that, born of the flesh according to Adam, he has contracted the contagion of that old death from his first being born."[31]

This is not the place to recall the numerous patristic statements to the effect that the sin of Adam and Eve was their using their sexual power before this was permitted them by God. Their punishment for their disobedience was, in Augustine's words, that they were "immediately embarrassed by the nakedness of their bodies. They even used fig leaves, which were perhaps the first things they could lay hands on in their confusion, to cover their *pudenda*, 'the organs of shame'. These organs were the same as they were before, but previously there was no shame attached to them. Thus they felt a novel disturbance in their disobedient flesh, as a punishment which answered to their own disobedience."[32] This is why he, with many other Church Fathers, held that it is through the concupiscence inherent in the act of generation that original sin is transmitted.[33]

Here the focus should be on the equally patristic perception that Christ's virginity (in its total sense) was demanded by the total holiness of his divine fullness. The point was best put by Leo the Great, the foremost articulator of the unity in Christ of two distinct natures in one person. And since that unity was needed that "the work of reparation be fully voluntary, just as Adam's fall was such, Christ had to be born free of Adam's erstwhile prevarication. But since this could not happen through a natural generation" and since the fallen nature could not be propagated without seed, "without male seed Christ was conceived of the Virgin, whom not human intercourse but the Holy Spirit made fruitful. And if in all mothers conception does not take place without stain of sin, this Mother drew purification from the Source whence she conceived. For the mildew of sin did not make its entry where the transferal of paternal seed did not obtain. Inviolate virginity knew no

---

[31] Letter to Fidus, quoted from Jurgens, vol. 1, p. 233.

[32] *Augustine. Concerning the City of God against the Pagans,* tr. J. Bettenson (Penguin Books, 1976), p. 512 (Bk. XIII, ch. 13). The same idea is expressed in his *Enchiridion,* cap. 26, in PL vol. 40, col. 245.

[33] Most explicitly and thematically in his *De nuptiis et concupiscentiis.*

concupiscence when it waited upon the substance. The Lord took from His Mother our substance, not our fault."[34]

The bearing of this on the articulation of a theology of priestly celibacy should be obvious. That theology must have original sin and its transmission for its empirical starting point or else it cannot cope with some very empirical problems of priestly celibacy. These problems can find some but not total relief in the married state. They ought to be differently overcome and kept under control in anyone who aims at sharing the priestly purpose of the theandric fullness embodied in Christ, the High Priest. It shows something of the theological lowlands to which some advocates of optional celibacy can sink when they express puzzlement over the question why Jesus remained a celibate.[35] But even some more sensitive minds can trap themselves in a conundrum of their own making. A case in point is Ida F. Görres, who introduced with the phrase, "Christ's virginity is a mystery," a series of questions, such as "*Why* did the Incarnation avoid this cardinal, apparently unavoidable, domain of human life? . . . Why is there not the slightest hint at any time during his life that he ever shared the physical experience of sex? Why does Tradition so firmly reject any such suggestion?" Yet Görres made the raising of such questions utterly futile by stating only a few pages earlier that "sex, while retaining much of its original glory, is somehow uniquely affected by original sin."[36]

Nothing new was, of course, said with this. Nothing new, as will be seen, can be added to what Saint Augustine has already said without becoming an unsavory sexologist. That original sin affected deeply man's sexual powers may, however, sound a novelty to many Catholics, who learned from some theologians to embrace sins of sex as virtues, and grow forgetful thereby of the impact which original sin exercises on the use of man's sexual

[34] Sermon 22,3, quoted from Jurgens, vol. 3. p. 276.

[35] For example, G. Soyen opined: "We do not know why Jesus remained unmarried but can deduce that, on his own principle, it was 'for the sake of God's reign' (Mt 19:12)." See W. Bassett and P. Huizing (eds.), *Celibacy in the Church* (New York: Herder & Herder, 1972), p. 17.

[36] Ida Friederike Görres, *Is Celibacy Outdated?* (Westminster, MD: The Newman Press, 1965), p. 33.

powers. This is but a particular facet of that broader predicament which claims many Catholics, conservatives and liberals alike: the liberals practically deny original sin, especially its role of unleashing man's concupiscence; the conservatives dream of programs that are feasible only if there had been no original sin.

They fully deserve the warning which Saint Augustine aimed at the Pelagians, who tried to defend what was indefensible. At the center of the problem was human nature, fallen in all empirical evidence and according to all basic theological considerations. Original sin alone explains, Augustine argued, man's rebellious concupiscence. Original sin alone explains, Augustine went on, the Church's practice of baptizing babies. For Augustine, a very realist theologian regarding that sin, the problem of Pelagians consisted in defending what certainly was defensible, namely, the Church's practice, and excusing its justification, the fallenness of human nature: "It is wounded, hurt, damaged, destroyed. What it needs is not false defense but true confession."[37]

What needs to be defended, if priestly celibacy is to be vindicated, is the fullness of divinity in Jesus and its very purpose. The former is under subtle attack along a broad front whose strategists engage in all sorts of scholarly ruses in exegesis and ecumenism, to reinstate in honor what Arius stood for: a reduction of Christianity to a religious humanism. The Church took no measures against Hans Küng when he stirred up his fellow priests to claim "their" right to marry. But the Church deprived him of his right to pose as a Catholic theologian after he had refused to endorse clearly and unequivocally the great christological dogmas, which he had questioned in his *On Being a Christian*.[38] The Church still has to bring to light the extent to which crypto-Arianism lies beneath the anti-Roman stance of many professors of theology in Europe and in the affluent Western World in general. Their simultaneous advocacy of optional celibacy makes perfect sense. Clearly, for a Christ who was just a creature, however supreme, only fools would sacrifice their lives in a way which for the

[37] *De natura et gratia,* cap. 53, quoted from Jurgens, vol. 2, p. 112.
[38] Translated by E. Quinn (New York: Simon and Schuster, 1976). See pp. 131-32.

modern mind is more inhuman and cruel than a self-sacrifice through a quick martyrdom.

This leads directly to the very purpose of Jesus's divine fullness. It alone made possible that he could offer the perfect sacrifice whereby alone man could be redeemed. Or as Saint Athanasius put it, the Word became incarnate so that "He might offer the sacrifice on behalf of all, surrendering His own temple to death in place of all, to settle man's account with death and free him from the primal transgression."[39] From this it was but a short step to anchor with Saint Augustine the purity of Christ's sacrifice, made possible by his fullness, in his virginal conception: "The Virgin did not conceive by the concupiscence of the flesh, and for this reason the flesh was propagated in Him without the propagation of sin."[40] On that basis Augustine could celebrate the utter perfection of Christ's highest priestly action as having the appropriate purity through the co-operation of the Virgin: "What priest is so just and so Holy as the only Son of God who needed no cleansing from his sins, whether original sin, or the sins of daily life? . . . What so clean to cleanse the sins of men as the Flesh born without any contagion of carnal concupiscence, Flesh nourished in and born from a Virgin's womb?"[41]

All this is a logical unfolding of the fullness of Jesus. It proved to be a most difficult proposition for man to accept, as is shown by the dogged reluctance of the Twelve. This happened in no small measure because of the infinite purity implied in that fullness. They showed the same reluctance, in anticipation of the instinctive reaction of all generations to come, to the implementation of the very purpose which that fullness was to serve. Yet Christ's supreme priestly action was also to be theirs to imitate.

---

[39] *On the Incarnation* (London: A. R. Mowbray, 1953), sec. 20.

[40] *Opus imperfectum contra Julianum*, 4, 79. In PL 44:1384. Quoted from Maurice de la Taille, *The Mystery of Faith*, vol. 1 (New York: Sheed and Ward, 1940), p. 37.

[41] *De Trinitate*, lib. 4, cap 14. PL 42:901. Quoted from de la Taille, *The Mystery of Faith*, vol. 1, p. 38.

# 2

# Ascent to Jerusalem

Priesthood is inseparable from altar. In stating, in his *The Eternal Priesthood,* that the priesthood of the Incarnate Son consists in his being "Altar, Victim and Priest by an eternal consecration of Himself,"[1] Cardinal Manning echoed long hallowed statements of Church Fathers and Scholastics. According to Saint Augustine Christ's altar was the cross where "on behalf of us he was, to you Father, the priest and the sacrifice, a priest precisely because he was the victim."[2] These words fully anticipated Thomas Aquinas' statement that "Christ Himself, as man, was not only priest, but also a perfect victim, being at the same time victim for sin, victim for a peace-offering, and a holocaust."[3] Saint Anselm merely gave a novel touch to an old conviction by saying that Christ's being and life were "so excellent and so glorious as to make ample satisfaction for the sins of the whole world, and even infinitely more."[4] For, even without using the word infinite, Saint Cyril of Alexan-

---

[1] H. E. Manning, *The Eternal Priesthood* (1883; reprinted, Westminster Md.: The Newman Press, n. d.), p. 4.

[2] A paraphrase of Saint Augustine's words: "pro nobis tibi sacerdos et sacrificium, et ideo sacerdos quia sacrificium," *Confessiones,* lib. X, cap. 43.

[3] *Summa theologica,* Pars III, qu. 22, art. 2. See English translation (New York: Benziger Brothers, 1947), vol. 3, p. 2143.

[4] *Cur Deus homo?* II, xviiia, in *St. Anselm. Basic Writings* (La Salle, IL: Open Court, 1962), p. 293.

dria had already said the same: "One died for all . . . but there was
in that one more value than in all men together, more even than in
the whole creation, for, beside being perfect man, He remained the
only son of God."[5] Thomas then made the use of the word "infinite" a standard procedure: "For an adequate satisfaction it was
necessary that the act of the one satisfying should have an infinite
efficiency, as being of God and Man."[6] The infinite value and eternity of Christ's priesthood are, of course, so many dogmas of faith.
It is equally a revealed truth that the sacrifice of Jesus is rendered
present whenever the Mass is celebrated, a priestly function instituted at the Last Supper. The Council of Trent left no room for
doubt on any of these points.

The eternity and infinite value of Christ's priesthood is a cor-
ollary to the fullness of divinity that resided in him in a bodily
form. As was discussed in the preceding chapter, the apostles found
this hard to accept. In that respect they foreshadowed a pattern,
which keeps manifesting itself even in priests and the faithful, let
alone in the world at large. Acceptance of that fullness means surrender to Christ's demands, which are hard demands in spite of his
assurance that his yoke is easy and his burden light. Only a full,
unambiguous, spirited acceptance of Jesus as *the* road, *the* truth, and
*the* life can save a priest from having his celibacy hang around his
neck like a millstone. The priest's acceptance of his celibacy is,
however, a task to be renewed every day throughout his entire life.
The observation—out of sight, out of mind—renders in an extreme form the general rule that human attention weakens from
the very moment when its object moves out of the range of the
senses. When attention is to be focused on someone who now ex-
ists for man only in spirit, nothing is more natural than a rapid de-
crease, at times almost to the vanishing point, of the intensity of
one's mental concentration.

Just as pertinent for a timely articulation of the theology of
priestly celibacy is the need to reflect on the fact that fallen human
nature has a built-in reluctance to focus on suffering and face up
to it unflinchingly. The shelves of books published in recent de-

[5] "Quod unus sit Christus," Migne PG, vol. 75, col. 1356.
[6] *Summa theologica*, Part III, qu. 1, art. 2, ad 2am.

cades on the priesthood have yet to come remotely close to the depths contained in the remark of a poor, hard-working woman, Margarita Bosco. The occasion was her arrival home, after hours of walking, with her son, following his first Mass. It was her custom for many years to light a candle, kneel down with her son, and pray. This time, when they arose, the mother took her son's hands in her own and said in a grave but sweet tone: "Well, now you are a priest, Johnny dear! Now you will be saying Mass every day. But be sure to remember this: beginning to say Mass means beginning to suffer. You won't notice it at first, but some day, in time, you will see that your mother is right."[7]

A priest must learn to accept this. If he tries to get around it, by feeding himself on highly regarded discourses on the priesthood that include not a word on suffering,[8] he will never have peace with his celibacy, an integral part of the lot of each and every priest. Such a loss of peace is all too natural. The first priests, or the Twelve, showed great reluctance along these lines, while Jesus had nothing so much at heart as to wear down slowly but resolutely their resistance to appreciate his utmost desire to perform his supreme sacrifice, an act of unusual suffering as well. Here again, let it be recalled that what is contained about this in the Scriptures was written down there for our admonition (1 Cor 10:11). On more than one momentous occasion Jesus tried to have the Twelve understand this, though apparently in vain. One such occasion came at about the mid-point of Jesus' public mission, when the apostles heard him exclaim: "I have a baptism to be baptized with; and how distressed I am until it is accomplished!" (Lk 12:50).

The word baptism could readily remind them of John the Baptizer and of Jesus' insistence to be baptized by him. But even then it must have appeared strange to them that Jesus chose to

---

[7] She went on: "Every morning, I am sure, you will pray for me. That is all I ask for. Henceforward, think of nothing but the saving of souls and don't worry about me." Quoted from the standard biography by A. Auffray, *Blessed John Bosco (1815-1888)* with a Preface by Cardinal Bourne (New York: Benziger Brothers, 1930), p. 60.

[8] Instead, there is a great deal on the "creative" rapport between priests and women. See *Sacramentum mundi: An Encyclopedia of Theology* (New York: Herder and Herder, 1970), vol. 5, pp. 97-101.

undergo the same rite of purification which John the Baptizer demanded from a sinful populace and especially from public sinners, such as publicans and soldiers (Lk 3:12,14). No less strange did the words of the Baptizer have to appear to them that Jesus was the one who, coming after him, would baptize "with the Holy Spirit and with fire" (Lk 3:16). The fire they were ready to consider only insofar as it was a fire brought down by the righteous on others. This was precisely in the mind of James and John when a year or so later, they asked Jesus' permission to bid fire come down from heaven on the Samaritans, who resented that Jesus' face was turned towards Jerusalem (Lk 9:53-55). Those two and the others were most reluctant to consider that the fire in question was the cauldron of suffering that waited for them precisely because their Master was resolved to continue his ascent to Jerusalem. Theirs was at first a total incomprehension of that possibility. It did not open their minds that Jesus denounced Peter as a scandal for him, a Satan in fact, for trying to dissuade him from that horrid business about being killed, after having been rejected by the elders, the chief priests, and the scribes. To them it appeared that it was not Jesus who was thinking the things of God, but Peter. Did not Peter seem to think in agreement with those leaders who in turn represented the things of God? Yet he was rebuked and no less were they in him.

It is not possible to say that the apostles remained attached to Jesus in view of his prediction, in the same context, that he would rise on the third day. They simply did not understand it (Mk 9:9). But whatever made them to cling to him, it was sorely tried. For right there and then Jesus laid it down that anyone ready to follow him should deny himself and take up his cross every day (Mt 16:24, Mk 8:34, Lk 9:23). In speaking of cross, he could only mean the most cruel form of execution ever invented, which at that time did not yet function as a gentle metaphor for mere inconveniences to bear with daily. Further specifications of this gruesome prospect came in quick order. Indeed, the three synoptics introduced with this vignette their account of Jesus' post-Galilean ministry: Jesus began to teach them about the necessity of his death, namely, his realization that he "must go up to Jerusalem" (Mt 16:21). Luke records this resolve of Jesus in the following words: "Now it came to pass, when the days had come for him to be taken up [to the cross], that he steadfastly set his face to go to Jerusalem" (Lk 9:51). The Twelve knew it bode ill.

Some Pharisees, who tried to change his mind, because they guessed Herod's evil intentions, were quickly rebuked. Jesus called Herod a fox and made it clear that no prophet could ever die out of Jerusalem (Lk 13:33). Thus the apostles felt that it was probably best not to ask him about any detail, because these would only make their prospects look even worse. Like so many ostriches, they thought that by closing their eyes to reality they could change it or perhaps even make it go away. Yet Jesus kept to his resolve and the Twelve willy-nilly had to fall in line.

In fact they let even much clearer words of Jesus fail to penetrate their minds. Somehow they dreamed about the immediate coming of the Kingdom of God as they were already near Jerusalem and saw Jesus go ahead of them, going up to Jerusalem (Lk 19:28). They did not recall that shortly beforehand they themselves reminded Jesus that the Jews in Jerusalem had tried to stone him (Jn 11:8). Still, they were not ready for some such eventuality even when Jesus began the Last Supper and referred to his innermost longing: "I have greatly desired to eat this Passover with you before I suffer" (Lk 22:18).

The Twelve certainly proved the human mind's imperviousness to plain words. They could not stomach the barter set by Jesus: one had to lose one's life in order to preserve it, because by trying to preserve one's life one would only lose one's very self (Lk 17:33). They could not grasp the warning that it made no sense trying to gain the whole world, if this meant the losing of one's very soul, because nothing could be offered in exchange for that soul (Mt 16:26, Mk 8:36–37, Lk 9:25). Indeed, two of them, James and John, wanted his assurance that they would sit next to him when he came in his Kingdom. They were given a fearsome warning which at that time they could not fathom: "You do not know what you are asking. Can you drink the cup I drink or be baptized with the baptism with which I am to be baptized?" This is why they answered enthusiastically: "We can" (Mk 10:38). Possibly they began to catch something of the awesome reality, which their answer implied, on seeing the Master in the Garden of Gethsemani begging his Father with a reference to his omnipotence that he need not drink this cup (Mk 14:36). For he knew that it was soon to be filled with his very blood shed on the cross.

Long before that, they were told, but apparently in vain, that it was better to lose one's eyes and limbs than to lose one's access to the Kingdom of God. This precept, gruesome in itself, had to appear all the more disturbing to them, because it echoed the warning that if one's eye made one look lustfully at a woman, it was better to pluck it out (Mt 5:28-29). A strange Kingdom indeed, they must have thought, in which enormous restrictions were placed on men's natural sexual exploitation of women: men no longer could divorce their wives at will and could only separate from them if they were found adulterous. They spontaneously remarked that this made wholly inexpedient the idea of marrying at all. In reply an even more astounding perspective was conjured up before them: the call for making oneself willingly a eunuch for the Kingdom of God and the challenge to grasp and implement that perspective (Mt 19:10-12).[9] What appeared to be the right set of values in the perspective of mere nature was also turned upside down by their Master when he warned them that nothing was more difficult than for a rich man to be saved. They were told to have contempt for riches, for first places, for exercising authority over others in the manner of this world's potentates.

All this meant for them not only utter puzzlement but also a frightful prospect. Of this Mark gave an account, both concise and gripping. He reports the moment when they started their way up to Jerusalem. They were in dismay, so much full of fear as to let Jesus walk on in front of them (Mk 10:32). Servants or officials of any master or ruler were supposed to precede, not to follow him. This time the greatest of all Masters did not have brave servants to march ahead of him. But Jesus was not to be deterred from his set purpose.

---

[9] It is wisely acknowledged in the article, "Celibacy," (*Sacramentum mundi,* vol. 1, p. 279) that this challenge is not the registering of a charisma, but a summons to which one has to respond with ever renewed dedication: "This is important to note for the preaching of celibacy" and, one may add, for writing about it.

About that set purpose they perceived nothing when Christ made a sudden and startling departure from the set rite of the Passover meal. The incomprehension of their Master's suffering characterized their attitude throughout that Supper. Not that they were not given, already at the very start of that Supper, two lessons, most germane to the true spirit of the sacrificial banquet which Christ meant that Supper to be in a sense far more demanding than anything they could think of. One was a lesson in humility. For the one who during that evening emphatically referred to himself as their Master, washed their feet, and told them to take this act of supreme humility of his for a pattern for them in the future. For the moment they did not perceive that this strange rite was to symbolize the utter denial of the self if one was to live up to the meaning of priesthood. In a typical anticipation of many a run-of-the-mill priest, they sought, by disputing the place of honor, their own aggrandizement. So Jesus served them a lesson in humility by washing their feet. One was not to approach the table of Christ with a sense of superiority over anyone, let alone with a mind that held itself to be superior to the reality of Christ himself. Critics, however biblical, may take note.

Another lesson, which Christ served them right there and then, was somewhat more hidden. On the face of it the washing of the feet could be taken for another ritual purification, customary with Jews before meals. But Christ then added that, although he washed the feet of all the Twelve, one of them did not become clean. Clearly, Jesus did not mean ritual cleanliness, but a spiritual one. He also meant something more than purity from inordinate attachment to money, which made Judas stumble. By then those among them who were married had to leave wife and family in order to achieve a purity characteristic of those who made themselves eunuchs for the Kingdom of God. At any rate, Judas was not to share that absolutely pure bread, the body of Christ.

In giving that bread (and the cup) Jesus gave something that, as he warned, was given up, that is, sacrificed. But Jesus did not wait until that supreme moment to suggest that the greatest drama of his was just about to unfold. Two days before that Passover meal he told his apostles that following that meal "the Son of Man will be delivered up to be crucified" (Mt 26:2). Then, as he finished his explanation of why he washed their feet, he became "troubled in spirit, and said solemnly: Amen, amen, I say to you, one of you will betray me" (Jn 13:21). This happened after the first cup of ritual wine had been passed around. Then the roast lamb was served, with wild herbs, unleavened bread, and special sauce. It was during that phase of the dinner that Jesus revealed the identity of his betrayer, who, after taking the piece of bread dipped in the sauce, was taken over by Satan. Judas rose and left, his ears ringing with the words our Lord spoke to him: "What you do, do it quickly." Clearly, Jesus was ready to die. John adds: "Now it was night" (Jn 13:30). No night was ever darker and yet more bathed in light.

It is not recorded what Jesus said after the second cup of ritual wine had been taken. The rite demanded that the head of the family should, with his eldest son, recall the deliverance from Egypt. Christ very well might have elaborated on this theme, so appropriate to the deliverance from the bondage of sin he was to accomplish. Then came the singing of Psalm 113, which was about that deliverance, followed by a general blessing. Then the ordinary supper began. The end of that supper was marked with the drinking of the third cup of ritual wine and a prayer of thanksgiving.

Somewhere during that closing phase of the Supper, during which food was no longer ritually distributed, Jesus did something that could not appear very novel, but it brought about the greatest novelty ever: "While they were eating" (Mk 14:22), "while they were at supper" (Mt 26:26), Jesus took a piece of unleavened bread, blessed it, broke it and gave it to them in pronouncing the words: "This is my body which is being given for you." Such is the Lukan and Pauline version of Jesus' words, whereas Matthew and Mark simply state: "This is my body." The subclause, "being given for you," would not have added anything to the meaning of the very act whereby Jesus gave that bread to them, had it not been a sacrificial giving. The subclause is in full accord with the words over the cup of wine as his very blood. For all three synoptics state that it is blood being shed, in clear indication of its being a sacrifice. Paul also states, in full agreement with the three synoptics, that it is the blood of a new covenant. The break with the Old Covenant was now complete, or rather the Old was being brought to completion.

This has been said so many times that it is apt to sound utterly trivial. Yet nothing could be more dramatic and more mysterious as well. For their Master did not just give each of them a piece of mere bread. Over that bread he had just said that it was his body. He did not qualify this astonishing statement of his. He did not say that they should take those pieces *as if* they were mere symbols of his body, or a gentle reminder of his readiness to give himself up. The statements—*this is my body*—and—*this is my blood*—could not be circumvented by taking them metaphorically or in any other way except in a plain direct sense.[10]

While this was not the time for speculative or linguistic reflections, those plain words must have struck them. Those words did not fail to do so as time went on. One wonders whether Saint Augustine could have ever offered his most stunning assertion about Christ's real presence in the Eucharist, had he not sensed that plain meaning in Jesus' very plain words. For Augustine endorsed that plainest sense in stating that whereas "we cannot find how could it be said literally of David [that he carried himself in his hands], we find it literally stated that Jesus was carried in his own hands, when he offered his very body in saying, 'This is my body'. For then he carried his body itself in his hands."[11] August-

[10] Efforts, that began with Zwingli, to give a merely significative meaning to Christ's words fail for two reasons. One is that no strictly parallel scriptural phrases can be found. The other relates to the distinct possibility to convey in Aramaic the meaning of mere signification, and this holds even more of Greek, the language of the four Gospels and of Paul himself. Further, the efforts initiated by Zwingli led to a bewildering variety of interpretations of a really plain statement.

[11] Enarratio in Psalmum 33, PL vol. 35, col. 306. The title of Psalm 33 gave an occasion to Augustine to expand on his favorite theme: The Old Testament, but especially David and his Psalms prefigure Christ and obtain their full meaning in him. After interpreting in this way David's victory over Goliath, Augustine turned to David's brief visit with Achis, king of Gath, during which David had to feign madness (1 Sam 21: 11-16). This the *Vetus Latina* translation, used by Augustine, rendered as "ferebatur in manibus suis" (carried himself in his hands), although the Hebrew text (with which Augustine was not familiar) merely stated that in order not to be captured by Achis' men, David had to feign madness, as he was al-

ine found this so instructive that after stating it in a sermon on Saturday, he repeated it on Sunday, lest those who could come only on Sunday might miss it.[12]

Eventually the apostles too looked back in some such way on that unique gesture of Christ. Perhaps at that moment some of them, John in particular, had recalled Jesus' insistence that he would give them his own body to eat and his own blood to drink, because only those fed in such a way would have eternal life. They now could see the moment of the fulfillment of that mysterious promise. John in particular could have had such thoughts, as he was the one who preserved the great eucharistic sermons preached by Christ that prompted the great parting of the ways among the disciples. Only the Twelve were left, in whose name Peter cried out: "Lord to whom shall we go? You have the words of everlasting life." One wonders, however, whether at the Last Supper Peter had recalled the rest of his enthusiastic words: "We have come to believe and to know that you are the Christ, the Son of God" (Jn 6:69).

The Supper itself was a supper and not an occasion for theological meditation. The latter came, of course, shortly, in a most authentic and authoritative form, or Jesus' priestly prayer. This in turn was preceded by his engraving on their memory two points: they would be forever locked in unremitting antagonism with the world, but they also would have the strength and light of the Holy Spirit to see this antagonism for what it is, and be able to endure it. For the moment there was no time to reflect on perhaps the strangest utterance made during a Supper full of such utterances. No sooner had their Master said those strange words over a loaf of bread and a cup of wine, and had them share both, than they were commanded: "Do this in remembrance of me."

---

ready "in their hands." In the phrase, "ferebatur in manibus suis," Augustine spotted a unique opportunity to state, in a truly graphic way, the Church's belief in the real presence of Christ in the Eucharist.

[12] The second time Augustine answered the question—In what manner (quomodo) was Christ carried in his own hands?—with an implicit reference to the sacramental reality of Christ's presence in the Eucharist: "When Christ offered his very body and blood, he held in his hands what the faithful knows all too well; and he somehow (quodam modo) carried himself when he said, This is my body." Ibid., col. 308.

By these words, reported by Luke and Paul, they were enjoined to re-enact the most central feature in Christ's mission, his total self-giving. Indeed, the entire mission of Christ aimed at leading them to receiving this commandment from him so that they would enjoin it on endless generations of priests to come. Awareness of this prompted François Mauriac to write: "May the Eucharist not deter us from being attentive to the other sacrament that was instituted on Maundy Thursday: the Sacrament of ordination."[13]

Mauriac would not, of course, have been Mauriac, had he left it at that and risked thereby offering a worn-out truth, however astonishing. Yet what he said immediately afterwards could still pass for a *déja-vu*: "This grace of Maundy Thursday will be transmitted to the end of time, until the last priest who shall say the last Mass in a half-destroyed universe. Maundy Thursday created these men; they were stamped by it; a sign was given to them. They are at one and the same time similar to us and yet so different—never more astonishing than in this pagan century."[14]

But Mauriac added what few theologians writing on the theology of priestly celibacy could match, even such among them who did not try to eschew the scandal of the cross that goes, for good measure, with ordination: "You will say that we lack priests. In truth, what an adorable mystery it is that there are still priests. There is no longer any human advantage in it: the chastity, the solitude, and very often the hatred and derision, with the indifference of the world in which there no longer appears to be any place for them, is the burden that they bear on their shoulders. Such is the lot which they have chosen."[15] Actually, what was true of the Apostles, whom Christ reminded of the fact that not they chose him but he chose them (Jn 15;16), was to remain true of all priests. The calling, the vocation someone feels to the priesthood has ultimately to become a call from the bishop, a choice made by him. And what a choice and for what end? To hear Mauriac: "For

---

[13] F. Mauriac, *Maundy Thursday*, tr. H. F. Kynaston-Snell (London: Burns Oates & Washbourne, 1932), p. 31.

[14] Ibid. pp. 32-33.

[15] Ibid., p. 33.

centuries now, ever since that Maundy Thursday, there have been men chosen to be hated and to receive no human consolation." Only because of this did it make sense for Mauriac to continue: "They choose to give up their lives, because, once upon a time, a promise which may seem foolish was made them: 'He that loseth his life for me shall find it'."[16]

Clearly, the task given to the Twelve, to repeat what Christ did, made sense only if it demanded on their part an utmost effort to achieve a total self-giving, in a strictly sacrificial sense. For the moment, if they reflected at all on that command of Christ, they perhaps thought that the Master would soon depart from their midst and they would have only a remembrance of him in a previously unknown ritual. But the more they thought of what they were supposed to do, the more it must have dawned on them what subsequent theological parlance designated as the rite of ordination.

They were now empowered to do something unheard-of before, namely, to render present the sacrifice of Christ, that infinitely perfect surrender to the will of God. This new power of theirs also demanded from them an unconditional renouncement of everything that makes one think the things of men, and not the things of God. Since this meant also the acceptance of martyrdom, to which Christ explicitly referred, why should any word have been wasted on much smaller sacrifices, among them celibacy, even though this was the kind of sacrifice that made one most effectively think solely the things of God.

Whatever instruction Christ gave them over forty days about their priestly status, it could not contain anything more than martyrdom waiting in the wings. But he most emphatically told them, after the conclusion of the Supper, that the Spirit would teach them about anything they needed to understand. This is indeed what happened. Otherwise the celebration of the Eucharist would not have become a massively attested rite in the early Church. By the same token, the Eucharist would not have been emphatically referred to, throughout Patristic times, as a sacrifice of Christ him-

---

[16] Ibid., p. 34.

self, a reenactment, however mysterious, that is, sacramental, of what Christ did at the Last Supper.[17]

For insofar as the bread and wine which Christ made them share at the Last Supper were Christ's Body and Blood given up for them, it was the highest conceivable sacrifice. Indeed, it mysteriously anticipated his death on the Cross.[18] In giving his own body and blood during the last Supper, Christ in a sense made it a foregone conclusion that he would indeed die on the Cross. In fact, he was as clear on this point as he could be. In handing around the first cup of ritual wine he uttered words which the three synoptics report almost identically, although Luke reports them with a most significant preamble. For Christ did not merely say that he would not drink again of this fruit of the vine, until the time when he will drink with the Apostles in the Kingdom of the Father. Christ specified the Passover meal, when he said: "For I say to you that I will eat of it no more until it has been fulfilled in the Kingdom of God" (Lk 22:16). He meant thereby that the deliverance symbolized by the Passover meal would soon become a full reality.

The process, his death on the cross, whereby this was to be achieved could seem outright scandalous or revolting. Already at the Supper he told them that still during that very night they

---

[17] On this point, very instructive remains the reaction of the Church of England to the episcopal charge (pastoral letter) issued in 1857 by the Anglican Bishop Forbes of Brechin, who declared: "The ancient doctors teach that the Eucharistic Sacrifice is the same substantially with that of the Cross." Quoted in F. Clark, *The Eucharistic Sacrifice and the Reformation* (London: Darton, Longman and Todd, 1960), p. 248. Ultimately, Brechin had to retract, but his judges could not, of course, change the Patristic record on the topic. It culminates in the letter of St. Cyril of Alexandria to Nestorius, a letter formally approved by the Fathers of the Council of Ephesus: "Proclaiming the death according to the flesh of the only begotten Son of God, that is, Jesus Christ, and confessing his resurrection from the dead and ascent into Heaven, we celebrate the bloodless sacrifice in our churches; and thus approach the mystic blessings, and are sanctified by partaking of the holy flesh and the precious blood of Christ the Saviour of us all. And we receive it, not as common flesh (God forbid), nor as the flesh of a man sanctified and associated with the Word according to the unity of merit, or as having a divine indwelling, but as really the life-giving and very flesh of the Word Himself." Migne PG, vol. 77, col. 113.

[18] This anticipation was asserted and articulated with particular force by M. de la Taille in his justly renowned work, *The Mystery of Faith* (New York: Sheed and Ward, 1940).

would be scandalized in him, that Peter himself would deny him three times, that the world would hate them, as it hated him, that those who kill them would take this for offering a service to God. He, of course, had words of encouragement as well. They would be sent by him into the world as the Father has sent him. They would have to be one as he and the Father were one so that the world may believe that he was sent by the Father. They would remain in this world but be not of this world. They would be sanctified in truth. They would be engulfed in that unity of love which streamed back and forth between the Father and Him. For he was giving them not a peace hawked by the world, but His peace, a peace welling up from the infinite depths of the Triune God himself.

Such was the broader perspective of the role for which they were ordained, a role pivoted on doing to the end of times what Christ did at the Last Supper. But first came the crucible of the Cross. They first saw Christ sweating blood and praying with loud cries in the Garden of Gethsemani. The supreme action was under way, but no sooner had it taken a concrete form with Jesus' arrest in the Garden, than they "left him and fled" (Mt 26:56, Mk 14:50). It seems that some of them drifted back. Peter thought he would not be recognized as he ventured into the High Priest's court, only to exit from there as one crushed by his own cowardice. The apostles were nowhere visible during the trial of Christ, during his condemnation by Pilate, during his flagellation, during his march to Golgotha. Not one of them but a passerby, Simon of Cyrene, had to help the Master carry the cross to the point where he would be nailed onto it. Only one of them, John, was mentioned as one present with that group of women, who looked at all this "from a distance" (Mt 27:55, Mk 15:40, Lk 23:49), though not so removed that they could not hear Christ's words to Mary and John and the good thief.

The rest of the Twelve must have wondered whether it was worth leaving everything for him. For he meant everything: house, brothers, sisters, father, mother, wife, children. Both Matthew (19:29) and Luke (18:29) have "wife" too in this sweeping list. Mark does not, simply to avoid incongruity. For he not only reports that in return one could expect a hundredfold as much but he goes on to specify it: "houses and brothers, and sisters and mothers, and children and lands." It would have been rankling to find a reference to "wives." Mark alone adds, "and persecutions besides," before saying with the two other synoptics, "and in the age to come life everlasting" (Mk 10:30). All this must have been in their minds, especially in the mind of Peter, whose enthusiastic outburst—"Behold, we have left all and followed thee; what shall we have?"—is reported by all three synoptics (Mt 19:27, Mk 10:28, Lk 18:28). Again, some of them were told to leave their nets because he wanted to make them fishers of men. But were not they to be caught rather than catching others? Soon they would be hiding for fear of men ready to seize them.

Nothing comforting came from the One agonizing on the Cross. He did not react to the taunting of the chief priests and the scribes and descend from the Cross. He was to prove in a different way that he was truly the Son of God. Of his seven brief utterances—the Canon of his Mass on the Cross—only one was aimed at his taunters, but only indirectly: He prayed down on them the blessing of forgiveness: "Father forgive them, for they do not know what they are doing" (Lk 23:34). His Mass was a supreme supplication for forgiveness, though not a facile glossing-over of human responsibility. Meanwhile his garments were divided among his executioners. He had left nothing behind except words that, unlike the world, shall not pass away.

Among these words were the ones making his promise to the good thief: "Amen I say to you, this day thou shalt be with me in paradise" (Lk 23:43). On learning about this promise and the thief's request that prompted it, the apostles might have first been puzzled by the discrepancy: Whereas the thief wanted to be remembered when Jesus was coming into his Kingdom, Jesus instead spoke to him of the paradise, which could mean only a place of refreshment for the soul immediately after death, if it meant anything concrete. No less clear were Jesus's words that confided his Mother to John, the beloved disciple, who leaned on his breast during the Supper, and him to his own Mother. She was a woman intensely loved but also strangely ignored by him. Yet her true valor was all too well known to him. He knew she would under-stand that he praised her above all when he extolled all those as his mothers, brothers, and sisters who heard his word and kept it. In-deed, if Mary had not kept the words of the Angel, the words of Elizabeth, the words of Simeon, the words of Anna—so many words from God—she would not have been able to cope with a motherhood whose true nature she had to hide among her neighbours and acquaintances at the permanent risk of becoming a social outcast. It was a motherhood that in the end forced her to follow in the footsteps of her son up to Golgotha, the place of skulls. He obviously wanted her to be there, the Virgin and Mother who made possible that he might have a body, his very instrument of redemption: "Sacrifice and offering you did not desire, but a body you have prepared for me . . . [for] I have come to do your will" (Heb 10:5-6).

Obviously, he wanted her to be present when the Spirit de-scended on the Apostles, so that they might fully perceive what that body of his really meant. They indeed perceived in full the fullness residing in that sacrificial body, with all its consequences for them. From that tangible fullness, so inseparable from the role of Mary, they gained insights and strength that were to astonish Jerusalem and then the *oikumene*. The strength was far more than the fearlessness with which they, previously so timid and hesitant, began to preach Christ. Their newborn fearlessness included an unflinching facing up not only to the enemy without, but to the far more fearsome one, the one within, that is, in their very selves. The name of the enemy within was Concupiscence writ large, a label for all disordinate urges in fallen man. Nothing would more thoroughly degrade the fullness of the gifts imparted on Pentecost than the assumption, however inadvertent, that the Apostles were given to understand everything, except what it meant to be eu-nuchs for the sake of God's Kingdom which they were to preach to the four corners of the world. Eunuchs in body, because they had to be above all eunuchs in soul.

Hence the unerring emphasis of the Apostolic tradition that Mary, who produced the sacrificial body of Christ, was herself utterly chaste. She had therefore to be unspotted by sin from the very moment of her existence, or else that absolutely chaste body of Christ would have been exposed in her womb to direct symbiosis with sinful existence. Long before this plain logic demanded by Christ's absolute holiness found itself expressed in the solemn definition of the dogma of the Immaculate Conception,[19] the Fathers kept asserting from the very start that Mary was a virgin. Subsequently, they looked upon the virginal conception of Jesus in Mary's womb as something made necessary by his absolute freedom from any sin. Or as Saint Augustine eventually put it: "The Virgin did not conceive by the concupiscence of the flesh, and for this reason the flesh was propagated in Him without the propagation of sin."[20]

Christ's was therefore a pure sacrifice, but also a most excruciating one. It is no accident that the word crux (cross) stands behind the word excruciating, as an indication of a suffering greater than which one can hardly imagine. Yet it could seem superfluous if indeed he was the fullness of a perfection which is total in the acceptance God's will. For it follows from the fullness of Christ's perfection that the smallest single conscious act of his would have been expressive of a total orientation of his life towards God the Father. Any such small act of his would have had an infinite redemptive value. But since sin brought, through the devil, death into the world, Christ chose a form of death which clearly showed the action of evil. Among such forms the crucifixion was not the only one. He could have become one of those who died while being scourged and be spared thereby of an even greater torture.

He could have chosen to be stoned to death right there when the Jews grabbed stones on noticing that he made himself equal to God. Certainly such a way of dying would have been far less painful than being crucified. Had he chosen to be stoned, the very first stone thrown at him might have knocked him uncon-

---

[19] "Ineffabilis Deus," Dec. 8, 1854, where Mary is accorded a degree of holiness greater than which "cannot be thought of apart from God."

[20] *Opus imperfectum contra Julianum*, 4, 79, Migne PL vol. 44, col. 1384; quoted from de la Taille, *The Mystery of Faith,* vol. 1, p. 37.

scious, or indeed have killed him instantaneously. But even if the stoning, as was the case with Stephen, had lasted a little while, it would have been immensely less painful than hanging on the cross for three full hours. Already the Romans, who were very fond of crucifying their enemies as well as their own recalcitrant slaves, recognized the peculiar cruelty involved in nailing someone on a cross.[21]

Details of that cruelty have been set forth in books written by experts in human physiology, of which Pierre Barbet's *A Doctor Looks at Calvary* is possibly the best known.[22] None of those authors have, of course, seen a crucifixion. The closest they came to it was to observe men condemned by military tribunals (and subsequently in Hitler's concentration camps) "to be tied up." The victim is hanged to a post so that the whole weight of his body pulls on his two hands. Soon violent contractions of the muscles set in, causing acute cramps, which from the lower arms spread to the upper arms, from there to the lower limbs and to the trunk of the body. Then the muscles of the chest and the diaphragm are hit. The lungs fill with air which they cannot expel. Consequently the oxygenation of the blood decreases and the victim feels strangulated. If the body is made to rest on a protrusion attached to the post (the *sedile* of the cross), the agony of the victim is greatly prolonged, perhaps for days. It seems that the cross on which Christ was nailed did not have such a support. This would explain why his agony came to an end within a relatively short time. But a horrible agony it was.

During all that agony Christ showed an extraordinary measure of resolve and presence of mind. This was all the more worthy of notice because by the time he had picked up his cross around 11AM or so, he could have collapsed several times. A full night spent on foot with uninterrupted exposure to enormous psychological stress, the scourging which caused not a few victims to die on the spot, the crowning with thorns, the weight of the cross—all

---

[21] One of them was Cicero. See note below.

[22] In Barbet's book, reprinted by Image Books in 1963, the long chapter 2, "Crucifixion and Archeology," is entirely based on the studies which Father Holzmeister published in *Verbum Domini* (May, July, August, September, 1934).

these demanded from Christ a superhuman effort to reach the place of his self-sacrifice, so that Scripture and his own prophecy might be fulfilled.

He felt totally alone and exclaimed: "My God, my God, why have you forsaken me?" Indeed, he could not help admitting: "I thirst." But he kept full control: it was he who had registered the *Ite missa est*, by saying: "It is consummated." Then his spirit signaled victory: his last words on the cross spoke of confidence in the Father, in whose hands he commended his spirit. Such was his Mass and such was his celebration of it. His Mass showed that only God counted, a truth which stands for the deepest principle in theology and for the only solid ground for priestly celibacy. He impressed by his example as much as by his words that those who continued his priestly office had to be such for whom only God counted. They were to show this in soul as well as in body, just as their Master did. But in order to live up to this standard, they have to recognize the full meaning of what the centurion and his guards merely guessed in saying: "This was truly the Son of God" (Mt 27:54). For the fullness of divinity in Christ could not have been more evident than in the moment of his supreme priestly act.

The one who died on the cross was not a better-grade Socrates. The latter asked others to act the priest on his behalf by enjoining them that, following his death, they offer a cock to Aesculapius.[23] Not that this had not shown some greatness of soul. Since Aesculapius was honored in such a way only after some bodily cure, Socrates must have thought of the cure of his soul which he did not let enter immortality with the taint of dissimulation.[24] But to compare the death of Socrates with that of Christ is an effrontery to the intellect which

[23] See *Phaedo*, 66.

[24] Such was Socrates' supreme motivation to decline his friends' scheme, who bribed the prison guard so that he might escape. At the same time, Socrates insisted that all bodies must have a soul if one was to gain rational certainty about having a soul that does not perish with death. This mixture of ethically heroic and intellectually misguided elements in Socrates' death left the scientific enterprise in quandary for almost two thousand years, as I argued in my various writings, most recently in the article, "Socrates or the Baby and the Bathwater" (1990), reprinted in my *Patterns or Principles and Other Essays* (Bryn Mawr, PA: Intercollegiate Studies Institute, 1995), pp. 50-62. Tellingly, the way out of that quandary was provided by belief in the only begotten Son as the Logos Creator

made even a Rousseau to exclaim: "What prejudices and blindness must there be before we dare to compare the son of Sophronisca with the son of Mary ... If the life and death of Socrates are those of a philosopher, the life and death of Christ are those of God!"[25]

In further proof of his divinity, which he best displayed in the hours stretching from the Last Supper to his death on the cross, Christ chose the breaking of the bread as one of his very first ways to make himself manifest after his resurrection. But the road to Emmaus was a means for him to set forth painstakingly all the passages of the Bible that showed that the Messiah had to suffer if he was to enter the Kingdom of God. The hearts of the two disciples were burning. Fortunate men, who were given to understand that the only road to the light was through the cross. No other road for happiness was left open for those who were to act the role of Jesus in the breaking of the bread.

Dreaming about other roads did not, of course, cease. The first to experience the pull of such dreams were indeed the ones who made up the first Christian Church, the Church in Jerusalem. They were the ones addressed by the elusive author of the Letter to the Hebrews, who, however, certainly wrote under the influence of Paul.[26] It is a wrenching document even today, if one does not take lightly its last two chapters. Only Jewish Christians literally on the run and hiding, and not those living in the relative safety of one of the great cities of the Mediterranean, could really appreciate the list of the heroes of the Old Covenant who were ready to suffer everything for their faith. But one wonders whether even they found it easy to follow the author of that Letter into a heavenly Tabernacle, where Jesus the High Priest entered to intercede for

---

of all. See my book, *The Savior of Science* (Edinburgh: Scottish Academic Press; Lanham, MD: Regnery Gateway, 1988).

[25] *Emile,* tr. B. Foxley (London: Dent, 1963), pp. 271-72. A noteworthy aspect of this passage is its being preceded with a reference to the portrayal by an early Platonist (whom Rousseau wrongly took for Plato) of the ideal just man, who suffers every indignity, including crucifixion, at the hands of his fellowmen, yet is never revengeful towards them.

[26] Since there is no reference in the Letter to the Hebrews to the destruction of the Temple, it is very difficult to assign this letter to Clement, bishop of Rome, regardless of the similarity of style between his letter to the Corinthians and the Letter to the Hebrews.

us. Its splendor had to be imagined, even more than the splendor of the tabernacle which Moses erected, whereas they could see with the naked eye, day after day, the Temple which Herod had brought to a level of unparalleled material splendor.

But they were not given false expectations. They were not given as much as a hint that somehow, sometime, their liturgical gatherings, centered on the breaking of the bread, would be surrounded (not necessarily an unmixed blessing) by the pomp and social respectability that characterized the Temple worship of which Josephus recorded stunning details. In going up to the Temple to pray, Christians could see from the outer courtyard, or the Court of Women, the front of the Sanctuary that "had everything that could amaze either mind or eyes. Overlaid all round with stout plates of gold, in the first rays of the sun it reflected so fierce a blaze of fire that those who endeavoured to look at it were forced to turn away as if they had looked straight at the sun. To strangers as they approached it seemed in the distance like a mountain covered in snow; for any part not covered with gold was dazzling white."[27]

From a closer range and still from that Court of Women, those Christians could see what particularly appealed to female eyes: "a curtain 82 feet high and 24 feet wide. It was a Babylonian tapestry embroidered with blue, scarlet, linen thread, and purple . . . The mixture of materials had a clear mystic meaning, typifying all creation: it seemed that scarlet symbolized fire, linen the earth, blue the air, and purple the sea." They could also see, on every sabbath and new moon, the high priest walking up to the Sanctuary, dressed "in an ankle-length blue robe, circular and tasselled; to the tassels were attached alternately golden bells and pomegranates, thunder being signified by the bells, lightning by the pomegranates. The sash that bound the robe to the breast was adorned by five bands in different colors—gold, purple, scarlet, linen, and blue."[28]

---

[27] See *Josephus. The Jewish War,* tr. G. A. Williamson (Harmondsworth: Penguin Classics 1959), pp. 394.

[28] Ibid., pp. 393 and 395.

There was also the frenzy and intoxication caused by the Pass-over, that drew, five years before the destruction of Jerusalem, well over two million pilgrims, sacrificing over two hundred thousand lambs during the long afternoon before the onset of the Passover meal.[29] Such and similar details represented an almost overbearing cultural pull, or temptation, towards backsliding. By contrast, a very weak attractiveness was posed by eucharistic banquets, held in se-crecy in dingy rooms. The author of the Letter to the Hebrews tried precisely to counteract that pull. He did so by stressing the unique grandeur of Christ's priesthood, its infinite, eternal perfec-tion, as against the imperfections of Old-Testament priesthood and rites, however splendid.

If one is to form an idea of the pull of the Temple-rites on the first Christians, almost all Hebrew Christians, it is enough to think of English Catholics, many of whom even today dream about having Mass in the big historical cathedrals dating back to the Catholic Middle Ages and, for good measure, also dream about becoming part of the Establishment and of all its pomp and circumstance. Those He-brew Christians certainly had to be protected against the pull of the sacrificial splendor of the Temple through that Letter, which if to make sense at all, had to be written some time before the na-tional catastrophe of 70 A.D., perhaps a few years before 68 A. D. when the siege began in a remote way and the Hebrew Christian community of Jerusalem removed to Pella, beyond the Jordan.[30]

Although the Letter to the Hebrews is the chief biblical docu-ment about the priesthood of Christ, it is almost devoid of refer-ences to Christ's life. About that life the author merely states: Jesus died outside the gate (Hb 13:12) and while "still in the flesh, he

---

[29] Ibid., p. 337.

[30] This escape of the Jewish Christians to Pella is also a clear indication that Matthew's Gospel had to be written before 66 A. D. Jesus' prediction reported in Matthew (10:23), "In truth I tell you, you will not have covered the towns of Is-rael until the Son of Man comes," would make no sense if that escape to Pella (a non-Jewish town beyond the Jordan) had already taken place. This point was al-ready made almost a hundred years ago by T. Zahn, in his *Das Evengelium des Matthäus* (1903; 4th ed. Leipzig-Erlangen, 1922; reprinted, Wuppertal/Zurich, 1984), p. 407. For further details, see C. P. Thiede and M. d'Ancona, *Eyewitness to Jesus* (New York: Doubleday, 1996), p. 12.

offered prayers and supplications with loud cries and tears to God" (Heb 5:7). The rather abstract reference to his birth is elaborated upon with thematic statements on his priesthood as the very purpose of his coming into this world: he came to do his Father's will, which meant that he should sacrifice his very body for the children of God (Heb 10:5-9).

Apart from this, much of the Letter to the Hebrews is a systematic elaboration of the claim that Christ's priesthood is infinitely superior to the priesthood of the Old Testament. This contrast is elaborated for one sole purpose: to help overcome the ever present pull to backslide into worldly categories and parameters. All the arguments in that Letter are purely spiritual, indeed, otherworldly, a point with enormous significance for a construction of a theology of priestly celibacy, a status or condition of life which is truly not of this world.

First came the presentation of Christ the Son, as one who was infinitely superior to the angels. Infinitely, because the encomium of the Son ended with an application to him of the concluding stanza of Psalm 102 (already referred to in the preceding chapter), which stated God's immutability against the background of the changing, transitory, decaying character of anything else, including the very heavens. This was followed up with a discourse on the abasement and suffering that had to precede the heavenly glory of the Son: "Indeed, it was fitting that when bringing many sons to glory, God, for whom and through whom all things exist, should make their leader in the work of salvation perfect through suffering." The suffering had to be the pain of death, because "since the children are men of blood and flesh, Jesus likewise had a full share in ours, that by his death he might rob the devil, the prince of death, of his power, and free those who through fear of death had been slaves their whole life long." Such was the role assumed by Christ, so that the children may clearly perceive him as a "merciful and faithful priest before God on their behalf." In this way they would vividly sense that "since he was himself tested through what he suffered, he is able to help those who are tempted" (Heb 2:9-10, 14, 17-18).

A further consideration against that temptation to backslide consisted in portraying Jesus as the faithful and compassionate High Priest who, to begin with, was superior even to Moses. With this the author of the Letter to the Hebrews made a point the cultural significance of which cannot be emphasized enough. But he saw as even more telling the self-sacrifice of Jesus, "who in the days when he was in the flesh, offered prayers and supplications with loud cries and tears to God," and "Son though he was, he learned obedience from what he suffered." Thus did Jesus "become the eternal source of salvation for all who obey him, designated by God as high priest according to the order of Melchizedek" (Heb 3:7–10).

The discourse on Jesus' priesthood as being eternal, because it is a priesthood according to Melchizedek, culminates in Jesus' being characterized as one "who remains forever, who does not pass away" because he is "holy, innocent, undefiled, separated from sinners." He is separated even farther from sinners than are the heavens from the earth; his sacrifice need not be repeated as were the sacrifices offered by the high priests, because Jesus is "the Son made perfect forever" (Heb 7:24, 26, 28). He is therefore in a heavenly sanctuary, present before God on our behalf as one who "through the eternal spirit offered himself up unblemished to God" and thereby "will cleanse our consciences from dead works to worship the living God" (Heb 9:14). That offering was his very body, prepared for him by God as a means whereby he could show full obedience in doing God's will. "By this will we have been sanctified through the offering of the body of Jesus Christ once and for all" (Heb 10:10).

Total submission of one's will to the will of God, full obedience, readiness to suffer to the point of death, such are the personal parameters of Jesus' priesthood. Consequently, those who wish to enjoy the benefits of that sacrifice must emulate him, "by holding unswervingly to our profession which gives us hope, for he [God] who made the promise deserves our trust" (Heb 10:23). This attitude implies the duty on the part of the faithful to keep rousing one another to strive without any let-up towards the highest ideals, or "to love and good deeds" (Heb 10:24).

Nothing would be more mistaken than to take this love and good deeds for sentimentality, domestic kindness, and glamorous social service. For immediately afterwards a long list of Old Testament heroes is recalled who "endured mockery, scourging, even chains and imprisonment. They were stoned, sawed in two, put to death at sword's point; they went about garbed in the skins of sheep or goats, needy, afflicted, tormented." And, as if to foreclose any backsliding to modernity, it is added: "The world was not worthy of them" (Heb 11:36-38).

Certainly, not that world of "critical" interpreters of the Bible, who from the comfort of well-endowed chairs pontificate as to what early Christianity was really like. They would be most pleased to seize upon the silence in that Letter about eucharistic celebration. Does not that silence indicate that the Eucharist was a late invention? Does it not suggest that the early Church was a body of faith, not of sacraments and therefore did not function through a priesthood, let alone a celibate one?

Such speculations are refuted by Paul's testimony. In his first Letter to the Corinthians, written in 57 A.D., he refers to the instruction he had given to the community there when he founded it in 51 A. D., concerning the celebration of the Eucharist. In a few years word reached him that the Corinthians' celebration showed features that undermined the true nature of the Eucharist. It gradually became a banquet, a supper, which anyone could have in his home, or a mere community meal that inevitably occasioned the selfishness of some of the participants. For this development Paul had only harsh strictures to offer: "Shall I praise you? Certainly not in this matter" (1 Cor 11:22).

He then laid on the line the full authority of his apostolic mission. Although he learned obviously from Kephas and the other apostles in Jerusalem the Lord's commandments about the Eucharist, he found their apostolic transmission so authoritative as to claim that he had received from the Lord himself the following instruction to be handed down no less authoritatively: "The Lord Jesus, on the night in which he was betrayed took bread, and after he had given thanks, broke it and said: 'This is my body, which is for you. Do this in remembrance of me.' In the same way, after the supper, he took the cup saying: 'This cup is the new covenant in my blood. Do this whenever you drink it, in remembrance of me'" (1 Cor 11:23-25).

As if all this were not clear enough, Paul added his own authoritative interpretation. It consisted in three points. The first was that the sharing of the bread and cup was equivalent to proclaiming the death of Jesus until he comes. Implied in this reference to Jesus' death was a warning against the temptation of reducing the Eucharistic meal into a "joyous" banquet. According to the second point, anyone who partook unworthily of the bread and cup sinned, right there and then, against the very body and blood of Christ. This foreclosed an escape into the vagaries of the future coming of Christ. Clearly, Paul's sense of the reality of Christ's body and blood in the form of the Eucharist was not something to be diluted by copious references to the second coming, a procedure so dear to modern biblical scholarship. The third point consisted in Paul's emphatic call for serious examination of conscience, a call hardly heeded today when the number of communicants has increased as much as the number of those going to confession has decreased. This has happened precisely because little attention is being given nowadays to the awesome reality of divine judgment! Yet, if there is one, and there will be one, would a chaste and celibate priestly life appear a burden and not a blessing to bear?

About Paul's Eucharistic instruction a further remark is in order. Had no abuses crept into the Corinthians' celebration of the Eucharist, Paul would not have written about it. Only the actual scandal in Corinth prompted him to write about the unspeakable sinfulness of an incestuous relationship. This alone shows that in writing his Letters Paul did not mean to give a systematic exposition of Christian faith and morals. But whatever he wrote on both subjects stands in total opposition to the spirit of dubious optimism and facile naturalism that has made heavy inroads into the ranks of Catholic theologians and the far more numerous would-be theologians, since Vatican II.

This remark should be kept in mind in order to appreciate the true weight of Paul's words that directly bolster the theology of priestly celibacy. Among such remarks of his is his emphatic praise of celibate, virginal life as something much above marital status (1 Cor 7:32-35). Another is his admonition to married couples that they should from time to time abstain from the conjugal act so that they may freely devote themselves to prayer (1 Cor 7:5). Coming as it does from the one who did his utmost to do away with the ritual precepts of the Law, this injunction had to be much more than a recommendation of ritual cleanliness. Paul did not go into details. But did not his list of pagan vices in the first chapter of his Letter to the Romans show his awareness of the moral havoc which the sexual urge could bring down on man? It is difficult to assume that Paul did not have in mind that havoc as he named Adam as the starting point of the sinfulness of all men, even of those "who had not sinned by breaking a precept as did Adam" (Rom 5:12-14).

On this latter point Tradition, especially the one as formulated by Augustine, seems to have brought out best the thrust of Paul's thinking.[31] A most precious thread in that Tradition, as the next chapter will show, did full justice to the range of his thinking in reference to his dictum that a bishop, a presbyter, and a deacon should be a "man of one wife," that is, "married but once" (1 Tim 3:2; Tit 1:6; 1 Tim 3:12). He flatly bars from the priesthood those who married again. Why? Was he a misogynist who looked askance at marriage? Did he not rather use marriage as a figure to describe that most exalted relation which is between Christ and the Church?

He did indeed, but only because he had a most exalted view of marriage, where sexual indulgence had to be under control.[32]

---

[31] Efforts aimed at showing an essential difference between Paul's idea and that of Augustine and, by extension, of the teaching of Trent on original sin, were rightly characterized as the efforts of those "inclined to quibble." See *The New Catholic Encyclopedia*, vol. 10, p. 777. This holds especially of the footwork of liberal Protestant students of the question, such as R. F. Tennant, who hardly recognize original sin, especially as something supernatural.

[32] And so did the Saints, such as Francis of Assisi. His mind is tellingly rendered in the sayings of Brother Giles. The latter said to a married man, who was taken aback by his high praises of chastity: "I keep away from all women except my wife—is [not] that enough for me to do?" Brother Giles answered: "Don't you think that a man can get drunk on the wine in his own glass?" *The Little Flowers of St. Francis*, ed. R. Brown (Doubleday Image Book, 1958), pp. 274-75.

Otherwise he would not have legislated that the Church's support of widows should be limited to those who were of "one husband" (1 Tim 5:9), that is, who never remarried. Paul did not have views on the legitimate use of sex that would even remotely match the present theological overemphasis on sexual fulfillment.[33] As for the illegitimate use of sex, he scathingly indicted those caught in it as ones "leading a life of living death." It is impossible to think that he meant this only in relation to the widow who gave herself up to "selfish indulgence" (1 Tim 5:6). Is it conceivable that from candidates to priesthood he did not expect much more than from those unmarried young women who recoiled from the prospect of remaining virgins? This would have been inconceivable to the early Church or simply the Church of the Fathers whose witness we must now hear on priestly celibacy.

One reason for doing this relates to the dislike of ecclesiastical authority nurtured on false ecclesiological grounds. Nothing creates so much opposition towards the invariable connection between priesthood and celibacy than its image of having been legislated, imposed from above, validly as it may be. But whatever it legislated about celibacy, the Church of the Fathers bore witness that it stood by an Apostolic injunction which in turn could come only from Christ. This chain of command matches fully the witness of the Fathers on behalf of the proposition that the priest (bishop) continues, especially with the celebration of the Eucharist, the mediation of Christ himself. They therefore went to great lengths to stress the purity which the priest must therefore have so that his prayer be properly heard. Such is the gist of the patristic theology of priestly celibacy to which we must now turn, especially in times that echo with loud protestations about the need of going back to the Church of the Fathers.

---

[33] Examples are a study commissioned by the Catholic Theological Society of America, published as *Human Sexuality: New Directions in American Catholic Thought* (New York: Paulist Press, 1977), or the writings of Dr. Jack Dominian, a frequent contributor to *The Tablet* (London), which eventually was disowned by the Bishops of England, Wales, and Scotland.

# 3

# Patristic Priesthood

The uphill struggle which Jesus had in shaping the mind and will of his own disciples was meant to convince them that theirs too would be a similar struggle, a struggle ever to be renewed. First they had to struggle against the leaders of their own people, who did everything to scuttle the New Way; shortly afterwards, against dissidents (heretics) within the flock itself; then against pagan society, which took them for the enemy of good order, in proof of their Master's word that those who put them to death would think that they were thereby doing service to God (Jn 16:2). Most importantly, the apostles engraved on the minds of those upon whom they entrusted their sacred mission, that they would never cease being engaged in similar struggles. The fight which Saint Paul enjoined on Timothy (1 Tim 6:12) did not cease to be a struggle just because it had to be done without ever losing one's patience (2 Tim 4:2). This was possible because of the Spirit which was in him through the imposition of hands (1 Tim 4:14; 2 Tim 1:6), ready to have its gifts stirred up in a weary recipient.

Indeed the very nature of the Master's message meant a struggle ever to be resumed, though with full encouragement. The Fathers of the Church understood this all too well. This should seem of utmost importance at a time, such as ours, when the thinking of the Fathers also carries so much weight, and rightly so, concerning a theology of priestly celibacy. Its truly theological character is tied to the Fathers because they are our link to apostolic origins, that supreme seal of genuine theology. That link is marked, as it should be, with unrelenting struggle. Even the great Church Fathers, who lived after the centuries of persecution, had plenty of struggle on their hands. Earlier, the struggle often meant martyrdom for the Fathers. As long as the persecutions raged, there was relatively little problem with those in the sacred orders. The continual prospect of martyrdom made promotion to those orders appealing mostly to such who had firmly set their eyes on a life to come. This could but make appear to them rather bearable sundry other privations, among them those of celibacy and, if they were already married, of continence.

Partly because of this, very little is contained on priestly celibacy in the patristic literature of the second and third centuries, which is silent, or fragmentary, or merely implicit even on some major points of faith and morals as well. Suffice it to think of the slow emergence of an explicit list, or canon, of scriptures with inspired character which meant above all direct ties with the apostles. It also had to be true of the law of priestly celibacy what obtains about any other law: long before the first formal statement of a law of priestly celibacy there had to be on hand a practice together with a set of relevant assumptions from which that law "necessarily follows." Indeed, such a prefiguration of the law of celibacy, so stated a prominent Protestant scholar, "is as naturally present in the writings of people like Cyprian, as are the universally known messianic utterances."[1] It could also be shown about some third-century passages that their grammatical construction does not necessarily imply something contrary to the law of celibacy. In sum, the

---

[1] The scholar in question is Heinrich Böhmer, who voiced this view in 1916 in his essay, "Die Entstehung des Zölibates," published in the Festschrift, *Geschichtliche Studien Albert Hauck zum 70. Geburtstag dargebracht* (Leipzig: J. C. Hinrichsche Buchhandlung, 1916), p. 17. The Festschrift, it is well to recall, was the combined effort of some thirty leading collaborators (including Harnack, Zahn and Loofs) of the *Realenzyclopädie für protestantische Theologie und Kirche.* Böhmer saw the ultimate origin of that law not so much in the biblical tradition as in pagan cults!

legal argument *ex prescriptione,* which Tertullian forged so effectively against various heretics, should seem valid about priestly
celibacy as well: the powerful legal formulations of a law of priestly
celibacy dating from the fourth century can only be explained if
they have their origin in some apostolic instruction.

Such is the view that came strongly into focus in the latest
stage of a controversy, whose modern phase began with the essay
which G. Bickell, famed for his studies of Christian Syriac poetry,
published in 1878 on the apostolic origin of priestly celibacy.[2] It
tells something of the strange twists and turns of the formation of
views prevailing among theologians that Bickell's powerful reasoning and meticulous documentation failed to receive proper attention. Particularly telling and unappreciated were Bickell's references to areas where during the fourth and fifth centuries
unobservance of celibacy was widespread, especially in the East.
They were areas controlled by Arians whose clergy, including their
bishops, did not refrain from marrying. Thus was a momentous
chapter written in the story of priesthood: here already one sees
firm belief in the absolute fullness of Jesus to invite priestly celibacy, whereas one sees any tampering with that belief to lead to
compromises with celibacy or simply to abandoning it completely.

The lack of appreciation shown towards Bickell's article
should seem all the more unscholarly and unfortunate, because the
initial responsibility lies with F. X. Funk, who had just earned fame
for his edition of the Apostolic Fathers. His "authority" became
further enhanced by his serving as one of the five editors of the
*Theologische Quartalschrift,* the flagship of the Catholic Faculty of
Theology of Tubingen. Funk immediately decried Bickell's essay as
a threat to a thesis still firmly adhered to in scholarly German theology.[3]

---

[2] G. Bickell's essay, "Der Cölibat eine apostolische Anordnung," appeared in
*Zeitschrift für Katholische Theologie* 2 (1878) pp. 26–64. Bickell's father was a prominent professor of Canon Law at the University of Marburg. He himself, a convert
from Protestantism, had just been ordained a priest at the age of 39. He was still at
the University of Innsbruck as professor of Christian archeology from where he
moved in the same capacity to the University of Vienna in 1891.

[3] F. X. Funk, "Der Cölibat keine apostolische Anordnung," appeared in *Theologische Quartalschrift* (1879), pp. 208–247; see pp. 210–11.

From the voice of such an "authority" it was not "wise" to dissent. In vain did Bickell come forward with a reply full of documentation as well as a devastating analysis of Funk's objections.[4] The imperious tone of Funk's rejoinder[5] made it clear to Bickell that further arguing was pointless. Others could but realize the perils of dissenting openly from Funk's view that clerical celibacy had a purely ecclesiastical origin in the fourth century. What followed was very similar to what obtains also in scientific circles. Indeed it was at that time that the inability (or reluctance) of most scientists to take an independent look at the evidence received a scathing indictment from an astronomer, S. P. Langley. His words have a graphic quality that cannot be improved upon. He compared scientific progress to the onrush of a pack of hounds, "where the loudmouths bring many to follow them; . . . where the entire pack even has been known to move off bodily on a false scent."[6] The false scent received a supreme ratification when in 1905 E. Vacandard published an article on celibacy in the *Dictionnaire de théologie catholique,* in which Bickell's reasoning was largely ignored.[7] The view that clerical celibacy was of purely ecclesiastical origin quickly became the "received" view.

A major monograph from 1970 still presented that false scent as the correct orientation.[8] This was all the more ironic, because Christian Cochini had just defended his doctoral dissertation,

---

[4] G. Bickell, "Der Cölibat dennoch eine apostolische Anordnung," *Zeitschrift für Katholische Theologie* 3 (1879), pp. 792-799.

[5] F. X. Funk, "Der Cölibat noch lange keine apostolische Anordnung," *Theologische Quartalschrift* (1880), pp. 202-221.

[6] S. P. Langley, "The History of a Doctrine," *Science* 12 (1888), p. 74. A hundred years later a voice from Tubingen, strengthened in its decibels by the media, effected a similar impact on theologians running like a pack of hounds.

[7] A chief merit of Vacandard's article, "Célibat ecclésiastique," (vol. 2 [1905], cols. 2068-2088), is its tone, restrained as it is in comparison with Funk's. Bickell, who died a year later, in 1906, could not have, of course, hoped to find a space for his view in the *Dictionnaire,* directed by Vacandard, who, tellingly, saw nothing really dubious in the Paphnutius story (see note 16 below). A rigorous presentation and analysis of the arguments in the Bickell-Funk debate and in its being "arbitrated" by Vacandard, would be all the more desirable as it became a pattern to refer to Bickell's studies without saying anything specific about his line of argument.

[8] R. Gryson, *Les origines du célibat ecclésiastique du premier au septième siècle* (Gembloux: J. Duculot, 1970).

which when published in an enlarged form in 1981 posed a major
challenge to the "received" view.[9] Added to the irony was the less
than adequate credit given by Cochini to Bickell's accomplish-
ment, which includes not only the importance to be attached to
the argument *ex prescriptione*, but also his tight argumentation
against the authenticity of the Paphnutius story, of which more
shortly. The close parallel Bickell drew between the acceptance of
Christological heresies and the laxity with regard to celibacy, especially in those parts of the orthodox East that had great troubles in
recovering from Arianism, is still to be duly appreciated and
worked out in full detail. Bickell was not mentioned when a hundred years later arguments against the authenticity of the Paphnutius story were marshalled again. Solid work in history and theology is often recognized only in heaven.

   Cochini showed in much greater detail than Bickell did that
patristic passages from the third century that suggest the practice of
married priests using their conjugal rights admit, from the grammatical viewpoint, a contrary interpretation more consonant with
the structure and meaning of comparable phrases. A case in point is
the passage in the *Stromata* of Clement of Alexandria, a teacher of

---

[9] C. Cochini, *Apostolic Origins of Priestly Celibacy*, tr. N. Marans (San Francisco:
Ignatius Press, 1990). The importance of this book, first published in French in
1981, cannot be emphasized enough. Marked as it is throughout with rigorous attention to the historical method, it exposed the thorough weakness of the position defended by Funk and Vacandard. Both failed to consider some important
grammatical nuances in patristic texts that seemed to support their position.
Needless to say, Cochini's book revealed the utter hollowness of the "standard"
work by H. C. Lea, *History of Sacerdotal Celibacy in the Christian Church*, first published in 1867, and re-edited and reprinted since many times as a "classic," and,
what is worse, mentioned with praise by champions of the "received" view. Most
importantly, reviews of Cochini's book that appeared in major theological peri-
odicals show its lasting merit in a roundabout way. Just as Funk did not care to report the (very solid) structure of Bickell's argumentation, critics of Cochini invariably picked on wholly secondary details. This fact, so revealing of some dubious aspects of the "new" theological scholarship, would deserve a special study, as
it replicates the typical reaction to Bickell's essays. Cochini's book clearly cannot
be digested by spokesmen of the liberal consensus who around Vatican II felt they
were in a commanding position and promoted with all possible means the cause
of optional celibacy. The charges that Cochini did not do justice to the historical
method can easily rebound on his critics. Gryson, who in 1970 still accepted the
historicity of the Paphnutius story, was hardly in a position to speak of Cochini's
disregard of the dictates of the historical method.

Origen, of which one rendering would be as follows: "The Apostle accepts easily the husband of an only wife, whether he be a priest, a deacon, or a layman; if he uses his marriage irreproachably, he will be saved by begetting children." Here the final subclause refers to all the three categories. But the passage admits another rendering as well, in which the subclause refers only to the layman: "The Apostle accepts easily the husband of an only wife, whether he be a priest, a deacon, or a layman using his marital rights irreproachably; because he will be saved by begetting children." [10]

But away from grammatical subtleties and back to theology, especially to its existentially practiced form. Problems of clerical continence came forcefully to the fore in the measure in which the Church enjoyed peace and, with it, a prosperity which readily made some clerics long for domestic comforts. Tellingly, right there and then the Church perceived that beyond the threat posed to clerical virtues there was a threat to the ideal of the priesthood itself. It was no coincidence that Arius' success occurred after the Church had suddenly become the object not of imperial persecution but of imperial favors. Had Arius had his way, Christian priesthood would have lost its meaning because Christ's fullness would have been reduced to what befitted an adopted Son of God, however perfect, but not God's true Son. Almost simultaneously with this threat to Christ's divine fullness, clerical celibacy, or the practice of total continence, seemed to be under threat as well. The threat evidenced that downward pull which nowhere appears more strongly than in man's sexual urges. To counter that threat many solemn decrees, instructions, rulings have since been issued in proof of the problem's permanent dynamics. They all manifest the awareness of a perennial need of striving upward in the sense of Paul's words: "Be intent on things above rather than on things on earth" (Col 3:2). The dubious advantage of following the line of least resistance was not given to the Church.

The date, 305 A. D., of the first known conciliar decree in support of priestly continence, is worth noting. It was then that the last great persecution was just blowing itself out after having

---

[10] Quoted from Cochini, *Apostolic Origins,* p. 151.

caused many defections precisely because it had been preceded by three or so decades of peace and growing prosperity for the Church. The bishops and priests who gathered in Elvira (near Granada, Spain) felt that a reminder in no uncertain terms was to be given to priests who did not observe full continence. Their Canon 33 was uncompromising: "It has seemed good absolutely to forbid the bishops, the priests, and the deacons, i. e. all the clerics in the service of the ministry, to have sexual relations with their wives and procreate children; should anyone do so, let him be excluded from the honor of the clergy."[11]

Canon 33 gives the impression that the number of offenders may have been large. The most striking aspect of the Canon is, of course, its uncompromising character. Were that Canon a sheer innovation, or even a drastic stiffening of not so strict rules already in force, it would have provoked protests and indeed vehement ones, given the nature of prohibition. The absence of any such protests, the absence of any qualification in that Canon, the absence of any justification on its behalf indicates that a long-standing, firm tradition lay behind it, which alone could justify its tone and range.[12]

The next document, Canon 29 of the First Council of Arles, held in 314, is noteworthy for two reasons. Constantine, who saw a threat in the Donatists to the peace of the Empire, wanted all bishops to attend; indeed about six hundred of them were present. Not one of them raised a word of protest against Canon 29, which threatens the recalcitrant with sanctions after exhorting them with a theological reason: "Moreover, [concerned with] what is worthy, pure, and honest, we exhort our brothers [in the

---

[11] Ibid., p. 159.

[12] This should be obvious to any historian, rightly suspicious of abrupt origins. In the absence of this suspicion any author who confronts the origin of priestly celibacy would find Canon 33 of Elvira to be a mystery. Thus, for instance, J. T. Noonan, Jr., concludes his essay, "Celibacy in the Fathers of the Church," on a note of puzzlement: "Why this legislation, why this compulsion occurred, is a question I find difficult to answer." Noonan's essay was published in G. H. Frein (ed.), *Celibacy: The Necessary Option* (New York: Herder and Herder, 1968). For quotation, see p. 151. Tellingly, Noonan offers no instances of compulsion, although he could have found much evidence to the point that the Church during the fourth century, and even more later, demanded free and clear consent on the part of the ordinand to live a life of continence.

episcopate] to make sure that priests and deacons have no [sexual] relations with their wives, since they are serving the ministry every day. Whoever will act against this decision will be deposed from the honor of the clergy."[13] The theological thrust of the Canon is in the words, "worthy, pure, and honest," as well as in the reference to the daily celebration of the Eucharist.[14] The canon indicates, as does Canon 33 of Elvira, that although the Church had to rely heavily on married men in order to recruit bishops, priests, and deacons, this did not deter her from expecting them to comply with the highest norms in a most difficult matter. Again, one should note the total absence of any legal justification for the Canon. This can only be explained if those who enacted it were aware of a long-standing, binding practice based on an unwritten rule.

A year later, in 315, the Council of Ancyra (Ankara) legislated concerning deacons who claimed that they had not given their consent to the law of continence at their ordination. The gist of the legislation is that silence on their part at the moment was taken for their consenting to a life of continence. In controversial cases the Council let certain deacons continue serving, but only as subdeacons. In the same year the Council of Neocaesarea stated in its first Canon: "If a priest marries, he will be excluded from the clergy; if he commits fornication or adultery, he will in addition be excommunicated and subject to penance."[15] Compared with the Council of Ancyra, this canon strengthened the punishment against offending priests, in clear recognition that priestly ordination conferred an even higher degree of sacredness than ordination to the diaconate.

The third disciplinary Canon of the famed Council of Nicaea aimed at what today might be best described as housekeepers in episcopal and priestly residences. Unless they were the clergyman's mother, sister, aunt, or "any other person above suspicion," their presence in those residences was absolutely forbidden. This Canon

[13] Cochini, *Apostolic Origins*, p. 161.
[14] Three generations earlier Cyprian in Carthage provided a telling witness about the daily celebration of the Eucharist in the African provinces.
[15] Cochini, *Apostolic Origins*, p. 177.

certainly witnessed the Church's concern that the chastity of the clergy be of the highest standard. Most importantly, the Council did not indirectly approve the use of conjugal rights by married priests as if it had been a recognized practice. This indirect approval would have consisted in the alleged yielding of the Council Fathers to the plea of Bishop Paphnutius that no censure be enacted against such priests.

This story about Paphnutius, an ace card in the hands of those urging the marriage of priests, should have long ago appeared a mere invention to anyone ready to add or subtract a few plain numbers. Socrates, the first to report that story in his *Church History* (written c. 439) names as his source a very old man. If the latter heard it at the Council of Nicaea, he must have been very old indeed, almost a centenarian by 400 or so when Socrates was a youth of twenty. Apart from this, the name of Paphnutius does not appear in the oldest lists of the participants at the Council. Moreover, the Fathers of the famed Council of Trullo (691) did not refer to it, although, as will be seen in the next Chapter, it would have provided them with a much needed argument. Most importantly, Eusebius, the principal historian of the early Church and a prominent figure at the Council of Nicaea, does not mention it in his *Historia ecclesiastica*. This is all the more telling, as in another work of his, *De Demonstratione evangelica*, written almost immediately after the Council, Eusebius contrasts the Levitic priesthood with the priesthood initiated by Christ. Eusebius does this in a way which runs counter to the moral of the story of Paphnutius: unlike the patriarchs and priests of the Old Testament, who were required to increase the number of the Chosen Race, the priests of New Testament generate new members in a spiritual way, in spite of the fact that, according to the Apostle, marriage is honorable and the bishop should be the husband of only one wife. Eusebius then concludes: "It behooves consecrated men, and those who are at the service of God's cult, to abstain hereafter from conjugal intercourse with their wives."[16]

---

[16] *De demonstratione evangelica*, I.9, PG vol. 22, col. 82. The Greeks did not refer to the Paphnutius story until Gratian included it in his *Decretum*, composed around 1140, where he argued that priestly celibacy had its origin in an ecclesiastically legislated vow attached to the ordination. The apocryphal character of the

Equally telling against the thrust of the Paphnutius story is Eusebius' reporting in his *Church History* a sermon which most likely he himself preached at the dedication of the basilica in Tyre in 330. In that sermon the preacher presents the composition of the community of the faithful in terms of the construction of the basilica itself. The sanctuary is occupied by the clergy living in purity.[17]

Indeed the concern of laity that priests should be paragons of continence could go to an extreme which the Church did not tolerate. The Council of Gangres (c. 340) rallied to the defense of married priests: The faithful should not suspect that priests were guilty of incontinence just because they had their wives with them. Thus the Council ordered the faithful not to refuse the Eucharist from the hands of married priests.

Here as elsewhere in the various references during the fourth century to Canon 3 of the Council of Nicaea, there is no trace of a relaxation of the strict standard that priests live in complete continence. Such a standard would have appeared nonsensical if indeed Paphnutius had intervened at Nicaea and successfully so, or if there had been no awareness about that standard's ancient, and indeed apostolic provenance. The first known case of explicit appeal to early times is all the more noteworthy, because in it nothing less is claimed than apostolic authority for legislation about strict continence for bishops, priests, and deacons, whether married or not.

One would only wish that we know details about the "previous council" to which Epigonius, bishop of the Royal Region of Bulla, in Africa, referred at the Council of Carthage in 390 in say-

---

Paphnutius story was reargued by F. Winkelmann, professor at the Martin Luther University in Halle-Wittenberg, in 1968, and an authority on the time of Constantine and Eusebius. (For a detailed summary of Winkelmann's reasoning, see Cochini, *Apostolic Origins,* pp. 197-99). Ironically, this happened at a time when agitation on behalf of optional celibacy for Catholic clergy reached its high-water mark with copious references to the Paphnutius story as an authentic evidence that in the early Church married priests legitimately used their conjugal rights.

[17] See *Eusebius. The History of the Church,* tr. G. A. Williamson (Harmondsworth: Penguin Books, 1965), pp. 399-400 (Book X, 4). Earlier (p. 328) Eusebius referred to the spread of moral decay among Christians prior to that final great persecution, in which he saw God's just punishment.

ing: "The rule of continence and chastity had been discussed in a previous council. Let it [now] with more emphasis be taught what are the three ranks that, by virtue of their consecration, are under the same obligation of chastity, i. e., the bishop, the priest, the deacon, and let them be instructed to keep their chastity." Then it was the turn of Genethlius, bishop of Carthage and well known to Augustine, to utter words that made history. In speaking of those three orders, it was fitting, he said, that "since they are in the service of the divine sacraments, they observe perfect continence." Then he added the theological reason: "so that they may obtain in all simplicity, what they are asking from God." There followed the canonical justification: "What the apostles taught and what antiquity itself observed, let us also endeavour to keep." After that the bishops present "declared unanimously: It pleases us all that bishop, priest, and deacon, guardians of purity, abstain from [conjugal intercourse] with their wives, so that those who serve at the altar may keep a perfect chastity."[18]

Twenty-seven years later two hundred and seventeen bishops of the African provinces gathered in Carthage, under the leadership of Aurelius, archbishop of Carthage, with Bishop Faustinus, the legate of Pope Boniface, presiding. Present was also Augustine, bishop of Hippo. The collection of a total of 113 Canons enacted at that Council is known as the *Codex canonum Ecclesiae africanae*. Five of its canons impose absolute continence on bishops, priests, and deacons, whether married or not. Canon 3 explicitly refers to the Council of 390 and endorses its rule of perfect continence, reminding all clerics of its rationale, namely, that thereby they may "obtain in all simplicity what they asked from God: what the apostles taught, and what antiquity itself observed, we also have to keep."[19]

Against this claim to apostolicity one may observe that the previous hundred or so years witnessed the production of not a few instructions, ordinances, as well as Gospels, Acts, Letters, and Apocalypses, that claimed to have been written by the Apostles and were suspect right there and then. Yet no suspicion arose

---

[18] Cochini, *Apostolic Origins,* p. 5.
[19] Ibid., p. 267.

about the apostolicity of the law reaffirmed at the Council of 390. This should seem all the more telling, because in view of the very existential nature of the law, heated questions would have been raised had it not been widely seen as firmly grounded in tradition.

That the legislation contained in Canon 3 of the Council of Carthage of 390 indeed represented apostolic teaching was not questioned even by the Fathers gathered at the Council of Trullo in 691. In fact, as will be seen, the Fathers of Trullo did their best to invoke that apostolic teaching, while they twisted its meaning. For only a reference to apostolic teaching was in their eyes suffi- cient to introduce a previously unheard of novelty, namely, that the Apostles allowed married priests to exercise their conjugal rights. The apostolic teaching invoked by Canon 3 of the Council of Carthage of 390 was to become the historic basis of the Gregorian Reforms; it figured prominently in the deliberations of the Coun- cil of Trent; it decided matters for Paul IV and for Pius V in turn- ing down the request of German princes to allow Catholic priests to marry.

The end of the fourth century was laden with crucial docu- ments concerning the apostolic origin of priestly celibacy, indeed its origin traced to Christ himself. The first to speak in this vein is Saint Epiphanius, a native of Gaza, Palestine, and bishop of Constantia in Cyprus for thirty-six years (367–403). A great pro- moter of orthodoxy, and perhaps excessively so in his wholly nega- tive attitude towards Origen, Epiphanius wrote the treatise, *Panarion* (or "Medicine Chest") against all heresies. There, in argu- ing against the Montanists who had rejected marriage, he defends marriage by rejoicing over virginity as the ideal set by our Lord's virginity. Moreover, he makes it absolutely clear that formerly monogamous men (obviously "the husbands of one wife" in Paul's Letter to Timothy) are practicing that perfect continence, once they have been elevated to the priesthood. The reason given speaks for itself: "As if he [Christ] prefigured precisely the charisma of the priesthood of former monogamists, practicing continence, or of men living continually in virginity, it is in the same way that his apostles regulated, with wisdom and sanctity, the ecclesiastical canon of the priesthood."[20]

Montanists and other extremists had indeed appealed to the total continence observed by the clergy in support of their opposition to marriage. If total continence was proper to one section of the believers, why not appropriate for all of them? In his rebuttal of this logic, Saint Epiphanius sheds precious light on the understanding of the Church concerning priestly continence. The understanding is rooted in the Church's understanding of the Incarnation itself! Deeper theological reason than this would have indeed been unimaginable. Then Epiphanius notes the difference between two kinds of monogamists, those who remarried after they had become widowers and those who never remarried: only the latter are accepted for the priesthood where "the ecclesiastical canons are exactly held and observed]." The former are not accepted to the priesthood "since the Incarnation of Christ, the Holy Word of God does not allow to the priesthood [these] monogamists . . . because of the exceptional honor of the priesthood."[21]

In the Preface to his *Panarion* Saint Epiphanius portrays the Church as a building of perfection: the basis is virginity, practiced by many and held in great honor. They support, so to speak, the ones living solitary lives, then those in marriages lived in sanctity. The crowning stage is constituted by the priesthood, that acts like a mother generating the rest and whose "dynamic force comes in great part from the virgins." In the same Preface Saint Epiphanius points out even more explicitly that priests are recruited mostly from among lay people who have dedicated themselves to perfect continence. If there are not enough of these, the Church turns to monks, and after these looks among married men who "observe continence with their wives or among exmonogamists who are

[20] This passage, quoted after Cochini (p. 227), is from Saint Epiphanius' *Panarion* against heretical doctrines and concerns Heresy #48 there. In view of the very legal sense of the word canon, which by itself may mean norm or ideal, given to it shortly afterwards by the African Councils, it is rather forced to argue that Epiphanius did not have in mind a legally binding norm.

[21] Here, in the same work, Saint Epiphanius argues against Heresy #59. Quoted from Cochini, *Apostolic Origins,* p. 227.

widowers." Further, in line with Paul's instruction about "husbands of one wife," Saint Epiphanius stresses that the Church does not allow to the priesthood a remarried man. In fact even if such a man "observes continence, or is a widower, [he is rejected] from the Order of bishops, priests, deacons and subdeacons."[22]

In view of all this, quite natural will appear chapter 7 of Pope Siricius' *Directa* to Himerus, metropolitan of Tarragone. No less importantly, the *Directa*, in which Pope Siricius answers, on February 10, 385, on behalf of his just deceased predecessor, Damasus, begins with the assertion: "We carry the burdens of all those who are laden; rather, Blessed Apostle Peter is carrying them in us, and we firmly trust that he protects and guards us in all things, as we are the heirs to his functions."

In the *Directa* Pope Siricius had to deal with the fact that many bishops, priests and deacons in Spain were bringing children into the world, "either through union with their wives or through shameful intercourse." Worse, they used as excuse the example of the priests of the Old Testament. The Pope first called attention to the fact that during the term of their priestly functions the Levites had to live in the Temple precincts, separated from their wives: "quite obviously so that they would not be able to have carnal knowledge of any woman, even their wives, and, thus having a conscience of integrity, they could offer to God offerings worthy of acceptance."

Something much more perfect was to be the norm in the New Covenant: "After having enlightened us with his coming, the Lord Jesus formally stipulated in the Gospel that he had not come to abolish the law, but to bring it to perfection; this is also why he wanted to bring the beauty of the Church whose Bridegroom he is to shine with the splendor of chastity, so that when he returns, on the Day of Judgment, he will find her without stain or wrinkle, as his Apostle taught." Then came, in the wake of this elevated theological consideration, the statement that the rule of priestly continence (celibacy) was inseparable from priestly ordination, as well as being unchangeable, because it went back to Christ and his Apostle Paul: "It is through the indissoluble law of these decisions

[22] Ibid., p. 232.

that all of us, priests and deacons, are bound together from the day of our ordination, and [held to] put our hearts and bodies to the service of sobriety and purity; may we be pleasing to our God in all things, in the sacrifices we offer daily."[23]

Clearly, the Pope saw something much more in the temporary continence imposed on the priests of the Temple than a mere means of securing ritual purity from a defect similar to various blemishes of the body, against which Moses legislated. Otherwise he would not have argued that the priesthood established by Christ had to be much more spiritual. Those modern commentators on priestly celibacy (some of them prominent post-Vatican-II theologians) who see in these fourth-century injunctions of priestly continence an untheological reversion to Old Testament ritualism are hardly doing justice to the record.[24]

And as if the contents of his *Directa* had not been enough, a year later Pope Siricius gave, in reference to a similar problem, a remarkable interpretation of Paul's dictum that bishops and deacons be men of one wife. Paul, the Pope argued in his Decretal *Cum in unum,* did not mean that those bishops could go on having conjugal relations. Rather, their having been faithful spouses (hardly a small matter then as now) in their marriage prior to their ordination, should be a guarantee that as ordained men they would live up to the much higher standard of perfect continence even though their wives should continue living in the same household.

---

[23] Ibid., p. 9.

[24] Such as E. Schillebeeckx, whose *Celibacy* will be discussed in Ch. 6. They overlook that the best orthodox Jewish tradition always considered masturbation, for instance, a serious moral deviation. See D. Biale, *Eros and the Jews: From Biblical Israel to Contemporary America* (New York: Basic Books, 1992), pp. 79-84. The same fact received a much wider notoriety through K. Menninger's book, *Whatever Became of Sin?* (New York: Hawthorne Books, 1973), where (p. 32) a passage is quoted in reference to masturbation from L. Epstein's *Sex Laws and Customs in Judaism:* "The Zohar ... accounts it the severest sin of all....The ethical literature of post-Talmudic days, down to the latest centuries, endlessly harps on the severity of this sin, exhorts its avoidance, points out its danger to health, threatens dire punishment in the day of reckoning, and pleads for penitence and expiation." It is beside the point that Menninger considers all this senseless and lets Rabbi Louis Finkelstein deny that the Jewish law has ever sanctioned that sin with capital punishment.

About the same time a Roman Synod answered, with the same Pope presiding, the concern of the bishops in Gaul over the fact that not a few bishops wanted to change the rules of priestly continence. In reply, the third of sixteen Canons promulgated at that Synod under the title *Dominus inter* declared: "Those [bishops, priests, and deacons] who have the responsibility of the divine sacrifice, and whose hands give the grace of baptism, and consecrate the Body of Christ, are ordered by divine Scripture, and not only ourselves, to be very chaste; the Fathers themselves ordered them to observe bodily continence." Then an explanation was given which should seem particularly relevant in this "pastoral" age: "How would a bishop or a priest dare preach continence and integrity to a widow or a virgin, or yet [how would he dare] exhort [spouses] to the chastity of the conjugal bed, if he himself is more concerned about begetting children for the world than begetting them for God?" Those pleading today for a married priesthood should take a look at the often cowardly compromising attitude which married ministers of non-Catholic Churches take in respect to those burning questions.

Sixteen hundred years ago reference could be made to the pagan priests, many of whom practiced continence prior to offering sacrifices, to the Levitical priests of the Temple, from whom periodic continence was demanded, but above all to Christian priests, for whom the perennial parameter was always the utmost holiness, as implied in their various functions. And since they had to perform them every day, and at times at a moment's notice, their observance of continence allowed no interruption: "If commixture is defiling, it is obvious that the priest must be ready to carry out his celestial functions—he who has to supplicate on behalf of the sins of the others—so that he himself is not to be found impure. If the lay people are told, 'Leave yourself free for prayer' (1 Cor 7:5), these men who put themselves first at the service of human procreation, might have the title of priests, but they cannot have that dignity."[25]

The same *Dominus inter* also had a most timely warning for these times that witness various efforts to relax the rule of priestly

<hr />

[25] Cochini, *Apostolic Origins*, p. 15.

celibacy for some part of the Church. It warned that the unity of
faith demands unity of tradition and this, in turn, a unity of discipline: "There must be one profession of faith for the Catholic bishops. This was decreed by the apostolic rule. Therefore if there is to
be one faith, there should also be one tradition. If there is one tradition, there must be one discipline observed by all the Churches.
Indeed the Churches were established in very diverse regions, but
throughout the whole world [the Church] is called 'one' thanks to
the unity of the Catholic faith. Thus we read: 'My dove is unique,
mine, unique, and perfect. She is the darling of her mother (Song
6:9)'."[26] These three Decretals, and the wholehearted espousal by
Rome of the Canon of the Council of Carthage of 390, attest to the
collegial co-operation between the bishops and the successor of Peter.
They also attest to the intimate connection between the See of Peter and the preservation of the rule of clerical continence as a most
precious bequest left by Christ and the apostles to the Church.

It is a bequest which every upright layman recognized as unconditionally binding. Such a layman was the Platonist philosopher, Synesius of Ptolemais, the seat of a small bishopric midway
between Alexandria and Carthage. As one who had rendered
important services to his town while pleading for it in the Imperial Court in Constantinople, Synesius, a mere catechumen, was
elected by plebiscite to be their bishop in 405. The result struck
him like thunderbolt. All of a sudden his pleasant, though virtuous
life seemed to fall apart. Some years earlier he had married a
woman he dearly loved and who had already borne to him three
children. He was far from ready to give up the legitimate pleasures
of married life. Indeed he wanted to have more children. But he
knew that as a bishop he had to live with his wife as if she were his
sister, something for which he was not ready at all. Deeply
troubled as he was, he wrote to Theophilus, bishop of Alexandria,
asking for advice. What Synesius wanted to know above all was
whether he should see in the plebiscite the will of God. To the
will of God he was ready to bow, even though it demanded that
he would give up the use of his marriage. He certainly did not

[26] Ibid., pp. 15–16.

want to live as a bishop in an adulterous state. But such would have been his case, if, as a bishop, he continued having conjugal relations with his wife. By his reasoning he tacitly recognized that a bishop (a priest) was married to the Church and through the Church to God. For as Synesius put it, the bishop is something "divine."[27]

Only a decade or so later, Germanus of Auxerre (378-448) provided a similar example. He was a married man, prefect of Gaul, when he was chosen bishop in 418. According to his early biographer, "he received the fullness of the priesthood under compulsion, as a conscript; but this done, immediately he made the change complete. He deserted the earthly militia to be enrolled in the heavenly. The pomp of this world was trodden underfoot; a lowly way of life was adopted; his wife was turned into a sister; his riches were distributed to the poor and poverty became his ambition."[28] Earlier, upon having been made bishop of Poitiers, Saint Hilary sent his wife away to Bordeaux. Still earlier, Urbicus, the first successor to Austremonius, the founder of the Church of Auvergne (c. 300), gave up his marital rights, only to fail to persevere. Once a daughter was born to his wife, he was compelled to retire to a monastery and do penance. In his *Exhortatio virginitatis*, Saint Ambrose speaks of a widow called Juliana, whose husband was called towards the end of his life to be a deacon and who thereafter lived with his wife in continence. Upon his death, Juliana exhorted their four children—one son and three daughters—to consecrate themselves to God in perfect chastity.[29]

The change of life was, of course, easier though no less obligatory when a bachelor was catapulted into the bishop's chair. Ambrose, the prefect of Milan and only a catechumen, was also elected by plebiscite. Whether he contemplated marriage, we do not know. But he knew that the sacred orders bound him to lifelong continence. He implemented this ideal with such a suggestive

---

[27] Ibid., pp. 303-05.

[28] Quoted from F. R. Hoare (ed.), *The Western Fathers* (New York: Sheed and Ward, 1954), p. 287.

[29] For the documentation of these instances, see Cochini, *Apostolic Origins,* pp. 97 and 99.

force that parents tried to prevent their daughters from hearing him preach. His treatise on virginity is one of the gems of patristic literature. It is to him that we owe an interpretation of Paul's words, "man of one wife" that runs parallel to Pope Siricius' interpretation of it. Behind that interpretation there lies a most exalted view of disciplined married life. The interpretation presupposes that married life can be a proper preparation to the discipline of full continence. For, clearly, it must have been a far greater trial at times to live with one's wife under the same roof as if she were his sister, than to live alone.

For the benefit of those priests who tried to justify their concubinage with reference to Old Testament priesthood, Ambrose coined one of his famed pithy phrases: "Si in figura tanta observantia, quanta in veritate?", that is, if the pre-figuration of truth demanded so much temporal continence, how much more the reign of truth demands its full measure? And with a reference to the Levites' ritual washing of their clothes, Ambrose exclaimed: "Learn, O priest, O deacon, what the washing of your clothes means, so as to present your pure body to the celebration of the mysteries. If it was forbidden to the people to approach their victim without having purified their clothes, would you dare, without having purified your spirit and body even more, to offer supplications for the others; would you dare exercise your ministry for the others?"[30]

Ambrose's sudden rise, against his will, from catechumen to bishop was most likely in Augustine's mind as he instructed the priest Pollentius about the art of persuading people to refrain from adulterous unions. When we try to persuade these men, Augustine writes, "for whom the superiority of their sex means freedom to sin," we refer not only to eternal death; we also "give them as an example the continence of these clerics who were frequently forced against their wills to carry such a burden [of perpetual continence]." The Doctor of divine grace shines through what follows: "Nevertheless as soon as they have accepted it, they carry it, faithful to their duty, until death . . . . If a great number of the Lord's ministers accepted all of a sudden and without warning the yoke

---

[30] Ibid., p. 235.

imposed on them, in the hope of receiving a more glorious place in Christ's inheritance, how much more should one avoid adultery and embrace continence, for fear, not of shining less in the Kingdom of God, but of burning in the Gehenna of fire?"[31] Of course, Augustine argued at a time when much reliance was put on the grace of God in the face of great challenges and even, if possible, greater attention was paid to the fact that life-long continence made sense only if what really counted was the eternal life to come. But in this age of theological emphasis on personal fulfillment in this life and of theological investigations into hell as an uninhabited place, even if it should exist, the arguments of Augustine may sound very strange indeed.

Saintly theologians, so rare in these days of theological "progress," alone provide, in most varied contexts, the proofs of the existence of the law of total priestly continence, together with most sublime theological reasons for it. Yes, it is upon the shoulders of the saints that falls much of the task of keeping alive what will forever remain an upward struggle. If there is a theological dynamic, it is there, in the saints' unrelenting support of priestly celibacy, which, let us not forget, is but a particular aspect of full continence for anyone, whether married or not, who is in the sacred orders. This point cannot be emphasized enough at a time when the picture of married, though fully continent men in bishops' seats has become a vague memory of a very distant past; at a time which produces dreamers among Catholics who envision their bishops and priests married as are their Anglican counterparts. Those dreamers are still to wake up to the real situation in the Church of England, where a bishop scoffed at the resurrection of Christ, another preached "honest to God" faith, and still another did his best to rescue Arius from his well-deserved disrepute. This tragedy of truth was followed with a comedy of morals when Richard Holloway, the Anglican bishop of Edinburgh, suggested that adultery need not be considered a sin and found considerable support for his stance among the faithless faithful.[32]

[31] Ibid., pp. 289-290.
[32] See Clifford Longley's report in *The Daily Telegraph,* May 18, 1995, p. 17.

Those Catholics, whether lay or clerical, should also focus on the true and saintly bishops of that great century, the fourth, or rather on the hundred or so years following the Church's exit from the catacombs. Those saints were the ones who had to steady a Church which, after over two centuries spent in the twilight of the catacombs, was part of public life for the first time. Saint Jerome should be particularly relevant today, in an age boastful of having a far fuller grasp of the Bible than any age before, in an age when a "biblical" in-depth understanding of sex is used to promote optional priestly celibacy. Jerome encountered an early trendsetter of this newfangled profundity in the person of Jovinian. In his refutation of Jovinian, who urged, with a reference to Paul's "man of one wife," that priests and bishops should beget children, Jerome pushed Jovinian into a corner by forcing him to admit the universal rule of priestly continence. Jerome was much more than a polemicist. He was a saint and a theologian, who as such quickly grasped the essence of Jovinian's contention: the abolition of a difference of dignity between the virginal and the marital status.

This abolition was in Jerome's eye a destruction of the saintly status of priesthood. The hierarchical Church was not merely a hierarchy of power and authority, but above all a hierarchy of states of sanctity. By defending that difference in his animated manner, Jerome provoked sharp protests. Then as now there were defenders of marriage who could not tolerate the specter of a higher form of Christian calling. But as Jerome noted, the rewards for each calling were different: "Marriage is permitted in the Gospel, but women, if they persist in accomplishing the duty that is theirs, cannot receive the reward promised to chastity. Let the husbands, if they grow indignant at this opinion, be irritated not with me but with Holy Scripture." There could be no compromise: "The virgin Christ and the virgin Mary have consecrated for each sex the beginnings of virginity; the apostles were either virgins or continent after having been married. Bishops, priests and deacons are chosen among virgins and widowers; in any case once they are ordained, they live in perfect chastity. Why delude ourselves, or get upset if, when we are constantly seeking the conjugal act, we are refused the recompenses promised to purity?"[33] The theology of priestly celibacy is therefore anchored in the virginal status of Christ and Mary. Any argument against celibacy is, according to Jerome, an argument against the states of life of those two.

Yet, all such considerations leave untold something that alone can explain what should seem a curious exception, given the truth of some assumptions. Suppose that it is right to assume, as some prominent theologians have done in recent decades, that priestly celibacy had its origin in a non-biblical misunderstanding on the part of the Church of the fourth century. The misunderstanding would have consisted in slighting love and its sexual use in favor of the rules of temporary continence imposed on the priests of the Temple. But why did the Church of the fourth century, or rather its great Fathers, make an exception with this sole ritual rule, while they did not try to reimpose any of the countless other rules of ritual purity? Did they act under the influence of a Platonism that frowned on the body, or were they crypto-Manicheans, full of hatred towards the body?

It is totally mistaken to look in that direction in our search for the deepest ground of the origin of clerical celibacy. This can easily be seen once one looks up certain pages in Augustine's *De civitate Dei,* pages that are hardly ever referred to in the vastly growing modern literature on priestly celibacy. Those arguing for its relax-ation or for its abolition would, of course, be the last ones to recall those pages. On the other hand, those who resolutely defend it, will have their theological argumentations hang in mid-air with-out thoroughly airing those pages. Of course, in this age that glori-fies the sexual act and tries to present its use in married life (and even outside it) as an unblemished source of greater perfection, it will hardly prove popular to call a spade a spade. Also, it goes against man's basic sense of modesty to be explicit, let alone prolific about an experience that is never void of shame, except for those who, in Paul's words, take their shame for their glory (Phil 3:19).

But even for an Augustine, who in his *Confessions* laid bare the full range of his sexual experience, the mere mention of the topic

---

[33] *Adversus Jovinianum,* quoted from Cochini, *Apostolic Origins,* pp. 296-97.

induced "a feeling of shame, under the present conditions." For him the mere "mention of this subject suggests to the mind only the turbulent lust, which we experience, not the calm act of will imagined in my speculation."[34] This he said towards the end of Book XIV, which dealt with the transgression of the first man and its consequences. The transgression consisted in an act of pride, in a refusal to be submitted to the command of the Creator. The punishment consisted in the refusal of man's various powers to remain subordinate to the right use of his reason and will. Consequently, man was engulfed in a wild variety of inordinate desires: lust for power, lust for food, lust for vengeance, lust for fame, lust for riches, lust for all sorts of pleasures. But there was one lust that touched man more powerfully than all the other kinds, the lust for sexual satisfaction: "This lust assumes power not only over the whole body, and not only from the outside, but also internally; it disturbs the whole man, when the mental emotion combines and mingles with the physical craving, resulting in a pleasure surpassing all physical delights. So intense is the pleasure that when it reaches its climax, there is an almost total extinction of mental alertness; the intellectual senses, as it were, are overwhelmed."[35] One wonders whether Freud or Kinsey, to say nothing of their crudely pornographic imitators, could have said it more tellingly, though hardly with Augustine's manly restraint.

As Augustine rightly knows, this disorder is experienced even by one mindful of Paul's injunction about "how to possess his bodily instrument, not in the sickness of desire, like the Gentiles who have no knowledge of God" (1 Thess 4:4). Yes, unlike some modern theologians of sex, Augustine knows fully that even in the holiest of marriages something inordinate remains attached to the act of procreation, and he is not ashamed of saying so. Of course, at that time he did not have to be concerned about a climate of opinion which today unleashes its storms on anybody who dares to say anything critical about man's sexual powers. For all its vices

---

[34] *Augustine. The City of God,* ed. D. Knowles; tr. H. Bettenson (Pelican Classics, 1972), p. 591 (Book XIV, ch. 26).

[35] Ibid., p. 577 (ch. 16).

and shortcomings, Augustine's times had more sanity than these progressive times of ours.

Today it might provoke protest even on the part of some theologians to report Augustine's restrained portrayal of man's natural shame in relation to the use of sex. He refers to the universal custom of the covering of the sexual organs and to the fact that "the sexual act itself, which is performed with such a lust, seeks privacy." Augustine knew of only one in Antiquity, the Cynic philosopher Diogenes, who in line with his defiance of all norms, performed copulation in public. It should not be difficult to imagine the reaction of Augustine, this great defender of redemption in Christ alone, if he were to see the supreme perversion of modern democratic society. The latter allows pornographic literature and videos to make a public farce of the conjugal act, on the ground that such a farce, in terms of the supreme unwisdom of the American Supreme Court, has a redeeming value. Yet Augustine even today could repeat that while all parts of the marriage ceremonies are a preparation for the conjugal act, the latter is performed in utter privacy. No parents would think of letting their own children witness the performance of the act by which they were begotten. Places for illicit use of sex shun the limelight, because "a natural sense of shame ensures that even brothels make provision for secrecy."[36]

It would be theologically most controversial today to quote Augustine on the transmission of original sin through precisely the inordinateness inherent in the sexual act. Not that he sees in that act something intrinsically evil. Far from it. He emphasizes that the task of procreation was given to man before his fall. But Adam's refusal to submit to God's command received its retribution in that he lost the perfect obedience of his various impulses to his will, which is most grippingly true of the sexual impulse: in the disobedience of that impulse, "which subjected the sexual organs solely to their own impulses and snatched them from the will's authority, we see a proof of the retribution imposed on man for that disobedience." Augustine therefore could rightly argue that the inordinateness, which, though not a personal sin, inheres in the sexual

---

[36] Ibid., p. 579 (ch. 18).

act, serves as a transmitter of the guilt of original sin: "It was entirely fitting that this retribution should show itself in that part which effects the procreation of the very nature that was changed for the worse through that first great sin."[37]

Had Adam not sinned, the seed of children would have been sowed "without the morbid condition of lust." Had man not fallen in Adam, "man would have sowed the seed and the woman would have conceived, when their sexual organs had been aroused by the will, at the appropriate time and in the necessary degree, and had not been excited by lust."[38] Augustine, of course, admits that all of man's experience shows the contrary. But he firmly holds up this scenario which he, the once misguided explorer of the joys of sex, gives with a sensitiveness totally lacking in sex manuals: "Then without feeling the passion of allurement goading him on, the husband would have relaxed on his wife's bosom in tranquillity of mind and with no impairment of his body's integrity." Again, he insists on the well-nigh unbelievable, namely, that "when those parts of the body were not activated by the turbulent heat of passion, but brought into service by deliberate use of power when the need arose, the male seed could have been dispatched into the womb with no loss of the wife's integrity."[39]

It would be useless to get bogged down in physiology. Augustine wanted to make an ethical point, and he did it irrefutably to anyone who has not blinded himself or herself to the general human experience that there is something deeply inordinate in the use of human sexual powers. It is that general and universal experience, about which decent people are as reticent as possible, which underlay even the Mosaic imposition of temporary continence of the Levites and prompted the Church to keep only that imposition from among countless others. Far from being a purely ritual blemish, incontinence, even in its marital context, was, is, and will forever remain a most palpable evidence of something deeply inordinate in man. Therefore those ordained for the things of God, the source

[37] Ibid., p. 582 (ch. 20).
[38] Ibid., p. 587 (ch. 24).
[39] Ibid., p. 591 (ch. 26).

of perfect order and tranquillity, should be as free as possible of that inordinateness.

Of those things of God, if they may be called things at all, none is so sublime as the body of Christ in the Eucharist. Christ's body is, of course, the body of the Incarnate Logos in whom God made everything, the point of theology on which Athanasius anchors his assertion that the created universe has to be fully ordered and harmonious.[40] In saying this, Athanasius merely gave a felicitous phrasing to an idea widely held. Otherwise, Augustine would not have brought to a close his account of the disorders of the sexual powers with a reference to the cosmic order resting in the Logos, which ultimately is the order of grace: God created man in the foreknowledge that man would sin, because that made it possible for God to show in the first parents and through them to us what "their guilt deserved and what his grace could give; and with God as creator and disposer of all things, the perverse disorder of transgression did not pervert the right ordering of the universe."[41]

All this would, of course, be greeted with a condescending smile on the part of those who trace their "spiritual" ancestry to the stance that found its first major disclosure in Jean-Jacques Rousseau's *Confessions*. While they go far beyond Rousseau's sexploits, far beyond his savoring at length his own initiation into manhood in the artful embraces of a woman almost twice his age,[42] they owe him this line of ephemeral logic: pleasure, especially of the sexual kind, is its own justification. Such is the true nature of post-Christian society, which reads that ephemeral logic even into Augustine's *Confessions*. But the gurus of this society have blinded themselves from seeing anything more than misguided sublimation of a male's frustrations in Augustine's vision of Continence writ large, just before the hour of truth, so divine and yet so human, struck for him: "While I stood trembling at the barrier, on the other side I could see the chaste beauty of Continence in all

[40] For details, see my *The Savior of Science* (Lanham, MD: Regnery; Edinburgh: Scottish Academic Press, 1988), pp. 76-77.

[41] *Augustine. The City of God*, p. 592 (Book XIV, ch. 26).

[42] J. J. Rousseau, *Confessions* (Penguin Classics, 1953), Book V, covering the years 1732-1738.

her serene, unsullied joy, as she modestly beckoned to me to cross over and hesitate no more. She stretched out loving hands to welcome and embrace me, holding up a host of good examples to my sight. . . . She smiled at me to give me courage, as though she were saying, 'Can you not do what these men and these women do? Do you think they find the strength to do it in themselves and not in the Lord their God? Cast yourself upon God and have no fear. He will not shrink away and let you fall. Cast yourself upon him without fear, for he will welcome you and cure you of your ills'."[43]

The rest, which came with an almost lightning speed, is well-known. Augustine learned that God's grace is supreme. Yet he never drew from this ever so slightly the inference that grace renders human effort futile and that man should consider hopeless the task of resisting the downward pull of the body. His advice given to Pollentius is a proof, among the many he provided, that to join the upward pull is very much possible for Christians, and in particular for those among them, priests, who have become especially configured with Christ. They above all should know that there remains a choice to make between two confessions: one by Augustine, the other by Jean-Jacques. There is no *via media* here. Some may prefer to listen to Jean-Jacques' plaintive moaning about the unattainable, or heaven on earth, be it the imaginary heaven of marriage. They may end up saying with him that "what is not is the only thing that is beautiful."[44] Jean-Jacques never came to the point of admitting that he was unfit for marriage, as shown all too clearly by the miseries he imposed on his children's mother. Those unable to make the choice between the two "confessions" on religious grounds should ponder Augustine's account of the frustration often brought about by indulging one's sexual impulse whether in or outside of marriage: "Sometime the impulse is an unwanted intruder, sometime it abandons the eager lover, and the desire cools off in the body while it is at boiling heat in the mind.

[43] *Augustine, Confessions,* tr. R. S. Pine-Coffin (Penguin Classics, 1961), p. 176 (Book VIII, 11).
[44] See P. M. Masson, *La religion de Rousseau* (Paris: Garnier, 1916), vol. 2, p. 270, and my book, *Angels, Apes and Men* (La Salle, IL: Sherwood Sugden, 1983), pp. 42-44.

. . . Thus lust arouses the mind, but does not follow its own lead by arousing the body."[45]

Prior to Augustine the Fathers of the Church did, out of a proper sense of modesty, only hint at all that. It fell to Augustine, whom God allowed to drink deep the cup of sexual gratification over many years, to spell out a plain reality. But once he did so, his words, so precise and tactful, should be appreciated all the more so as they might spare others from trying to say it even remotely as well as he did. To forget the lessons of Book XIV of *De civitate Dei* is to add further pages to a book to be written perhaps under the title, "De confusione hominis." To forget those lessons would deprive any discourse on the theology of priestly celibacy of a basis, which, precisely because of its concreteness and experienced truth, remains the only solid basis for that discourse. Otherwise that discourse may sublimate itself into sheer abstractions, if not unreality, as to the basic rationale for priestly celibacy. This sublimation sets the tone of a new theology which loudly invokes Kant as its philosopher, although he roundly rejected original sin,[46] and which takes Teilhard de Chardin for a chief inspiration, although he denied by silence the same basic Christian dogma.[47]

Attention to what Augustine said would also save to that discourse its dynamics, namely, that celibacy is not so much a status as an ongoing rededication to an uphill struggle both in the individual and in the community which that celibacy is to serve. It should seem remarkable that the Church articulated all this within one century, that very century when the Church first came to grips with the world in an open contest. In that world nothing needed, then or now, more healing than man's sexual urge. This is why that century is, in a sense, the beginning of an explicit ruling about priestly celibacy, a ruling that goes back to the apostles, and indeed to Christ himself.

---

[45] *Augustine. The City of God*, p. 577 (Book XIV, ch. 16).

[46] The pertinent material is fully presented in C. Simm's dissertation, *Kants Ablehnung jeglicher Erbsündenlehere* (Münster: Lit Verlag, 1991).

[47] Since there is no reference to this in Father de Lubac's *Teilhard Explained*, tr. A. Buono (New York: Paulist Press, 1968), the book, for other reasons as well, should have carried the title: "Teilhard Explained Away."

During that century and during the three previous ones, there were many who were called to the priesthood though already married. There is not a single documented case that such priest or bishop carried out his ministry while having the considered consent of the Church that he might have conjugal relations with his wife. On the contrary, time and again it was requested from the spouses of such clergy that they give up their conjugal rights. There were, of course, infringements, human nature being what it is. The struggle began now in the open. In the early fifth century Pope Innocent I joined the struggle in letters to three different bishops. Still later, Saint Leo the Great instructed bishop Anastasius of Thessalonika that he should demand full continence from subdeacons as well. To bishop Rusticus of Narbonne, the Pope wrote that when married men become either bishops or priests, they become subject to the law of continence: "In order for their union to change from carnal to spiritual, they must, without sending away their wives, live with them as if they did not have them, so that conjugal love be safeguarded and nuptial activity be ended."[48]

A century and a half later Gregory I, the only other pope who earned the epithet Great, engaged anew in that struggle. From among the dozen or so of his instructions concerning the continence to be observed by the clergy, let only two be recalled here. In May 594 he instructed John, the bishop of Cagliari, that he should deprive of the sacred order anyone who after his ordination fell into the sin of flesh and violated thereby "the holy canons." The bishop should also prevent those already ordained from perishing through the same weakness. Therefore he should "take thought and check those who are candidates to Orders; first let it be examined whether they have led a continent life for many years, whether they have demonstrated a taste for the study [of Holy Scriptures], whether they like giving alms. One must also find out if they were not, by chance, bigamists [married again after they had become widowers]." To Chrysanthes, bishop of Spoleto, Gregory drew up a most spiritual picture of the ideal shepherd of souls: "A shepherd must, by obligation, give a good example in all

---

[48] See Cochini, *Apostolic Origins,* pp. 255–63.

things, he must, dying to all the passions of the flesh, already live
here below in a spiritual life, and having said goodbye to the ad-
vantages of this world, he must not be afraid of any adversity and
desire only interior goods."[49] Here was in a nutshell a good deal of
the theology of priestly celibacy as well as the call for courage in
upholding it in the face of any adversity, a call to which another
pope, also called Gregory, was to respond half a millennium later in
a way that made Church history.

Undoubtedly the foregoing rules and instructions were difficult to live up to, and especially in centuries that saw mostly social
and cultural confusion following the collapse of the Roman Empire. Abuses began to creep in; at times they came as a flood. Still
the Church kept insisting and struggling, and especially in that part
of it that kept its essential vitality through its union with the Rock,
or Peter's See. That struggle took on a gigantic proportion with the
coming of another saintly pope, the Seventh of the Gregories. His
engagement in the battle was the high point of a heroic and humanly unexplainable resistance to the forces of evil, as if to prove
once more that they will not prevail even when they concentrate
on the humanly weakest point of those who constitute the sacred
orders.

[49] Ibid., pp. 374–75 and 382.

# 4

# Ex Oriente Lux?

Those who plead for a relaxation of compulsory priestly celibacy in the Roman Catholic Church never fail to hold high the example of the Eastern Orthodox Churches. This strategy, which reasserted itself with particular force during these past decades,[1] makes much of the Council of Trullo, also called Quinisext, because it wanted to complete the legislation of the Fifth (553) and Sixth (680-81) Ecumenical Councils. While the Council of Trullo, convoked by Emperor Justinian II (685-711) in 691, reasserted the rule that priests cannot marry, nor can they remarry once widowed, it also allowed married priests to use their conjugal rights. About this latter policy it is hardly ever noted by the champions of that strategy, that it represented a *drastically* new version of a rule that had by then been publicly proclaimed for three hundred years and challenged by no Council, ecumenical or provincial.

They are just as unwilling to point out that Trullo had a sharply anti-Roman (and anti-Armenian) thrust. Against Rome

---

[1] Rather restrained is Ida Friederika Görres' report in her booklet, *Is Celibacy Outdated?*, tr. B. Waldstein-Wartenberg (Westminster MD.: The Newman Press, 1965, p. 70), that a group of Catholic laymen in Germany asked the Fathers of Vatican II to introduce the Eastern discipline in the Roman Catholic Church. Most advocates of the same idea are distinctly dreamy-eyed, as if the Eastern discipline had no serious problems of its own.

Canon 36 of Trullo reiterated Canon 28 of Chalcedon that as-
cribed to Constantinople, "the New Rome," rights and privileges
identical to the ones possessed by the old Rome. Obviously, this
could not be acceptable to Pope Sergius II (687-701), a Syriac by
birth, who formally disavowed the decisions of the Council. His
successor, John VII (705-707), returned the Acts of the Council
unsigned. Only almost a century later did a pope, Adrian I (772-
795), accept with qualifications those Acts, which he attached to
the Sixth Ecumenical Council. He did so, however, only after he
had received the profession of Faith from the Patriarch of
Constantinople which implied a recognition of the primacy of
Rome. In another hundred years or so, Pope John VIII (872-82)
reiterated the stipulation of Adrian I, namely, that the recognition
cannot include the anti-Roman Canons.

But here to be considered are the theological aspects of a development, which, because of the erstwhile involvement of political power, did not bode well for theology in general and for the
theology of priestly celibacy in particular. Political power always
aims at compromises and, given its involvement in matters relating
to the Church, it may dress its intentions, even if worthy, in references to Christian virtues. One of the problems the Emperor
wanted to be discussed by that Council, gathered in a domed hall
(Trullo) of the Imperial palace, related to irregularities apparently
widespread within the clergy. First, in Canon 3, the question of
unlawful marriages entered into by some of the clergy were taken
up at the urging of "the Pious and Christian Emperor." Some of
the clergy were married to widows, some others to servants, to
actresses, and even to harlots, or married again after they had become
widowers. The remedy aimed at enabling "those who are in the list
of the clergy, through whom the graces of the sacraments are
transmitted, that they be pure and blameless ministers, and worthy
of the spiritual sacrifice of the great God, victim and high priest at
the same time, and that it may purify them from the stains of unlawful marriages."[2]

---

[2] Quoted from R. Cholij, *Clerical Celibacy in East and West* (Herefordshire:
Flower Wright Books, 1989), pp. 9-10. The present chapter owes much to this excellent work.

Such would have been a most worthy statement had it not been followed immediately by a dubious manoeuvering about virtues. One kind of virtue, Rome's observance of ancient rules that such offenders should be barred from functioning as priests, was declared to be very strict. The other kind of virtue, followed by "those who are under the throne of this heavenly protected and Imperial City," was declared to be "the rule of humanity and condescendence." Then the Council claimed that its relaxation of those strict rules would merge the two policies into one so "that gentleness may not degenerate into licence, nor austerity into harshness."[3] Such a pious (and anti-Roman) rhetoric was not, however, needed to justify the indulgence to be shown towards those of the clergy who prior to their ordination had contracted, with no sufficient information, canonically forbidden unions.

This was not the first of the illogicalities in which the Trullo Fathers embroiled themselves. Why, one may ask, their insistence that the priest's wife should be absolutely above any suspicion as a paragon of virtue? Did not this insistence echo the rule that married priests, as well as their wives, had to observe perfect continence? The Trullo Fathers were not, of course, to be blamed for not suspecting the apocryphal character of the so-called Apostolic Constitutions that included 85 disciplinary Canons. But they honored logic in the breach as they read more into its Canon 6 than it actually contained and ignored that the same Canon forbade not only deacons and priests but also bishops to send away their wives "with the excuse of piety."[4] The Fathers of Trullo took this prohibition for permission that married deacons and priests may use their conjugal rights. In doing so, the Fathers of Trullo simply ignored that they had thereby deprived themselves of the right to impose absolute continence on bishops and, in addition, as will be shortly seen, to command them to send away their wives to a distant monastery. It was just as illogical on the part of the Fathers of Trullo to suggest, however implicitly, that a universal validity

[3] Cholij, *Clerical Celibacy*, p. 31.

[4] "Let no bishop, priest, or deacon send away his wife with the excuse of piety; if he sends her away, let him be excommunicated, and if he persists, let him be deposed." Quoted from C. Cochini, *The Apostolic Origins of Priestly Celibacy*, tr. N. Marans (Sam Fancisco: Ignatius Press, 1990), p. 263.

should be accorded to Canon 6 of the Apostolic Constitutions but not to the African Canons' emphatic reference to the apostolic rule.

Certainly, nothing new was contained in Canon 6 of Trullo which declared, with an eye on the Apostolic Canons (Constitutions), that "in no wise is it lawful for any subdeacon, deacon or presbyter after his ordination to contract matrimony, but if he shall have dared to do so, let him be deposed." Again, it had been by then an old rule that marriage must precede ordination, if it was to take place at all.[5] Canon 12 of Trullo dealt with the case of those who were elevated from priesthood to the rank of bishop. This Canon began with reporting that in Africa, Lybia and elsewhere some bishops (already married as priests) continued to have conjugal relations with their wives, a custom which the Canon reprobated in no uncertain terms while it upheld the ideal: "Since therefore it is our particular concern that all things are to be done for the edification of the people committed to our care, it has seemed good that henceforth nothing of this kind should ever occur again. And we say this not to abolish and overthrow what things were established of old by apostolic authority, but as caring for the spiritual health of the people and their progress in virtue, and lest ecclesiastical discipline suffer any reproach." Then, after quoting Saint Paul, though not directly to the purpose,[6] the Canon ordered that all offending bishops be deposed.[7] Moreover Canon 48 ordered that the wife of a priest elevated to be bishop should be immediately separated from him and enter a monastery situated at a distance from the bishop's residence. Obviously this ordinance could not be obeyed easily. It was easier to restrict the dignity of bishop to monks, celibate forever by their vows of chastity.

In all this one can see an effort to comply with universally accepted norms that were honored as having apostolic origin. The

---

[5] Ibid., p. 35.

[6] "Do all to the glory of God, give offence to no one, neither to the Jews nor to the Greeks, nor to the Church of God, even as I please all men in all things, not seeking my own profit, but the profit of many that they may be saved. Be ye imitators of me, even as I am also of Christ" (1 Cor 10:31-32).

[7] Cholij, *Clerical Celibacy*, p. 106.

Canons so far reviewed reflect, for the most part, a resolve to live up to long accepted ideals and norms. With Canon 13 this resolve suddenly changes, a fact which the Fathers of Trullo tried to dissimulate. Tellingly, Canon 13 begins with a contrast set up between the rule set by the Roman See and the rule of Apostolic perfection. According to Canon 13 the Roman rule demanded that "those who are deemed worthy to be advanced to the diaconate or presbyterate should promise to no longer cohabit with their wives." Against this the Fathers of Trullo set themselves up as the ones who were "preserving the ancient rule and apostolic perfection and order." Therefore, they continued, "we will that the lawful marriage of men who are in holy orders be from this time forward firm, by no means dissolving their union with their wives, nor depriving them from their mutual relationship at a convenient time."[8]

The idea of married priests with the right to use their conjugal rights "at a convenient time," demanded, precisely because of its novelty, some justification. The drafters of Canon 13 offered two. One was a reference to the indissolubility of marriage as a tie that foreclosed an unconditional prohibition of the exercise of marital rights. This, however, raised a disturbing question. After all, if it was legitimate, that is, virtuous for a priest to have conjugal relations with his wife, on what grounds was that right to be restricted to suitable times? But once the drafters of the Canon entered a logically dubious ground, it was clearly tempting to them to change a fact as well, namely the written record. A change it was, indeed a willful tampering with a well known document. For even if that tampering had taken place some time before the Council of Trullo convened, it is difficult to assume that none of the Fathers of Trullo had been ignorant of the genuine text of the African Canons, discussed in the preceding chapter. They, however, went on quoting a radically changed text in order to justify the previously unheard-of novelty they now proposed and indeed ordered.

The fact is that there is not a single example of that tampered text from the three centuries that separate the African Canons

---

[8] Ibid., p. 116.

from the Council of Trullo. Yet the Fathers of Trullo sorely needed
those Canons because of the reference in them to apostolic tradition. But whereas that tradition as contained in the African Canons
stood for an absolute continence, the Fathers of Trullo twice less-
ened that prohibition to "proper times," that is, the days of the Eucharistic celebration. Thus the famed Canon 13 of Trullo claims
that according to apostolic tradition it was right for married priests
to use their conjugal rights "at convenient times," because "we
know, as they who assembled at Carthage said, caring for the honest life of the clergy, that subdeacons who wait upon the Holy
Mysteries and deacons and presbyters, should abstain from their
spouses *during the periods particularly (assigned) to them,* so that what
has been handed down through the Apostles and preserved by ancient custom, we too likewise maintain, *knowing that there is a
time for all things and especially for fasting and prayer.* For it is
proper that they who assist at the divine altar should be absolutely
continent *during the time when they are handling holy things,* in order
to obtain in all simplicity what they ask from God." Having in-
serted the phrases (given in Italics), of which there is not a trace in
the Carthaginian Canons, or in any Canon (including the ones in
the Canons of the Apostolic Constitutions) enacted prior to Trullo,
the Fathers of Trullo could thunder: "If therefore, anyone shall have
dared, contrary to the Apostolic Canons, to deprive any of those
who are in holy orders, presbyter, deacon or subdeacon, of cohabi-
tation and relations with his lawful wife, let him be deposed. In
like manner also if any presbyter or deacon on pretence of piety
has dismissed his wife, let him be excluded from communion; and
if he persist, let him be deposed."[9]

The new legislation involved the Eastern Churches in stark illogicalities as well as serious practical problems. The former is best
illustrated by the defense of Trullo which C. Knetes, Archivist of
the Great Church, Constantinople, offered early in this century in
the pages of *The Journal of Theological Studies,* a circumstance that as-
sures it some significance. Knetes acknowledged the obvious,

---

[9] Cholij gives (pp. 119-121) in parallel columns the text of Canon 13 and of the
corresponding ruling of the African Canons, using bold-face type to show the
differences and underlining for the similarities.

namely, that the Council of Trullo "evidently modified the canons of Carthage and, by adding a few words, changed their original meaning, so that they were made to accord with the Council's own views on the subject." But then he claimed that "the decisions of the Synod of Carthage referred only to local practice, while those of the Council of Trullo are of general application."[10] But if it was legitimate for Trullo (and Knetes) to invoke the Canon of Carthage precisely because it professed to present the apostolic tradition, how could it have a purely local bearing?

The expression "general application" hides another, no less serious illogicality, from the Orthodox perspective. By taking, as does Knetes, the Council of Trullo for an Ecumenical Council, the Orthodox Church, now consisting of fully independent (autocephalic) Churches, is depriving itself for all practical purposes of its ability to modify that famed Canon of Trullo. Their problem is not merely whether it is necessary or not to "enter into interminable and subtle discussions as to how far the Western Church was or was not right" in questioning that ecumencial character. Their problem goes beyond the need to prove that the ecumenicity of that Council is assured by the fact that it "has always been acknowledged throughout the Eastern Church." Their problem peaks in their inability to change that law which, according to Knetes, "indisputably proves that the Eastern Orthodox Church followed faithfully the gradual development of the question, and the last official enactment fixed her discipline." For according to Knetes, that discipline "can only be changed or superseded, in case of necessity, by an authority similar to which it owes its establishment."[11] Yet, as will be seen, necessity to change that discipline raises its dubious head, although nothing indicates the coming of another ecumenical Council. Instead of a liberation, Trullo appears more and more as a straitjacket within the orthodox perspective.

---

[10] C. Knetes, "Ordination and Matrimony in the Eastern Orthodox Church," *Journal of Theological Studies* 11 (1910), p. 355. Knetes' two-part article (pp. 348-400 and 481-513) begins with quotations from 3rd- and 4th-century Church Fathers concerning priestly marriage, a list, which, like many similar efforts, lost much of its scholarly force following the publication of Cochini's book.

[11] Ibid., pp. 508-09.

Meanwhile there began a steady flow of insinuations and accusations from the Greek side that according to Rome the law of continence dissolved the priest's marriage, or implied a rejection of marriage itself, or at least that in Rome's eyes marriage was something impure by itself. The Fathers of Trullo ignored that the consent of wives to live a life of continence had always been requested prior to the ordination of their spouses. The Fathers of Trullo failed to consider above all two theological points. One, a dilemma, implied that not Rome, but the Fathers of Trullo were guilty of those insinuations: if conjugal relations were honorable, why then bar them during the day preceding and following the Eucharistic celebration? The other was also a dilemma: if the bishop, because of his office, had to live a life of perfect continence, why not the priest? Was not the priest equal to the bishop with respect to his Eucharistic powers? Did not the Canons of Carthage speak of bishops too in the same breath that they spoke of priests and deacons? By keeping this detail under cover, the Fathers of Trullo flagrantly abused of the Council of Carthage. In doing so they provided a most powerful reason for posterity to look upon their reasoning as patently inconsistent, in fact contradictory, not only in respect to bishops but to priests as well.[12]

There was the further problem, which became acute in modern times, for Orthodox priests who became widowers. What reason was left by Canon 13 against their remarrying? Could the spirit of that Canon be reconciled with animated declarations that no valid marriage could be contracted by a priest? A mere century after the Council of Trullo a Syrian theologian, John Dara, denounced the attempt of a priest to marry as being as bad as when a father tries to marry his own daughter.[13] The theological reasons given by John Dara are certainly revealing as they run counter to the "moderate" approach advocated by Canon 13. He begins with saying that Moses separated from his wife after receiving his call

[12] "All the arguments used by the Trullan Fathers," wrote H. Crouzel, "can be turned against them, since they impose on bishops not only continence, but a complete separation from their wives as well." See his "Celibacy and Ecclesiastical Continence: The Motives Involved," in J. Coppens (ed.), *Priesthood and Celibacy* (Milano: Editrice Ancora, 1972), p. 492.

[13] Cholij, *Clerical Celibacy*, p. 49.

from God, and even more so was this the case with the apostles after Christ had called them: "Peter and the other married apostles did not approach their wives again after having followed the Lord: just as priests ought to abstain from carnal union and unite themselves only to God. . . . It is through virginity that priests are to please God, like monks . . . ; furthermore the priest is the father of all the faithful, men and women. Whoever occupies this dignity among the faithful and then marries a woman, is like someone who has married his own daughter. And this is a great scandal."[14]

One may, of course, agree instinctively with this reasoning. But if one looks for a theological rationale, one looks in vain for it in Canon 13 of Trullo, which in fact blocks the theological perspective for a satisfactory resolution of the problem posed by it. The strain was already apparent in Canon 3 of Trullo, where continent priests are described as proper intercessors. It is continence, wrote John Zonaras, one of the great Byzantine canonists of the 12th century, that enables those in the sacred orders to carry out with no impediment their intercessory role with God on behalf of the people: "But if these same men deprive themselves, through their own fault [incontinence] of their freedom of speech, how could they fulfill their role as intercessors for the good of others?"[15]

Another instance of this perplexity was provided by the Coptic Jacobite writer, Ibn Saba'ibn Zakarya, who flourished towards the end of the 13th century. In chapter 43 of his "The Precious Pearl of Ecclesiastical Sciences," he takes up the problem posed by the priest who wants to marry a second time, after the death of his first wife. The peremptory answer of Ibn Saba'ibn Zakarya is that a priest who remarries renders himself unworthy of fulfilling any priestly function: "The dignity of the priest is extremely great: it is like that of the inhabitants of heaven, namely the angels and the twenty-four Elders who, standing before the throne of the Majesty, intercede for all creatures." As an intercessor the priest ranks with the angels, "a terrestrial angel, a celestial man."

[14] Ibid., p. 49.
[15] Ibid., p. 7 (PG 138, col. 32c).

As such, if he "gives himself to the passions of the body and to carnal commerce, he falls from the society of men to that of ani-
mals."[16] Such a reasoning was already difficult to reconcile with
the practice of ordaining one who had already been married, and
it certainly ran counter to the thrust of Canon 13 of Trullo that
practically forced marriage upon priests.

Indeed not so much the theological myopia of Canon 13 but
the ecclesiastical practice generated by it cast the strongest doubt
on its merit. The "convenient time" and its converse the "appropriate time," as stipulated by that Canon, varied from place to place
and from time to time, involving ever more problems and tensions.
The early practice of one-day continence grew eventually to three
and even to longer periods in some Oriental Churches. Thus in
the 18th century the period was a week in the Chaldean Church,
whereas in some parts of the Armenian Church it could extend to
forty days. Infringements of this rule entailed severe punishments.
In the Syrian (Jacobite) Church the punishment was that given to
adulterers. A priest of the Slav churches who approached his wife
on the same day after celebrating the Eucharist had to fast on
bread and water for forty days.[17]

Who could, however, ever prove that a married priest did not
sleep with his wife during the night immediately preceding the
celebration of the Eucharist? Thus, to keep the practical effective-
ness of Canon 13, it was soon decided in the Orthodox Churches
that priests should not celebrate the Eucharist every day, for a daily
celebration would obviously scandalize the faithful! Here was another departure from at least the custom of Africa, where daily celebration was a rule already in Saint Cyprian's time. Balsamon, the
12th-century Greek canonist, reports, in a tone suggesting he was
scandalized, that in Constantinople priests were celebrating daily.
Elsewhere priests were divided into groups, each given the right to
celebrate the Eucharist daily for a week.

No wonder that celibate secular priests were less and less tolerated. Canon 13 was fully responsible for the imposition of marriage on all priests, except the monks, of course. By the 11th cen-

---

[16] Ibid., pp. 49-50.
[17] Ibid., p. 157.

tury no celibate could expect to be ordained to priesthood in the
secular clergy of the Greek and Slav Churches. Moreover it was
also claimed that apostolic rulings prohibited such ordinations.[18]
Celibate priests were soon removed to the bishop's house to oc-
cupy themselves with administrative functions. As late as 1923 civil
legislation in Greece prohibited the assignment of a celibate priest
to a parish post in the countryside. Other Orthodox churches too
required marriage as a pre-condition that a priest be given a pastoral ministry.[19] All this did not fail to establish a chasm between the
secular clergy and the monks in the Oriental Churches. Within the
clergy itself there emerged a hereditary priesthood, with the unwritten rule that sons of priests should become priests whether
they felt a calling or not. In fact it became a custom to attribute to
such children the right to be ordained. In Russia special schools
were set up for them which further strengthened their presumed
right to ordination.

    The gradual elimination of the daily Eucharist, the develop-
ment of a poorly trained and spiritually unmotivated priestly caste,
the holding under suspicion of lifelong continence by priests—
such were some of the hardly beneficial results of Canon 13 of
Trullo. Little attention has been paid to this in the Oriental Orthodox Churches. In fact these problems seem to be wilfully ignored,
especially in "ecumenical" contexts. Very typical in this regard is an
essay by D. Constantelos, which has the further weakness that the
author was unaware of the inanity of invoking the Paphnutius
story as a proof that the Eastern Churches have always resisted the
compulsory imposition of full continence (and celibacy) on
priests.[20] Not a word in that essay about the apocryphal character
of the Apostolic Constitutions and of its Canons, nor is there any
attention paid to the fact that just because many bishops were married, this does not mean that they could (or did) legitimately use
their marital rights. Constantelos overlooks the fact that a bishop's

---

[18] See ibid, pp. 134–35.

[19] Cholij notes (p. 137) that as far as he could ascertain, this is a universal rule in
Eastern Orthodox Churches.

[20] See W. Bassett and P. Huizing (eds.), *Celibacy in the Church* (New York: Herder
and Herder, 1972), pp. 30-38.

married status does not necessarily mean that he sired children while a bishop.[21] Forced comparisons between the "puritanical" and "rigid" Latin discipline and the "very humane" Eastern discipline, full of respect for the mystery of the Incarnation, are revealing enough about a thwarted theological logic. This comes even more sharply to the fore in Constantelos' roundabout recognition that there is something very defective about Canon 13 of Trullo and the practice it imposed in the name of humaneness. For modern Orthodox priests want in ever larger numbers a change of the rule that restricts them to one marriage per life. This question cannot be resolved with a facile reference to the fact that most Orthodox bishops are "conservative." The use of such words denotes escapism from theological categories to politically or "humanly" correct ones. When such categories replace the genuinely theological ones, even the authority of bishops, by which the Orthodox set so great a store in their resistance to the papacy, will degenerate into a purely sociological category to be readily manipulated by publicity pressures.

These points will hardly be appreciated even by uniate Eastern Orthodox who are obsessed by a sense of ecclesiastical nationalism. This can also blind one to some obvious historical facts, as shown clearly in an essay by Petro B. T. Bilaniuk.[22] For even prior to the publication of Cochini's book it was simply not true that there was an airtight case in favor of the view that priestly celibacy was purely optional prior to the early 4th century and that married priests could use their conjugal rights. The claim that Eastern Orthodoxy represents the biblical approach to sexuality is at best an inept handwaving, but not theology. Again the

---

[21] Constantelos should have recalled the case of Gregory the Enlightener (died c. 328), the first Catholicos of Armenia and the originator of a family dynasty of bishops. Gregory's two sons were born in his youth. His immediate successor, Aristakes, was a celibate. His other son, Verthanes, occupied the throne when an old man, and the latter's son Yousik was a widower by the time of his elevation. It can also be shown that chronological data indicate that Gregory of Nazianzus, the Younger, was born to his father before the latter became a bishop. See Cholij, p. 73. Constantelos also misconstrues the statement of Synesius, as if his letter were a proof that as a bishop he lived with his wife. Quite the contrary!

[22] "Celibacy and Eastern Tradition," in Frein, *Celibacy: The Necessary Option,* pp. 32-72.

Paphnutius story is paraded as an ace-card, although even prior to 1968 strong reasons could be marshalled against its authenticity. It is a howler to claim that "in the fourth and fifth centuries there were no strict laws in the Eastern Churches concerning celibacy and married clergy."[23] Further, it is hardly an exercise in the theology of priestly celibacy to claim, as Bilaniuk does, that Rome took a deplorable approach towards priestly marriages once the use of the Greek language was dying out there. The same is true of his claim that "as long as Rome was closely linked to the Eastern Churches, everything was perfect there" because there was no mention of celibacy but only of virginity.[24] For Bilaniuk this means that Rome was "Westernized." By whom? Or should one say that the Greeks and all nationalities under Eastern Orthodoxy have the right to be themselves, but Rome and the Latins have no such right?

Fortunately, Bilaniuk's torrid Ukranian nationalism does not represent the standard of theological perception of Catholics of Eastern Rite united with Rome. They perceived early on the seriousness of the defects, enumerated above, in Canon 13 of Trullo. Their perception is largely ignored by those Catholics who, with a reference to the Orthodox example (left in studied vagueness, of course), push for the relaxation of the law of celibacy in the Catholic Church. A good example of that keen perception was provided in the prominent context of Vatican I. There the Armenian archbishop Melchior Nasarian called attention to the marked increase in the number of Armenian Uniate Catholics since Benedict XIV, who had promoted the education of celibate clergy there. Celibate priests, the Archbishop argued, were able to give themselves wholly to the service of their flock.[25] The Archbishop also urged the Council that it openly address itself to problems to

---

[23] Ibid., p. 44.

[24] Ibid.

[25] Just before Vatican II, a Catholic Archbishop reported the following remark, which a uniate priest, as they were flying to Rome, addressed to him: "One celibate priest can do the work of four married priests." Unfortunately I no longer have the report which I read, I believe in 1958, in *The Monitor* of the Archdiocese of San Francisco.

which a *lack* of a law of celibacy in the Uniate Oriental Church had given rise.[26]

One step the Council took in that direction consisted in re-affirming the directions given in 1858 to the Rumanian Archbishop of the Ruthenian Province of Alba-Julia and Fogaras (Transylvania). The Synod held in 1872 by that Province was the first to implement those directives that included a tactful promotion of celibacy for those to be ordained henceforth. Other Uniate Churches followed suit. The Fathers of the Syrian Synod of Sharfeh decided in 1888 that all their clergy should be celibate, leaving intact the rights of clergy already married. Ten years later the Coptic Church adopted obligatory celibacy, with the proviso that orthodox Coptic priests who rejoined their uniate brethren might continue in their married state.[27] There much was also made of the conflict that obtains between the duties of a priest as the spiritual father of his congregation and his duties as a father of a family and as a husband.

Further impetus in that direction was given through the instructions of Pius X about the daily reception of the Eucharist, which was not at all the norm considered by Canon 13 of Trullo. Much less notice has, however, been given to the fact that the same instructions indirectly nullified previous counsels whereby married lay couples were advised to abstain from conjugal union for one or several days before communion. Clearly then, the celibacy required from priests implies more than to secure proper spiritual disposition for the reception of the Blessed Sacrament. One has therefore to consider, as Cholij aptly notes, priestly ordination as a consecration which is "qualitatively different" from the one conferred by baptism.[28]

But this question, which has a bearing on the theology of priestly celibacy even within the Latin rite, becomes all the more complex as Rome, in order to facilitate reunion, often made statements that amount to much more than a mere toleration of the Eastern practice, established in Trullo. Particularly relevant in this

---

[26] Cholij, *Clerical Celibacy*, p. 175

[27] See ibid., p. 177.

[28] Ibid., p. 178.

respect are statements made by popes in this century. They went much further than to praise the exemplary, heroic priests of the Oriental rite. In his Encyclical *Ad Catholici sacerdotii* Pius XI leaned over backward, lest his encomium on priestly celibacy would be taken for an indirect slighting of the Oriental discipline: "We do not wish that what we said in commendation of clerical celibacy should be interpreted as though it were our mind in any way to blame, or, as it were, disapprove the different discipline legitimately prevailing in the Oriental Church."[29] Of course, this claim may appear to be offset by what immediately follows: "What we have said has been meant solely to exalt in the Lord something We consider one of the purest glories of the Catholic priesthood; something which seems to us to correspond better to the desires of the Sacred Heart of Jesus and to his purposes in regard to priestly souls."[30]

Very recent official utterances of Rome have come close to attributing ecumenical validity to the Trullan legislation on married priests. Vatican II's Decree on the Ministry and Life of the Priests states: "While this most sacred Synod recommends ecclesiastical celibacy, it in no way intends to change the different discipline which lawfully prevails in the Eastern Churches. It lovingly exhorts all those who have received the priesthood after marriage to persevere in their sacred vocation, and continue to spend their lives fully and generously for the flock committed to them." In his Encyclical *Sacerdotalis caelibatus*, Paul VI declared: "If the legislation of the Eastern Church is different in the matter of discipline with regard to clerical celibacy, as was finally established by the Council in Trullo, held in the year 692, and which has been clearly recognized by the Second Vatican Council, this is due to the different historical background of that most noble part of the Church, a situation which the Holy Spirit has providentially and supernaturally influenced."[31]

---

[29] From the English translation published by the National Catholic Welfare Conference (Washington D. C. 1935), pp. 31-32.

[30] Ibid., p. 32.

[31] Quoted from the English translation, *Encyclical Letter on Priestly Celibacy of Pope Paul VI* (Washington: United States Catholic Conference, 1967), pp. 16-17 (#38). The Pope referred to the Decree on priesthood, #16.

It should be noted that this statement is not really a recognition of the Council of Trullo as such. Nor should the reference to the presence there of the providential and supernatural influence of the Holy Spirit be taken incautiously. For in the same Encyclical Paul VI makes a pointed reference to the unconditionally celibate status required from bishops in the Eastern Churches and to the fact that there priests cannot contract marriage after their ordination: "This indicates that these venerable Churches also possess to a certain extent the principle of a celibate priesthood, of which the bishops possess the summit and fullness of the observance of celibacy."[32]

The qualifier, "to a certain extent," and Pius XI's reference to the desire of the Sacred Heart, would hardly satisfy those Orientals (and their Western admirers) who hold the Eastern discipline of celibacy to be far superior to the one in the West. Apart from this the statements of both popes leave unanswered the question so well formulated by Cholij: "Should not the priests even of the Oriental Churches be celibate if celibacy is indeed the most adequate and fruitful way of living the priesthood of Christ? If the celibate priesthood is related closely to the priesthood of the Gospel, and infused with the Gospel spirit, and the Church has always desired the best for the priesthood, namely strict celibacy, how is it that the 'Eastern' priesthood is in effect excluded from this vision and these ideals?"[33]

Yet, it is the East that produced some of the most soaring praises of priestly celibacy. A leader in this respect was Saint John Chrysostom, whose erstwhile renown in the East as *the* Church Father *par excellence* went into eclipse in later times obviously because of his encomiums of the See of Peter,[34] but perhaps also because he assigned a superlative dignity to the priesthood in terms of priestly purity. His *De sacerdotio* gives the lie to sundry claims that Eastern Orthodoxy gave equal dignity to married and non-married priesthood. Chrysostom would certainly not have

---

[32] Ibid., p. 17 (#40).

[33] Cholij, *Clerical Celibacy*, pp. 195-97.

[34] A point well made by Dom John Chapman in chapter IV, "St. Chrysostom on St. Peter," in his *Studies on the Early Papacy* (London: Sheed and Ward, 1928), p. 73.

countenanced the notion that married priests would have conjugal relations with their wives, however intermittently. In the section where he describes the glory that devolves on the priesthood on account of the celestial work performed by the priest, he immediately refers to the angelic purity the priest must therefore possess. Further, the section ends with a comparison between the power of earthly parents and the fatherly power of the priest: "Parents bring us into this life; priests into the life to come. Parents cannot avert bodily death nor drive away the onset of disease; priests have often saved the soul that is sick and at the point of death, by making the punishment milder for some, and preventing others from ever incurring it. . . . Again, natural parents cannot help their sons, if they fall foul of the prominent and powerful, but priests have often appeased the anger of God himself, to say nothing of rulers and kings."[35]

Had Chrysostom endorsed in advance the perspective of Trullo, he would not have listed the dangers posed to the priesthood by certain women, whom "the divine law excluded from this sacred ministry, yet they forcibly push themselves in, and since they can do nothing personally, they do everything by proxy."[36] Among the duties of the priesthood the saint enumerated the fearless preaching of God's law, regardless of the resentment and persecution the priest might thereby invite upon himself. Did not the married priesthood, inaugurated by Trullo, prove particularly weak in that respect?

Further, the saint described the purity befitting the priesthood in terms that would hardly have fallen within the perspective of Trullo. According to the saint the purity demanded from the priest should be far greater and more robust than the one a hermit may muster, because the priest is constantly in the midst of temptations, which can only be mastered "by the practice of unremitting self-denial and strict self-discipline." In what follows we have one of the finest of those graphic passages that render an unsurpassed quality to Chrysostom's eloquence: "There is enough to upset the

---

[35] *Saint John Chrysostom. Six Books on the Priesthood,* tr. with introduction by G. Neville (Crestwood, NY: Saint Vladimir Seminary, 1984), p. 74 (III, 4–5).

[36] Ibid., p. 78 (III, 9).

priest's spirit—unless it is desiccated by the very exacting demands of self-control—in pretty faces, affected movements, a mincing walk, a silvery voice, eyes dark with shadow, painted cheeks, complicated hair styles, tinted hair, expensive clothes, gold ornaments in plenty, fine jewelry, sweet perfumes, and all the other tricks of womanhood."[37]

But the saint would not have been a true observer of reality, if he had not noted the opposite. Only in these very days of postmodern decadence, when fashion promoters hawk studiedly sloppy jeans, rumpled blouses, and nonfunctional boots, can one really flavor the saint's warning about priests, who, though successful in escaping the snares of luxurious sex appeal, have been caught by the opposite: "Even a neglected appearance, unkempt hair, slovenly clothing, absence of make-up, simple behaviour, artless language, an unstudied gait, a natural voice, a life of poverty, and despised unprotected lonely existence, have led the beholder first to compassion and then to utter downfall." And in this age which pushes women into all sorts of leadership positions, there is an eery touch to the saint's registering the sad, dangerous consequences for priests arising from the honor some women bestow on them: "Those bestowed by women damage the sinews of self-restraint and often destroy them altogether, when a man does not know how to keep continual watch against such insidious temptations."[38] One wonders whether the Fathers of Trullo would not have done better if, instead of drawing up new Canons, they would have ordered thousands of copies to be made of the saint's not too long work on priesthood. This way they would have powerfully contributed to that upward pull which all the saints of the Oriental Churches considered their prime duty and calling to strengthen. Were there any among the well over two hundred bishop-signatories of Trullo whom the Eastern Orthodox Churches, let alone the Churches in the West, eventually venerated as saints, that is, Christians always pulling heroically in the upward direction?

[37] Ibid., p. 138 (VI, 2).
[38] Ibid., p. 138.

For that greatest doctor of the Oriental Church minced no words about the duty of strengthening that upward pull precisely because he had so high a view of the ministry to be fulfilled by priests. The ministry consisted in a manifold intercession for mankind before God: "I do not think that even the confidence of Moses and Elijah is adequate for this great intercession . . . . He must so far surpass all those for whom he intercedes in all qualities as one in authority ought properly to surpass those under his charge. But when he invokes the Holy Spirit and offers that awful sacrifice and keeps on touching the common Master of us all, tell me, where shall we rank him?" While contemplating that awesome summit of priestly dignity the saint refers to purity: "Consider how spotless should the hands be that administer these things, how holy the tongue that utters these words. Ought anyone to have a purer and holier soul than one who is to welcome this great Spirit? At that moment angels attend the priest, and the whole dais and the sanctuary are thronged with heavenly powers in honor of Him who lies there."[39] It was on this note that the saint began his consideration on the priesthood: "The priest must be so pure, that if he were to be lifted up and placed in the heavens themselves, he might take a place in the midst of the Angels."[40]

Of the many other similar voices from the East let us here briefly recall only a few. According to Saint Ephraem (c. 306–373), "it is not enough for the priest and the name of the priesthood, it is not enough, I say, for him who offers up the living body [of Christ], to cleanse his soul and tongue and hand and make spotless his whole body; but he must at all times be absolutely and preeminently pure, because he is established as a mediator between God and the human race. May He be praised who made His servants clean!"[41] Saint Epiphanius of Salamis (c. 316–403) spoke of the "incredible honour and dignity" of the priesthood.[42]

---

[39] Ibid., pp. 140–41 (VI, 4).

[40] Ibid (III, 4). This statement is also quoted in the Encyclical of Pius XI.

[41] *Carmina Nisibaena,* carm. xviii. ed. Bickel p. 112. Quoted ibid.

[42] *Panacea against all Heresies,* 59, 4 (PG vol. 41, col. 1024), a work written between 374 and 377.

Such voices of the East are hardly the voice of Trullo. The ideal of priesthood as proclaimed by Trullo is not something that would strengthen the credibility of the motto, *Ex oriente lux,* whatever its dubious provenance. The light needed by the Orientals can come to them only from what is "the West" to them. Of course, Rome too is subject to the pastoral rule followed already by Saint Paul, as well as to the latter's recognition that there is an inexorably logic to the fullness of truth. It was not possible to feed the neophyte Corinthians forever on milk (1 Cor 3:2). Before long he had to resort to dispensing them solid food, that is, telling them the truth plainly and fully. And so it is with the present-day ecumenical concern of Rome. Sooner or later, the question of plain and full truth forces itself onto the center stage.

This happened when Rome had to point out grave defects in the final ARCIC (Anglican Roman Catholic Interfaith Commission) report on ministry. In an age when nobody is willing to be treated otherwise than as a mature adult, it did not make a good psychological impression that Rome did not seem to treat the Anglicans in this way. In excusing its policy of not spelling out early enough the points that cannot be "negotiated," Rome referred to the need of a friendly atmosphere to be first established. To create such an atmosphere demands, of course, much tactfulness, especially when the task is to cope with centuries of hostile feelings. Still, truth will come out, and at times in the not too long run. This had to be experienced in a memorable way by John Paul II, who, more than any of his recent predecessors, made stunning symbolic gestures towards the separated brethren. He did not refuse, only a mere five months before the Church of England ordained its first women priests, to accept from the Archbishop of Canterbury a chalice as a symbol of an eventual reunion. Yet only two months after that wholly misguided "ordination" of some thirty women in Bristol, John Paul II was forced to declare infallibly that the Church has no authority to ordain women.[43] Rome had to recognize that its policy, supported by many signal gestures of good-will, of seeking to find in the Church of England a bridgehead towards

[43] For details, see my report, "Authoritatively No Authority to Ordain Women," *The Wanderer,* June 30, 1994, pp. 1 and 8.

the less liturgically inclined Protestant Churches might not bring the expected result.[44]

Something similar may be in store for Rome's cultivation of most friendly relations with Eastern Orthodox Churches. During the Council of Trent many thought that the granting of the use of the chalice and even of marriage to priests could be the means to bring Protestants back into the true fold. It was Protestants who perceived most forcefully that such concessions did not touch on the essentials. Of course, Eastern Orthodoxy possesses in full the priesthood and with it the full sacramental system, both of which Luther roundly rejected in his *On the Babylonian Captivity of the Church*. But the same Eastern Orthodoxy could not effectively oppose the penetration, into its theological academies, of the Protestant principle of private judgment as something superior to the voice of its hierarchy, which itself stands hopelessly divided into national units.[45]

Very recent denunciations by Eastern Orthodox patriarchs and Synods of the primacy and infallibility of the Bishop of Rome, reveal the root of the problem, which is ecclesiological. This ecclesiological root pushes itself very visibly above the surface in the defense which E. Meyendorff wrote on behalf of the Eastern Orthodox practice of ordaining married men to the priesthood. The defense was prompted by the unconditional condemnation of artificial birth control in the Encyclical *Humanae vitae* of Paul VI. Meyendorff did not go along with that condemnation, although "local [orthodox] Church authorities may have issued statements on the matter identical to that of the Pope." Then follows his admission which shows, to anyone with open eyes, the deep penetration of the Protestant principle of private judgment into Orthodox theological circles: "In any case," Meyendorff states, as if it were something far from being debatable and controversial, "it has *never* been the Church's practice to give moral guidance by issuing stan-

---

[44] This became all too clear on the occasion of the visit of the Archbishop of Canterbury to Rome in early December 1996.

[45] This process gained strong impetus with the Slavophile movement spearheaded by S. Khomiakov in the middle of the 19th century. For details, see my *Les Tendances nouvelles de l'ecclésiologie* (1957; Rome: Herder & Herder, 1961), pp. 103–110.

dard formulas claiming universal validity on questions which actually require a personal act of conscience." Therefore Meyendorff
has to state that "the question of birth control and of its acceptable
forms can only be solved by individual Christian couples."[46]

The claim that the Church, that is, the Orthodox Eastern
Church never issued guidance, nay strict rules with universal
validity flies in the face of facts. The Council of Trullo, which is the
basis of Meyendorff's defense of his Church's almost dictatorial
practice of ordaining only married men to serve as parish priests,
contains more than one strict precept of universal validity, to say
nothing of ecumenical councils, held before and after, and recognized as such by the East. But the real rub in Meyendorff's position
is that he implicitly takes married sexual morality out of the hands
of an ecumenical council. He cannot therefore hold that an ecumenical gathering of bishops can speak with an authority against
which there is no further appeal, an outcome very destructive for
the cogency of the orthodox ecclesiological position. This is far
more revealing about it than the unlikelihood that such a Council
would ever be held again. It is by voicing that unlikelihood that
Meyendorff concludes his sympathetic discussion of the growing
desire that bishops should be selected also from the ranks of married clergy.[47]

Compared with these points, rather unimportant should seem
Meyendorff's defense of the Trullan legislation. According to him,
the Orthodox rule of ordaining men already married is justified by
the distractions and instability that go with courting: "Dating, pref-
erential treatment, preoccupation with externals cannot be considered legitimate for a man [aspiring to be] in charge of human
souls, and who is supposed to be dedicated *only* to bringing them
into the Kingdom of God" (Italics added). Apparently Saint Paul
got it all wrong in saying that "the married man is busy with the
world's demands and occupied with pleasing his wife. This means
that he is divided" (1 Cor 7:33), that is, he cannot be dedicated

---

[46] E. Meyendorff, *Marriage: An Orthodox Perspective* (New York, St. Vladimir
Seminary Press, 1970), p. 84.

[47] Ibid., p. 55.

*only* to the task specified by Meyendorff. Sensing the horns of the dilemma on which he has impaled himself, Meyendorff defends with an ecclesiological argument the Eastern Orthodox rule that forbids a widowed priest to remarry: "While in the first case what is involved is only pastoral propriety and discipline, in the second case the Church, by requiring absolute monogamy of the clergy, protects the scriptural, doctrinal and sacramental teaching on marriage."[48] His sudden shift from priesthood to marriage should seem telling. Those among Catholics who still appreciate consistency will know what to think. The others will keep invoking the example of the Oriental Churches on behalf of their push for optional celibacy and ignore the salient point: saddled by an inconsistent ecclesiology, Eastern Orthodoxy cannot argue consistently about the marriage of those who are the beneficiaries of the sacrament of priesthood. The inconsistency of Trullo casts indeed a very long shadow.

Ecclesiological is indeed the ultimate ground of the celibacy of the priesthood and apostolic has to be the ground of a sound ecclesiology. To talk of celibacy's apostolic origins is to stake out an ecclesiological ground, the only ground on which it can be justified. Only within such a perspective will priestly celibacy appear as an ideal that calls for the highest respect and deserves to be protected by an unremitting pull upward. The moving devotion toward the Mother of God in Eastern Orthodox Churches is rightly looked upon as a most powerful source of grace in matters where arguments seem to fail. The Virgin Mother of God embodies undying ideals of purity and continence that have a logic reaching far beyond ordinary reasoning. She is the woman clothed in the sun (Rev 12:1), because her womb was the depository of the One the prophet called the Sun of Justice who spreads healing rays (Mal 3:20). Immediately before that Sun appeared, Zacharias pictured him as the *oriens ex alto,* the source of eternal light that "will shine

---

[48] Second enlarged edition, 1984, p. 67. One may, of course, despair of a meeting of minds between Rome and Constantinople as long as an Orthodox theologian of repute, such as Meyendorff, writes that while in the Roman Church marriage cannot be dissolved because it is a legal contract, in Orthodoxy the indissolubility of marriage rests on viewing it as a sacrament (1st ed. p. 42).

on those who sit in darkness and in the shadow of death" (Lk 2:79). Wherever He rises, be it in the East or in the West, He rises on high so that man may rise with Him from his fallen state and be no longer a Jew or a Greek but the new creature. It is this process which is most effectively served by priestly celibacy according to the very best testimony of the Eastern Church.

# 5

# Celibacy Legislated

The slightest reminder of a connection between priestly celibacy and ecclesiastical law gives a very negative impression in an age that boasts of its distaste for organized religion as well as for secular legislation. The grounds for that distaste deserve a brief scrutiny, if for no other reason than to notice its rank inconsistency. To dislike the law just because it imposes restraint on one's behavior can hardly be reconciled with demands for legal protection. Nor can it be claimed consistently that all forms of behavior should be protected by the law, for in that case conflicts alone would be legalized. This outcome is increasingly noticeable in the legislatively sanctioned rush toward sheer pragmatism. Beneath that pragmatism there lurks a radical relativism, which, with its utter illogicality, does not fail to invite anarchy. This self-defeating nature of relativism does not necessarily dawn on its champions. Auguste Comte, the father of positivism, was fond of stating in a most positive tone, "Nothing is absolute, all is relative," as if he had not thereby made an absolutist claim.[1] In declaring that "Everything absolute belongs to pathology," Nietzsche could not, by the very

---

[1] See E. Gilson, *The Unity of Philosophical Experience* (New York: Charles Scribner's Sons, 1937), p. 278.

125

nature of the matter, offer an accurate self-diagnosis.[2] So much for the logical wages of divorcing positive law from natural law, its indispensable foundation embodying absolute truths.

No less illogical is the thinking of those who dream about a non-organized religion. A religion that embraces only the individual can hardly justify the effort to propagate itself through the organism known as society. A strictly individualistic religion implies a solipsism whose advocates have no other right than enjoying absolute privacy. As long as religion embraces not only the individual but also his or her relation to others, religion will take on some organizational aspects. The more a religion is about one's duties toward one's neighbors, the more it will entail some legislation. For even if one's religious duties towards one's neighbor are purely negative, the effort to avoid hurting others or giving them any offense will have to conform to some very positive rules. Such rules are present in all branches of Buddhism, perhaps the least organizational of all religions.

Therefore, on a purely logical ground it should seem obvious that to the extent in which a religion implies positive obligations, its organizational character becomes prominent in a legislative sense. No higher or more sweeping positive obligations can be thought of than the two great commandments: to love God from one's whole heart, and to love one's neighbor as oneself. A revelation summed up in such a way had to be replete with laws. This is certainly true about biblical revelation from its very inception on. Abraham received not only a special call from God but also some laws. They aimed at perpetuating the tangible, societal continuation of the Covenant between God and Abraham as well as his progeny. That Covenant was not a pact that man could initiate at will, but the expression of God's absolute will about man.

Underlying the vastness of the Mosaic legislation is the perception that religion is man's recognition of his duty to show unconditional obedience to God's will. Christ referred to the sacredness of that will when he said that he came "not to abolish

---

[2] This aphorism (#154 in Nietzsche's *Beyond Good and Evil* ) begins as follows: "Objection, evasion, joyous distrust, and love of irony, are signs of health."

the Law and the Prophets, but to fulfill them" (Mt 5:17). In the same breath he conjured up the entire future of the Kingdom of God he was bringing about as the gradual fulfillment of law: "Of this much I assure you: until heaven and earth pass away, not the smallest letter of the law, not the smallest part of a letter shall be done away with, until it all comes true" (Mt 5:18). No higher praise could be accorded to "the Law and the Prophets" or the will of God about man than Christ's declaration that they are summed up in the two great commandments, the love of God and the love of neighbor (Mt 22:40). The divine will expressed a supreme justice and order which man had to make his own if he was to live and live eternally. This is why Christ insisted that if his followers were to enter the Kingdom of God, they should possess a "justice" surpassing that of the Pharisees and of the Scribes (Mt 5:20).

This superior kind of justice included not only the love of one's neighbors, but also the love of one's enemies. One even had to pray for one's persecutors (Mt 5:44). Clearly, the love in question, whereby Christ wanted his followers to be made perfect as their Father in heaven is perfect (Mt 5:48), was not a matter of sentimentalism. Christ therefore could not encourage anti-law sentiments when he set a stunning standard, totally at variance with accepted norms of behavior: Whereas "the rulers of the Gentiles lord it over them [their subjects], and their great men exercise authority over them, . . . whoever wishes to be great among you shall be your servant and whoever wishes to be first among you shall be your slave." But he himself immediately clarified the paradoxical nature of this startling injunction. All that self-abasement and self-denial had to serve the same purpose which was the very purpose of his own self-abasement: "The Son of Man has not come to be served but to serve and to give his life as a ransom for many" (Mt 20:28, Mk 10:45). Whatever else they were supposed to preach authoritatively, this was certainly to be included in their message. They had already been told that only those would be called great in the Kingdom of Heaven who while teaching those commandments also practiced them (Mt 5:19).

It is therefore most justified to see something very biblical in efforts to legislate comportment within the Church. Only if Christ had been a dreamer would he not have spent much of his efforts on the selection and education of the Twelve, whom he ultimately entrusted with the task of preaching with authority in his name. By then he had also given them a power of binding and loosing, a power of which every exercise would be upheld in heaven. He also warned them of the awesome measure of their responsibility: "Of everyone to whom much has been given, much will be required; and of him to whom they have entrusted much, they will demand the more" (Lk 12:48).

It should seem therefore not surprising that the fate and fortunes of priestly celibacy waxed and waned in the measure in which bishops and popes had truly deep notions of the incomparable dignity and crucial importance of God's sovereign dispensation about man, or the Kingdom of God, the Church. Moreover, to have that notion truly in depth demanded a profoundly committed life from them, the life of saints. This unity between in-depth ecclesiology and commitment to the demands of the Gospel has a most revealing and instructive instance in Pope Gregory VII, a saint also known as Hildebrand.

The name of Pope Gregory VII is the first to come up in almost all discourse about priestly celibacy as legislated into a law, and a rigid law at that. Of course, Pope Gregory VII did not legislate that law. He was fully conscious of a long-standing legislation in which he was fond of singling out the acts of Leo the Great and especially of Gregory the Great that imposed on him the duty to reaffirm the rule of priestly celibacy.[3] As a close advisor to five popes—Leo IX (1049-54), Victor II (1055-57), Stephen IX (1057-1058), Nicholas II (1059-61), and Alexander II (1061-1073)—Hildebrand saw the papacy committed to a reform of the Church of which the bishops and priests were the chief targets: Occupants of

[3] Thus in his letter of December 1074 to Otto, bishop of Constance, and in the instructions he gave to the legates he sent to Normandy. See *The Correspondence of Pope Gregory VII. Selected Letters from the Registrum,* tr. with an introduction by E. Emerton (New York: Columbia University Press, 1932), pp. 53 and 183. This work will be quoted hereafter as *The Correspondence.*

ecclesiastical offices were not to remain in bondage to the sins of simony and incontinence.

Such a reform could only be implemented by a Church totally independent of the secular power. This is why Hildebrand, a monk not yet thirty, prevailed upon bishop Bruno of Toul, whom his relative Emperor Henry III had just "elected" pope in Worms, to ask for his true election from the clergy and people of Rome. Otherwise, Hildebrand argued, Bruno would have "seized hold of the Roman Church, not in accordance with ecclesiastical statute but by royal and secular force."[4] This was the voice of the future crusader against investiture. To Rome they went as two simple pilgrims, after Bruno prevailed on Hildebrand to accompany him. Hildebrand would have preferred to stay in Cluny following the death of Clement II, whom he had accompanied from Rome to Germany after Clement had been deposed by the Emperor. Hildebrand, who did not even go to Worms, was not driven by ambition. Bruno had to find him in Besançon in the company of Abbot Hugo of Cluny.

What Bruno and Hildebrand talked about on their way to Rome will be no secret to those who ponder what is meant by their eventual canonization. Leo IX, canonized by Victor III in 1087, was venerated as a saint immediately upon his death. Didier, abbot of Montecassino, echoed the voice of multitudes as he wrote: "Heaven has opened for the pontiff that this world was not worthy to keep: the glory of the saints is his."[5] Nothing commends more the saintly virtues of Hildebrand than that he was canonized at a time, in 1627, when Rome had already become particularly cautious in canonizing anyone, especially if he was a pope.

Both Bruno and Hildebrand must have been deeply agitated by the obvious spread of sin all over the Church. Only half a century had gone by since the Council of Trosly deplored the fact that "bad priests, rotting on the dung-heap of an unchaste life, bring

---

[4] F. Gontard, *The Popes,* tr. from the German by A. J. and E. F. Peeler (London: Barrie and Rockliff, 1964), p. 210.

[5] *Butler's Lives of the Saints,* ed. H. Thurston and D. Attwater (New York: P. J. Kenedy and Sons, 1962), vol. 2, p. 127.

with them into disrepute all those who have kept themselves pure, for the faithful are only too easily inclined to say to each other: 'Such are the priests of the Church'."[6] Other Councils in France, most likely under the influence of reforms initiated from Cluny, spoke in the same vein. Cluny was not, however, responsible for the idea arising in some that "the Church can thrive and prosper as the pillar and foundation of truth without a visible head. Perhaps it might thrive better so than in the shadow of such scandalous events as have occurred through the last centuries at the instigation of the Antichrist in Rome."[7]

No decent churchmen could be oblivious to the fact that the rule of Sergius III (904-11) was plain pornocracy and that some of his immediate successors behaved as if there were no difference between virtue and vice. John XII (955-63) committed incest with his sisters, used Castel San Angelo for orgies during which he even drank to the devil's health. Six hundred years later the great church historian, Cardinal Baronius, portrayed the tenth century as "the iron age of the Church in view of its barrenness of virtue; a leaden age because of the overflow of evil deforming it; . . . an obscure age as well because of the penury of written documents." It was a time, Baronius continued, when "the abomination of desolation appeared in the sanctuary itself." But according to Baronius this was the source of great consolation for true believers, because more than any other age, the tenth century evidenced with more "persuasive experiments" that the Church, like another Ark of Noah, remains safe above all those waves, although "the bark of Peter seemed to flounder in a deluge of sin," deprived as it was of "almost all governance."[8]

Worse, Baronius went on, papal elections were governed by "powerful dirty harlots; . . . libido claimed everything; . . . Christ himself, so it seemed, was fast asleep in that bark, which, being tossed around by high winds, was taking water heavily amidst huge waves. Still worse, there were no disciples around to awaken the

[6] Gontard, *The Popes,* p. 210.

[7] Ibid., p. 211.

[8] C. Baronius, *Annales ecclesiastici* (Antwerp: Ex officina Plantiniana, 1618), vol. 10, p. 629.

Lord with loud cries, because "everybody seemed to be snoring."
But there was in all this "a great consolation for the pious: although the Lord slept, he did so in the same bark, the very bark
that bears the type of the Church; he remained in it; owing to his
promise to Peter, he did not abandon it."⁹ Eventually Christ let
such men gain leadership of the bark of Peter who did not cease to
call out loudly to him, as well as to the clergy and the faithful
within that bark.

In fact the picture was not as dark as painted by Baronius.
There was, for instance, the zeal and success of Saint Dunstan (c.
910-988), archbishop of Canterbury, who had the English clergy
live up to the norms of celibacy. Clearly, a saint like Dunstan did
not need to be discouraged just because he had received the pal-
lium from a pope like John XII, a moral wretch, who also ap-
pointed him papal legate in England. Nor could the forces of evil
in his own country prevent Dunstan, who upon his death was immediately venerated as a saint, from becoming, in an Anglican
historian's judgment, "one of England's makers."¹⁰ Less than a
hundred years after the sad pontificate of John XII, something
casting it in a superior light was aptly recalled by Abbot Leo of
Spain. He gave a never untimely instruction in basic ecclesiology
to French bishops and potentates gathered in a Synod in Rheims
in 1049: "In the times of Pope John [XII], son of Alberic, whom
you wantonly besmirched, Julian, Archbishop of Cordova, sent [to
the pope] by envoys a letter on many difficult matters. He wanted
guidance, and—not asking about the character of the reigning
pontiff, but expressing his respect for the Apostolic See—he sought
for what was useful for himself. From this incident," concludes the
Abbot, "you should learn that the Roman Church is still honoured
and venerated by all the churches."¹¹

In Leo IX's traveling pastorate the Synod of Rheims was the
first major stopover. With the pope was Hildebrand, who indeed

⁹ Ibid., p. 663.

¹⁰ J. Armitage Robinson, *The Times of Saint Dunstan* (Oxford: Clarendon Press,
1923), pp. 81 and 91.

¹¹ Quoted by Horace K. Mann, *The Lives of the Popes in the Early Middle Ages,* vol.
IV (St Louis: Herder, 1910), p. 272. Clearly, good Christians even in bad times
could distinguish between the office and the person.

stole the show by upbraiding "the traditional pretensions of the
French bishops," who tried to remove from the agenda the subject
of Rome's primacy. But Leo IX, who by nature was mild and
yielding, persisted. Hildebrand began to cast a long shadow indeed.
Thus the Synod had to listen to a recital of passages from the Fathers about the pre-eminence of the See of Peter, including the
statement of the Greek bishop of Patara to Emperor Justinian:
"There can be many rulers on the earth, but there is only *one* pope
over all the churches in the world."[12]

At any rate, the French were no longer able to denounce
Rome, as Leo was succeeded by four other popes of tested virtue,
all assisted by Hildebrand. They turned the tables around. The See
of Peter shone with virtue, whereas the episcopacy had much to
reproach itself with in France as elsewhere. While Gregory VII saw
that there were "some good monks, priests, and knights, and not a
few good poor people," he did not mince words as he appraised
the bishops: "When I review in my mind the regions of the West,
whether north or south, I find scarce any bishops worthy of their
positions by their lives or by the manner in which they acquired
their offices, or who rule Christ's flock from love and not from
worldly ambition."[13]

He could not say anything much better about the princes,
with the exception of King William of England, and even there
he had to overlook a number of things. In Philip I, king of
France, Gregory VII faced a young ruffian in his twenties in
whose almost half-a-century reign modern historians find little to
praise. In an impassioned letter to the French clergy, Gregory VII
denounced the king as "the cause and fountainhead, under the
inspiration of the Devil," of the fact that in France "everyone, as if
smitten with some horrible pestilence, is committing every kind
of abominable crime . . . . They regard neither divine nor human
law; they make nothing of perjury, sacrilege, incest or mutual be-
trayal."[14] In the equally youthful Henry IV of the Holy Roman

[12] Gontard, *The Popes,* p. 224.

[13] Letter of Jan. 22, 1075, to Hugo, abbot of Cluny. Here I follow the translation
by Mann, *The Lives of the Popes,* vol. 7, p. 30, and not that by Emerton, p. 65.

[14] Letter of September 10, 1074, *The Correspondence,* pp. 39-40.

Empire the pope faced someone whom a younger contemporary, the great Saint Anselm, characterized as "a successor of Nero and Julian the Apostate."[15] For one modern historian Henry was "intelligent, though violent, given to extremes, and of irregular morality," whereas another has called him "a monster of immorality."[16]

Gregory VII may have exaggerated in directly seeing the Antichrist in so many instances, but the opposition he faced was commensurate with the highest standards he had set and, most importantly, wanted to implement. One dismisses by implication the revulsion Christ felt on seeing the Temple's courtyard turned into a market place, if one looks askance at Gregory's resolve to let no priestly immorality taint the sacredness of the altar on which the holiest of holies, Christ's very body, is immolated anew. Only by seeing the saint in Gregory is it possible to do justice to the determination with which he turned, right at the very start of his pontificate, to the eradication of simony as well as of clerical incontinence. He considered both as sins utterly incompatible with the very essence of the priesthood and of its source, the Church, the bride of Christ.

Gregory VII did not introduce new legislation about celibacy. Nor was he the first of popes, not even of eleventh-century popes, to take with utter seriousness the sacred duty of priests to cultivate a chastity proper to their sacerdotal function. Gregory merely did what counted most, namely, helping fellow bishops stir up the grace which was in them through their episcopal consecration. This was a thoroughly biblical program, that may be given an even more biblical hue by referring it to the duty enjoined by Jesus on Peter to strengthen his brethren. It was a classic exercise of what is today spoken of as the principle of episcopal collegiality, unless the latter is debased into a scheme of endless evasions. By galvanizing the faith and moral courage of his fellow bishops, Gregory aimed at rekindling the spiritual forces in a laity that did not fail to stand in awe of what was done on the altars. This is why Gregory made

---

[15] *De tribus Wallerani quaestionibus, ac praesertim de azymo et fermentato,* PL vol. 158, col. 541.

[16] Mann, *The Lives of the Popes,* p. 26.

energetic steps to remind the faithful of the obligation which Nicholas II had urged on them: to abstain from attending masses celebrated by priests living in concubinage. Of course, Nicholas II also forbade such priests to celebrate parish masses and live in parish houses.

Not that Gregory achieved immediate success. But he certainly set in motion a relentless effort that could not fail, within two generations, to produce what since has become the capstone of ecclesiastical legislation about priestly celibacy: as decreed by the First and Second Lateran Councils (1123 and 1139), marriages contracted by priests were no longer considered gravely illicit but intrinsically invalid. Gregory succeeded in giving an elemental push towards that result mainly because he united in himself an unusual measure of saintly courage and a similar measure of consciousness of being Peter's successor. The saint in Gregory responded to the saint in Peter. This comes through in many ways in Gregory's lengthy Register of letters to all parts of Christendom. Although those letters still have to be studied systematically as documents illustrative of Gregory's saintly spirituality,[17] the salient points can readily be stated and ought to be stated as an important part of the dynamics working within the Church's law about priestly celibacy.

Notable, first, is Hildebrand's utter disinterestedness about gaining ecclesiastical promotion. Had he been consumed ever so slightly with a hunger of power, he could have easily had himself elected following the deaths of Stephen IX or Nicholas II. More than anyone was he stunned by the plebiscite that declared him during the funeral of Alexander II to be the pope. Gregory himself described the scene the next day in a letter to Desiderius, abbot of Montecassino. There he tells of the plan of the cardinals to spend three days in fasting and prayer before proceeding to the election of the new pope. "But then, suddenly, while our lord the pope was

[17] Perhaps because of Pope Gregory's enormous involvement in matters that on account of their political nature retain too much interest for his historians, the saint in him has not received adequate attention even in works whose authors certainly had no blind spot in that respect. I mean *Saint Grégoire VII* (Paris: J. Gabalda, 1920) by A. Fliche, and *Saint Grégoire VII* (Paris: J. Vrin, 1934) by H. X. Arquillière.

being carried to his burial in the church of Our Savior, a great tumult and shouting of the people arose, and they rushed upon me like madmen, so that I might say with the prophet: 'I am come into deep waters where the floods overflow me. I am weary with my crying; my throat is dried.' And also: 'Fear and trembling came upon me and darkness hath encompassed me about'." Then he begged the prayer of his brethren monks that the Lord who kept him until now from danger, that is from being put in the papal chair, "may at least protect me now that I am in danger." And he implored the abbot, who eventually became his successor, to come as soon as possible, "for you know how greatly the Church of Rome needs you and how much it depends on your good judgment."[18]

As Gregory came, three days later, to the end of the same story in a letter to Wibert, archbishop of Ravenna, he spoke of the sudden piling on him of so many cares "that I cannot well dictate, and so I pass over my misfortunes." But he had strength to beg for prayers that God "may give me strength to bear this burden imposed upon me against my will and with great reluctance on my part."[19] Two years later he wrote to Hugo, abbot of Cluny, that he would never have come back to Rome with Bruno, not yet a lawfully elected pope, had he not been under obedience. There "as God knows, I have lived under compulsion for the last twenty [-five] years." And were it not for his belief "in a better [eternal] life and one more useful to the Holy Church," he would not now remain in Rome. But he knew that his duty was that of St. Peter. There was indeed a veiled reference to the famed legend of "quo vadis?" in Gregory's agonizing appraisal of what it meant for him to be a pope: "Between the suffering daily renewed and the hope none too plain before me, I am crushed by a thousand woes, and suffer a living death waiting for him who bound me in his chains, led me back to Rome against my will and has beset me there with a thousand anxieties. I cry out to him repeatedly: 'Hasten and delay

[18] Letter of April 23, 1073, *The Correspondence*, p. 2. The prophet in question is the author of Psalm 73.
[19] *The Correspondence*, p. 3.

not! Hasten and die not, and deliver me for the love of blessed Mary and of St. Peter'."[20]

To the monks of Marseille he spoke of the "unspeakable mercy of the Queen of Heaven."[21] He invoked, in 1081, his blessing on king Alfonso, of Castile and Leon, with a reference to "the merits of our supreme mistress, Mary, Mother of God."[22] The finest document of his profound devotion to Mary is, of course, one of his letters to Matilda, Countess of Tuscany, whom he directs to trust herself "wholly to the unfailing protection of the Mother of God." Later in the same letter, he writes: "Concerning the Mother of God—to whom above all I have committed you, do now commit and shall never cease to commit you until, as we hope, we shall meet her face to face,—what can I say of her whom earth and heaven cease not to praise, though never as her merits deserve? May you believe beyond all doubt that, as she is higher and better and more holy than all human mothers, so she is more gracious and tender toward every sinner who turns to her. Cease, therefore, every sinful desire and prostrate before her, pour out your tear from an humble and a contrite heart. You will find her, I surely promise you, more ready than any earthly mother and more lenient in her love for you."[23]

His letters show many instances of a saint's devotion to St. Peter. In the letter just quoted, he calls Matilda "the best beloved daughter of St. Peter." He commended to Empress Agnes the devotion which her daughter and granddaughter, Beatrice and Matilda, showed at the tomb of St. Peter as similar to the one which the holy women had shown at the tomb of our Lord. And though he felt that through his own merits he could little commend his prayers to God, he hoped that, "aided by the virtues of Peter, whose servant we are, they may not be wholly worthless in the sight of God."[24] He commanded Anno, archbishop of Co-

[20] Letter of Oct. 16, 1074, to Beatrice and Matilda concerning Italian affairs, ibid., p. 45.

[21] Jan. 2, 1079, ibid., p. 138.

[22] Only the year, 1081, is certain about the date of this letter; ibid., p. 178.

[23] Letter of February 16, 1074; ibid., p. 24.

[24] Letter of June 15, 1074; ibid., p. 37.

logne, in the name "of our common lord, St. Peter," and assured
him that he would find him "prepared at every moment and
armed with the shield of St. Peter" to hold back his enemies.[25] In
his case deep devotion was the fruit of profound insight into
dogma, namely, that God stands by Peter, and that Peter stands by
his successor. No wonder that even in his most fateful action, his
excommunication of Henry IV on March 7, 1080, he began with
a humble supplication: "O blessed Peter, chief of the Apostles, and
thou, Paul, teacher of the Gentiles, deign, I pray, to incline your
ears to me and mercifully to hear my prayer." He prayed not so
much that he might be obeyed, but above all that he might be
found truthful in the eyes of those two great saints: "Ye who are
disciples and lovers of the truth, aid me to tell the truth to you,
freed from all falsehood so hateful to you, that my brethren may be
more united with me and may know and understand that through
faith in you, next to God and his mother Mary, ever virgin, I resist
the wicked and give aid to those who are loyal to you."[26]

Yes, Pope Gregory undertook the task, as befitting a saint, to
resist evil and serve holiness. This is the gist of his struggle on behalf of priestly continence. He knew it was his God-given duty, as
he stated at his very first Synod in Rome, to champion a "pure and
obedient Christendom." It was at that Synod that what is most
mistakenly called the "legal imposition" of celibacy came about.
The Synod reiterated the decrees of the Lateran Synod (1059),
presided over by Nicholas II: the faithful were forbidden to take
part in Masses celebrated by married priests; the latter were forbidden to perform any ecclesiastical function and obligated to lead a
*vita communis,* as monks do. In addition, the Synod of 1074 imposed a suspension of twelve years on any priest who took a wife
and a suspension for life on any who publicly defied this ordinance.[27]

But such decrees did not represent the deeper gist of the
Synod of Gregory. It is not possible to read its record without

[25] Letter of March 29, 1075; ibid., p. 73

[26] Ibid., pp. 149–50.

[27] See Mansi, *Sacrorum conciliorum nova at amplissima collectio,* vol. 20, col. 414.

being struck by the zeal with which Gregory marshalled the decrees and reasoning of the first four Ecumenical Councils, and cited the teaching and examples of the saints. Clearly, only a saint could see much point in citing Saint Augustine's refusal to stay with his sister's fellow nuns: "Those who are with my sister are not my sisters." Most importantly, Pope Gregory wanted to leave no doubt that celibacy and priestly continence were an apostolic rule which "imposes perpetual silence on the defenders of priestly incontinence."[28] This rule he corroborated with his own apostolic authority.

Gregory knew, of course, that he could not implement those decrees unless he galvanized the support of all laymen and laywomen who longed for a chaste Church. The refined (and the corrupt) called these zealous Christians the "rubble" (*pataria*), but for Gregory they were the glory of the Church. Possibly he thought of the reminder which Paul served to the refined, the rich, and the well-born among the faithful in Corinth: they were far outnumbered by the poor, the lowly and the despised. Gregory most emphatically endorsed the rubble. That his Synod also decreed that henceforth all those presenting themselves to major orders must take the oath of perfect chastity is most understandable. In a rude age, when recourse had to be taken time and again to oaths, the oath in question aimed at nipping in the bud any misunderstanding about the spiritual status demanded by priestly ordination. The oath was also a reminder, a badly needed one, that the Church would, in the future, be even less willing to tolerate priestly concubinage than ever before.

Unfortunately, toleration had reached an unusual degree. Not that during those dark centuries popes and Councils had not thundered against what had by then been denoted as the heresy of the Nicolaitans.[29] Clerical marriage, let alone concubinage, was rejected in 868 by Pope Nicholas I in his letter to the Bulgarians; in 868 by the Synod of Worms; in 938 in the letter of Leo VII to the Gauls and Germans; in 952 in the decrees of Augsburg; in 1020 in

[28] Ibid., col. 417.

[29] A reference to the Nicolaitans reproved in Apocalypse (2:5 and 16), possibly because they may have practiced fornication as a form of worship.

Benedict VIII's address to the synod of Pavia and in the canons adopted there.[30] But these decrees were not followed up energetically, not even by those five very worthy popes who preceded Gregory VII in the See of Peter. It remained to Gregory to write a decisively new chapter in the always uphill struggle on behalf of priestly celibacy. A crusader saint, crusading for holiness, was all the more needed as widespread toleration of priestly concubinage was creating the impression that it was somehow lawful, or, if not lawful, at least a custom that, owing to its being tolerated to no end, would eventually claim legitimacy.

The chapter which Gregory VII opened in the history of priestly celibacy was, significantly, full of theology and of the best kind, which is the direct involvement of theology in the struggle for daily mercies. The first thing to note is Gregory's sense of responsibility as a shepherd who has to lead souls away from sin to the state of grace. Time and again Gregory refers to the deadly responsibility which God made his prophet Ezekiel feel about warning the sinner. In his letter to Duke Wratislaw, he thus defends the instructions he had given to his legates: "We are forced unwillingly to this action, nor dare we hide the boldness of it. For we are driven on by the word of the Prophet Ezekiel [33:8] upon peril of our own ruin. 'If thou dost not speak to warn the wicked from his way, that wicked man shall die in his iniquity but his blood will I require at thine hand.' And elsewhere [Jer 48:10] 'Woe to him who keepeth back his sword from the incorrigible sinner'."[31]

The same quotation from Ezekiel occurs in his rallying to the support of the bishop of Carthage whom the Saracens severely punished after some Christians had falsely accused him: "Are we to keep silence about these things or are we to cry aloud and to reprove them with tears? It is written, 'Cry aloud, and spare not'." Then, after quoting the foregoing passage from Ezekiel, he continued: "I am bound, therefore, to cry aloud; I am bound to reprove

[30] See J. W. Bowden, *The Life of Gregory the Seventh* (London: J. G. F and J. Rivington, 1840), vol. 1, p. 142.

[31] July 8, 1073, *The Correspondence*, p. 15.

you, lest your blood be required at my hand and lest I be punished at the bar of a fearful, just, and avenging God."[32]

No wonder that Gregory was impatient with footdragging bishops, especially if they occupied pivotal positions. A classic case was that of Siegfried, Archbishop of Mainz, primate of Germany and unworthy successor of St. Boniface, who hesitated to convoke a Council of German bishops. The Pope granted that humanly speaking "it does indeed seem a reasonable explanation that the kingdom is in confusion, with wars, rebellions, hostile invasion, ruin of your property and the fear of death which seems to threaten our brethren from the hatred of the king." Even more weighty could seem the prospect of a violent conflict with Henry IV. But only a deeply spiritual pope could raise the decisive point: "But what if we consider the wide difference between divine and human judgments"? Then "we find scarcely any pretext that we could safely offer in that last day for drawing back from the rescue of souls." For mere pretext is any reference to "the loss of property, the assaults of the wicked, the wrath of the mighty and even the sacrifice of our safety or of life itself." All this was theology at its best and very biblical indeed. And no less did such a theology inform the pope's immediate reference to the difference between a shepherd and a hireling, and their respective attitudes toward the sheep threatened by the wolf.[33]

Again, it was very much a biblical theology that made Gregory refer to his own duty to watch over the flock and made him recall the fate of the sons of Eli. One could disagree with the interpretation which Gregory gave to the words of the prophet, "cursed be he who holds back his sword from blood,"[34] that is, "who holds back the word of preaching from destroying the carnal things of life." Yet the idea itself was Gospel truth and biblical theology, pure and simple. The pope grew impatient with Siegfried's reluctance to look into the simoniac status of the bishop of Strasbourg. And to the argument that the king [Henry

---

[32] Sept. 15, 1073; ibid., p. 17.

[33] Sept. 3, 1075; ibid., pp. 81–83.

[34] Jeremiah 49:10. The verse is likely a gloss. The context is a call on the Jews to take revenge on Moab.

IV] is busy with opposing invading enemies, the pope noted that evil spirits suggest to the king "to lay waste the Church of Christ with the flames of their vicious lives." Therefore the pope could rightly ask: "What ought those royal soldiers, the holy priests, to do, but to rise up against their fury, armed with the shield of priestly charity and girded with the sword of the divine word?" Again the Pope exhorts Siegfried to be courageous, and appeals to the courage and readiness of earthly soldiers: "We ought to regard it as a shameful thing that the soldiers of this world daily stand up to fight for their earthly prince and shrink not from deadly conflict, while we, who are called priests of God, will not fight for our king who created all things out of nothing and has promised us an eternal reward." Investigation of the case of the bishop of Strasbourg and a convocation of a German Council were not to distract from a proper housecleaning in Siegfried's own diocese: "This also we enjoin on you, my brother, that you make diligent inquiry into the simoniac heresy and fornication of your clergy, as you have been instructed by the Apostolic See, and that whatever you find has been committed in the past you punish according to law and thoroughly root it out, and give strictest orders that it shall not occur in future."[35]

Half a year earlier Gregory, in his letter to Archbishop Anno of Cologne, reversed the respective spaces he had allotted to simony and concubinage in his instruction to Archbishop Siegfried. In the name of their common Lord, St. Peter, he commanded the archbishop to apply himself "with more zeal and energy to preaching and enforcing the celibacy of the clergy according to the edicts of the fathers and the authority of the canons, together with all your subordinates, so that the service of a pure and unspotted family may be offered to the bride of Christ who knows no spot or wrinkle." Gregory insisted that he did not invent those orders. He was proclaiming them "as decrees of the ancient fathers, taught to them by the inspiration of the Holy Spirit." He also referred to his duty to obey those ancient orders for, "in the words of Solomon, 'obedience is that without which one who seems to be loyal is

[35] The Correspondence, pp. 81–83.

convicted of disloyalty'."[36] Then Gregory urged Anno to bring together as large a Council as possible and "there make a clear statement of the canon law and the authority of the Apostolic See as
well as your own and that of the assembled brethren. Expound at
length, as God shall give you knowledge, how great is the virtue of
chastity, how necessary it is for all grades of the clergy and how fitting for the chamberlains [priests and bishops] of the virgin bride-
groom [Christ] and the virgin bride [the Church]."[37]

Then the proper measures should be announced against those
who do not comply: "They should rather completely resign their
offices than to impose upon the Savior a criminal and grievous
servitude and thus heap up wrath for themselves from the very
source which ought to bring them a reward." In case of fierce opposition Anno should recall the words of the Savior, "Be of good
cheer; I have overcome the world," and be assured that Gregory,
"armed with the shield of St. Peter," would stand by Anno at every
moment to hold back his enemies. Then Gregory recalled the action taken at the Roman Synod against concubinage, namely, that
at no price should it ever be tolerated. Offenders ought to be removed from celebrating the Mass and from reading the Gospel,
"and we lay upon you the strictest orders to observe these directives."[38]

It was not hunger for power or domination that motivated
Gregory, but an utter devotion to the highest spiritual ideals.
Otherwise he would not have rushed to the defense of a woman
falsely charged with adultery. He did so in a letter to the bishop
and people of Genoa which shows his utter reverence for the sacredness of sacraments: "We learn that the sacrament of marriage,
consecrated by divine commandment and laws, is being viciously
profaned among you."[39] Such was a saint's reaction to what most
others would have written off as a minor detail.

[36] March 29, 1075, ibid., p. 72. The name, Solomon, is debatable. Perhaps the
passage, "Obedience is better than sacrifice" (1 Sam 15:22), is meant, or perhaps
some passage from Proverbs or The Wisdom of Solomon.

[37] March 27, 1075; ibid., p. 73.

[38] Ibid., p. 73.

[39] Feb. 26, 1074; ibid., p. 24.

Sacraments he revered because they, especially the sacrament of the body of Christ, were channels of divine grace. Gregory had to experience deeply the saving effects of that sacrament in order to write in the following vein about frequent communion to Matilda of Tuscany. His instruction to her about devotion to the Mother of God is preceded by the exhortation that she should find time to devote herself solely to the salvation of her soul: "Among the weapons against the prince of this world which, by God's grace, I supplied to you, the most potent is, as I have suggested, a frequent partaking of the Lord's body." He showed further his role as spiritual advisor by quoting St. Ambrose, Gregory the Great and Saint Chrysostom about frequent communion. "This, then, I have written to you, best beloved daughter of St. Peter, that your faith and confidence in receiving the body of the Lord may constantly increase. This treasure and these gifts [spiritual advice], and not gold or precious stones, your soul requires of me, in love of your Father, the prince of Heaven [Christ]."[40]

Such a spiritual perspective could make it all the easier for Gregory VII to rely on the political support of Matilda. The same perspective dominates his request from others for similar support. As he recalled to Empress Agnes her visit in Rome, he compared it with the visit of the holy women at the sepulchre of the Lord and drew a parallel most expressive of his spiritual vision of the Church. Here in Rome "the Church of Christ is laid in the sepulcher of affliction before many others—nay, before almost all the princes of the world in pious service. You strive with all your strength that she may rise again to her state of freedom and, taught as it were by angelic answers, you call others to the support of the struggling Church. Wherefore await without anxiety the revelation of supreme glory and eternal life which is in Christ Jesus, and in the company of those women you shall enter the presence of our Savior with the angelic host and enjoy peace forever with him as your leader."[41]

When Gregory saw a glint of spirituality in Henry IV, he eagerly seized on the opportunity to act as a spiritual counselor as

[40] Feb. 16, 1074; ibid., pp. 23-24.
[41] June 15, 1074; ibid., p. 37.

befitted his pastoral office. He expressed his rejoicing on receiving repeated assurances from Henry's mother, the empress Agnes, that her son was determined "to root out completely the heresy of simony . . . and to use every effort to cure the inveterate disease of clerical unchastity." In return, Gregory VII offered his prayers in a tone which reverberated with profound faith in the grace of God channelled through the sacraments: "And so, sinner that I am, I have kept and shall keep you in mind in the solemn service of the Mass above the bodies of the Apostles, humbly beseeching that Almighty God may confirm you in your present good intentions and may grant you still better things to the advantage of the Church."[42]

Nothing of this spiritual perspective transpires in most of the countless references to Hildebrand as the legislator of compulsory priestly celibacy. A good illustration of this is Henry C. Lea's notorious "classic," *A Historical Sketch of Sacerdotal Celibacy in the Christian Church*.[43] There Gregory's motivations are reduced to his shrewd perception that nothing secures so effectively the obedience of priests as the bondage of celibacy whereby they become willing soldiers on behalf of papal politics. Although Lea granted that the popes' struggle for celibacy helped promote their cultural efforts,[44] he found little if anything to admire in the virtue of continence. He saw in Gregory a thwarted puritan, just because the latter felt remorse of conscience for having touched the neck-

---

[42] Dec. 7, 1074; ibid., p. 55.

[43] First published in 1867. My references are to the second, revised and enlarged edition (Boston: Houghton, Mifflin and Company, 1884). An edition, without almost all the notes and references, was published in 1932 (London: Watts). The latest reprinting, from 1965, of the book is useful only for those who have no eyes for priestly celibacy as a virtue and do not wish to be reminded of the various exposures of Lea's cavalier handling of facts and issues. Among those exposures was H. Thurston's pamphlet, *How History is Miswritten* (London: Catholic Truth Society, 1938, 32pp.), the text of his two articles originally published in the January and February 1937 issues of *The Month*. The pamphlet originated in Thurston's assertion, made to Dr. G. G. Coulton, a virulently anti-Catholic medieval historian, that he would find ten blunders in any ten pages of Lea's *History of Auricular Confessions and Indulgences,* which he did after Coulton deigned to select the pages. The relevance of this to the quality of historical scholarship in Lea's work on the history of sacerdotal celibacy should be obvious.

[44] Ibid., p. 225.

lace of his niece who came to visit him in his grave sickness.[45] Lea's sympathies, in line with his Unitarian naturalism, were with those concubinary priests whom Gregory's zeal drove from their livelihood.[46]

Even more significant is Gibbon's silence on Gregory's campaign on behalf of sacerdotal celibacy. To understand it, it is enough to recall some cursory remarks of Gibbon's in his famed *The Decline and Fall of the Roman Empire*. In speaking of the resurgence of the papacy from the moral disasters of John XII and other 10th-century popes, Gibbon warns against following the Protestants, who "have dwelt with malicious pleasure on these characters of antichrist." A strange advice, one is tempted to think, on the part of one who turned a Catholic, then reverted to Protestantism, only to abandon finally the Christian faith altogether. But Gibbon showed his true color as he continued, no longer a Protestant but a *philosophe*: "To the philosophic eye the vices of the clergy are far less dangerous than their virtues."[47] A more revealing as well as more pertinent phrase can hardly be found in the entire literary production of those who loathed priestly celibacy. No wonder that Gibbon had no use for the saint in Gregory VII, whom he praised as "undoubtedly a great man, a second Athanasius, in a more fortunate age of the church." For in Gibbon's portrayal of Athanasius, which he held to be "one of the passages of my history, with which I am the least dissatisfied,"[48] there was no room for the saint either.

Gregory fared better at the hands of non-Catholic historians who had appreciation for the supernatural. Thus John William

[45] Ibid., p. 226.

[46] See "The Religion of Henry Charles Lea," by E. A. Ryan, in *Mélanges. Joseph de Ghellinck* (Gembloux: J. Duculot, 1951), vol. 2, pp. 1043-51. As shown in J. M. O'Brian's essay, "Henry Charles Lea: The Historian as a Reformer," *American Quarterly* 19 (1967), pp. 104-13, Lea engaged his vast researches on the history of celibacy and of the Inquisition on behalf of a culture of tolerance. He would never consider the question why tolerance was not supposed to tolerate intolerance. Had he pondered that question he might have perceived that it was illogical to attack inquisition and celibacy with disregard to the problem of whether there could be some absolute truth and norm.

[47] See the edition in *Great Books of the Western World*, vol. 41, p. 215 (ch. 49).

[48] Ibid., p. 715 (ch. 66, note 85).

Bowden acknowledged that the real issue for Gregory VII and the popes immediately before and after him was not a question of power: "The battle which they undertook . . . was, unquestionably, that of purity against impurity, of holiness against corruption." As an Anglican, and a Tractarian at that, Bowden could not help suggesting that the adoption of the Greek policy concerning clerical marriage might have produced better results. But he also recognized that "a line like this, circumstanced as they [the popes] were, can scarcely be said to have been open to their adoption. Seizing the means in their power, they set themselves to achieve,—and did achieve,—a most important reformation; and we may not think lightly, either of their principles or of their labours, because that reformation was imperfect."[49]

Bowden failed to note that one of the circumstances limiting the option of the popes (even if any of them had wanted to introduce the Greek pattern, which they certainly had no intention of doing),[50] was that the laity was far from being reconciled to the quasi-marriage of priests. For many of the laity those priests were plain sinners. Therefore Gregory could urge the laity to refuse their services as part of his campaign against concubinary priests. At any rate, the real lesson of Gregory's struggles lay far deeper than the question whether clerics could marry or not. The real lesson was glimpsed by John Henry Newman, still an Anglican, as he wrote a lengthy review of Bowden's work. Newman took the view that the whole struggle was feasible only because the corruption of priests, bishops and popes did not go beyond the surface. The essence of the Church remained intact and this is why the Church could perform what to a mere historian may appear unbelievable. The Church rose as the proverbial phoenix rises from the ashes: "Taking the corruptions of that day at the worst, they were principally on the surface of the Church. Scandals are petulant and press into view, and they are exaggerated from the shock they communicate to the beholders. Friends exaggerate through indignation, foes through malevolence. In the worst of times there is always a

---

[49] Bowden, *The Life of Gregory the Seventh*, vol. 2, pp. 143-44.

[50] On Cardinal Humbert's disputes with the Greeks, see R. Cholij, *Clerical Celibacy in East and West* (Herefordshire: Fowler Wright Books, 1988), p. 61.

remnant of holy men out of sight, scanty perhaps in numbers, but great in moral strength, and there is always even in the multitude an acknowledgment of truths which they do not themselves practice."[51]

And so came about what Baronius called a miracle that should have been obvious even for those who willfully blinded themselves. He meant the Reformers, who "by focusing on the waves threatening the boat, fail to see Christ inside. . . . Blind are they and leaders of the blind who do not see Christ sleeping in the boat, nor perceive the presence of God in such a great miracle."[52] By the time Baronius wrote this, the early 1600's, the Church at the Council of Trent had reaffirmed, in its last session (1563), the decision of the First and Second Lateran Councils that marriages attempted by priests were intrinsically invalid. In the four ensuing decades a miracle took place contrary to all worldly wisdom. In a Germany where, in the 1560's, priests were scarce, priests were everywhere again by 1600 or so, except, of course, in the lands controlled by Lutheran princes, who limited their Catholic subjects' freedom of conscience to moving "freely" elsewhere. Further, the legislation of Trent was part of the Church's defense of the state of virginity, which Luther held to be no more noble than marriage, while actually despising it. He certainly failed to inspire anyone to embrace that *equally* noble state.

The result, within Protestantism, was all too plain, although, like almost everything in history, it took some time to unfold. In registering the absence of religious vows, especially that of chastity, within the Church of England, Newman, still an Anglican, spoke of its Judaizing tendency, by which he meant the yielding to natural instincts: "There is one virtue which of old time good men especially had not. Indulgences were allowed the Jews on account of the hardness of their hearts. Divorce of marriage was allowed them. More wives than one at once were not denied them. If there is one grace in which Christianity stands in especial contrast to the old

---

[51] The essay, "Reformation of the Eleventh Century," first published in the *British Review*, became ch. XIII in Newman's *Essays, Critical and Historical* (London: Longmans, Green & Co., 1897), vol. 2, pp. 249-317; for quotation, see pp. 269-270.

[52] Baronius, *Annales ecclesiastici*, p. 664.

religion, it is that of purity. Christ was born of a Virgin; He remained a virgin; He abolished polygamy and divorce; and he said that there were those who for the kingdom of heaven's sake would be even as He." To be sure, Newman referred to Paul's remark that the gifts of God are different. But he made no secret of the fact that "the way of the world is to deny that there is such a gift" of virginity. And he wondered aloud why within the Church of England "none have it." Was this not a proof that "we have fallen into a Jewish state?"[53]

Nothing more incisive than this could have been objected to the claim of Horace Bushnell, the leading Congregationalist minister of the 19th century, who is remembered today for the consistency with which he naturalized and domesticated supernatural Christian faith. His *Christian Nurture*, first published in 1846, was all nurture, that is, nature and no Christ. He looked forward to the day when "the sporadic cases of sanctification from the womb of which scripture speaks, such as that of Samuel, Jeremiah and John [the Baptist], are . . . finally . . . the ordinary and common fact of family development."[54] He shied away from noting that the birth of John announced the birth of the One who was by nurture, taken for nature, Jewish, though only on his mother's side.

Protestantism still has to face up to its predicament or rather logic that pushes it into naturalism. It was a Protestant, Friedrich Wilhelm Foerster, who a hundred years ago called that process an enslavement within the natural. He warned: "If Protestantism does not energetically withdraw from such slavery to the natural instincts, then it will be lost beyond recall. Religion is being beyond and above nature in every sense."[55] Is Protestantism capable of

---

[53] In a Sermon, "Judaism of the Present Day," in *Parochial and Plain Sermons* (London: Longmans, Green and Co., 1897), vol. VI, p. 187.

[54] Originally published in 1861, it saw numerous re-editions, the latest of them in 1979.

[55] F. W. Foerster, *Sexualethik und Sexual Pädagogik* (Kempten: J. Kösel, 1907), p. 53. Foerster introduces this devastating judgment by pointing out that arguments against celibacy as being unnatural and impossible to observe strike at monogamous marriage as well: "If celibacy is a physiological impossibility, then so are many marriages where sexual relations have to be broken off for a fairly long period or perhaps altogether, out of consideration for the life or the health of the

such withdrawal, except in fits and starts? More than four hundred years after Luther and Calvin, any frank Protestant observer must agree with the observation of the Lutheran theologian J. C. Hampe, that "it is inconceivable that the [Protestant] clergy should abstain from marriage."[56]

One may ask, has God not granted to the Protestant Churches the gift of continence? Or should not one rather ask whether there is something in Protestantism that blocks the reception of that gift? Was not this spelled out in a roundabout way by Luther himself, who confessed that if in his time priests had observed celibacy as they did in the time of Jerome, Ambrose and Augustine, he would have made little headway, because "celibacy was something remarkable in the eyes of the world, a thing that makes a man angelic."[57] Protestantism came to block another spiritual gift, as Voltaire noted with an eye on the Sisters of Charity: "Perhaps there is nothing greater on earth than the sacrifice of youth and beauty, often of high birth, made by the gentle sex in order to work in hospitals for the relief of human misery, the sight of which is so revolting to our delicacy. Peoples separated from the Roman religion have imitated but imperfectly so generous a charity."[58]

The sporadic appearance of religious communities within one or two Protestant denominations, during this century, is less than a drop in a bucket that was radically emptied almost five hundred years ago.[59] There arose no significant echo within Protestantism to an observation of Roger Schutz, the Prior of Taizé: "In its rejection of monasticism the Reformation struck a blow at the celibate. It is surprising to discover that for centuries the Churches that is-

woman, or where a journey separates the married couple for a long period of time." In fact, he prefaces all this with the declaration: "Celibacy is the greatest safeguard of marriage." Quotations are taken from M. Pfliegler, "Celibacy," in *Life in the Spirit* (New York: Sheed & Ward, 1968), p. 145.

[56] See F. Bökle (ed.), *Der Zölibat* (Mainz: 1968), p. 23.

[57] Quoted by P. Delhaye in his article, "Celibacy, History of," in the *New Catholic Encyclopedia,* vol. 4, p. 373.

[58] Quoted in H. Daniel-Rops, *The Church in the Eighteenth Century* (Doubleday Image Books, 1964), p. 358.

[59] A classic in the art of exaggeration is the title of F. Biot's book, *The Rise of Protestant Monasticism,* tr. W. J. Kerrigan (Baltimore: Helicon, 1963).

sued from the Reformation have erected a conspiracy of silence
around the scriptural texts that relate to celibacy."[60] Karl Barth spoke
of a process that, starting with the erstwhile reaction of the Reformers "to the Roman doctrine of the excellence of celibacy" over marriage, led them "to seeing Christian joy in marriage . . . to know no
limits. And this hardened itself into a doctrine of universal obligation of marriage on the basis of a supposed order of creation."[61]

Worse, Barth also notes, the Reformation, in order to avoid
the Scylla of monasticism (celibacy), sparked a trend that made it
run aground on the Charybdis of secularism and naturalism.[62] The
chief victim of that shipwreck was the image that Protestants form
of Jesus Christ himself. "In its glad affirmation of marriage born of
the conflict against the priestly and monastic celibacy of Rome,"
the Protestant ethic, Barth continues, ignored that "Jesus Christ
himself, of whose true humanity there can be no doubt, had no
other beloved, bride or wife, no other family or domestic sphere
but this community of disciples."[63] Yet Barth could not, even theo-
retically, redress the balance, in spite of quoting all the sayings of
Jesus that are so many praises of and invitations to a celibate life.
He could not, because he refused to concede, in spite of quoting
Paul too about the superior excellence of full continence, that virginity (celibacy) represented a religious calling superior to marriage. For Barth neither do Jesus' words "contain any suggestion of
the superiority of celibacy," nor does Paul proclaim "a celibate and
as such a higher status."[64]

---

[60] R. Schutz, *Dynamique du provisoire* (Les Presses de Taizé, 1965), p. 164. This
praise of celibacy is part of a portrayal of marital union as a realization of the
unity of the Church. Needless to say, the Prior of Taizé feels it necessary to defend
himself against the suspicion that any praise of celibacy undercuts the esteem in
which marriage ought to be held: "What is stated here represents a discovery
made here in Taizé and may appear foreign to marriage. But one can never repeat
often enough: celibacy can only revitalize the appreciation of marriage" (p. 167).
Why, one may ask, have Protestants to rediscover, again and again, truths that have
been known and held all along by Catholics?

[61] K. Barth, *Christian Dogmatics. Vol. III. The Doctrine of Creation* (Edinburgh: T. &
T. Clark, 1961), p. 141.

[62] Ibid., p. 602.

[63] Ibid., p. 144.

[64] Ibid., pp. 144 and 146.

This is why Barth's brief recommendation of monasticism is full of caveats. No amount of biblical references and lessons of history could stir up real enthusiasm in Barth for a monasticism construed on Protestant principles. To fathom this puzzle it may be enough to read carefully Barth's recognition of the fact that monasticism (and priestly celibacy too) must have what is best called an institutional character, regardless of the legalistic flavor of that word. They must have that character if they are part of that *communio sanctorum* which is the Church: "And if it is incontestable that the *communio sanctorum* can be achieved only in the distinctive triangle of God, a man and a fellow man—the two latter being united in a definitely ordered relationship—we cannot reject out of hand the recognisable purpose of the *vita monastica,* for all the questions and objections which we may have to level against its theoretical and practical existence."[65]

Here, in this reference to "definitely ordered relationship" lies the stumbling block for a monastic (and celibate) dispensation to be set up in a Protestant manner. Such a relationship, if it is to be real and lasting, calls for some legal framework, which in turn cannot become operative without legislation and a power that can legislate. But can Protestantism legislate? Can it claim authority to do so? Is not Protestantism the repeated registering of an evershifting consensus? If indeed Protestantism had been more an action than a reaction, it would have inspired a zealous imitation of that Christ, who, though not having wife and children of his own, still had the fullness of humanity in him.

By contrast, there has always been in Catholicism a steady inspiration in that direction. No less importantly, it could be and has been controlled by a power that could and did legislate. Lacking this power, indeed having denounced and renounced it, Protestantism deprived itself of a vital factor in the Christian dispensation. It is precisely this factor that produces, time and again, those turns in Church history that befuddle historians, but which loom large as well-nigh miraculous instances of the enduring presence of Christ in Peter's bark. It is this factor that enables the Church, the Catholic Church, never to relent in its effort to sustain an ever

---

[65] *Christian Dogmatics,* Part IV. vol. 2, p. 18.

uphill struggle in respect to celibacy and in many other respects as well. The new Canon Law and its reaffirmation of priestly celibacy witness not so much the persistence of institutionalized oppression as the abiding presence of a living power, the Holy Spirit, within an institution that derives its strength from having been instituted by Christ, the eternal High Priest. Hildebrand was but a memorable and saintly instance of this priesthood. Otherwise his enemies would not have branded him a "false monk" while grudgingly recognizing his holiness. A close collaborator was tempted to see in him a "holy Satan."[66] Satan received indeed a powerful blow as this wholehearted, single-minded, chaste priest of the Lord, Pope Gregory VII, saw to it that the law of priestly celibacy did not decay into a mere letter, but served the Spirit of Christ which has been the source and inspiration of that law since Apostolic times. Such is an age-old theological point that, as will now be seen, became ignored in a so-called new theology, though only by casting doubt on the thinking of some of its chief champions.

---

[66] See Gontard, *The Popes*, p. 233.

# 6

# A New Theology?

Next to distrust with anything legislated, it is the craving for everything new that poses nowadays the principal obstacle to a theological understanding and appreciation of priestly celibacy. The skill of giving the impression that one came up with something new has become the ticket of admission into the inner circles of theological progress. The dangling of some novelty passes for a "more profound" approach, which all too often is but a shallow cavorting in faddish expressions. Novelty for novelty's sake has become a theological *l'art pour l'art* which, as happened in art proper a century ago, imposes in theological discourse a brazen selectivity. Not surprisingly, the spokesmen of this new theological trendiness ignore or slight the views held on priestly celibacy by those great 19th-century theologians whom they love to expropriate as their forerunners.

The first to come in mind is Johann Adam Moehler (1796-1838), who in the 1940's and 1950's was re-discovered by the trendsetters of a new Catholic ecclesiology. Moehler's early monograph (1825) on Saint Cyprian's idea on the unity of the Church suddenly loomed large as a model for ecumenical theology. Yet hardly anything was said at that time about his later and far sounder work *Symbolik* (1832), which by 1902 was in its 13th edition and came out in English in 1906, although it had a no less important message for ecumenism.[1] No wonder. In an age of new ecumenism, when some Catholic theologians began to discourage conversion to the Catholic Church, it must have been embarrassing to speak of this work of Moehler's that prompted, at least on the Continent, more Protestants to convert to Catholicism than any other theological work published during the 19th century. Of course, that was an age when people preferred to noble rhetoric solid intellectual arguments, such as the ones set forth by Moehler in his *Symbolik*. There he effectively contrasted the endless variations of Protestant formulas of faith, with the steady consistency of Catholic credal formulas.

No wonder that Moehler came in as a whipping boy in the context of recent efforts aimed at giving a theological underpinning to optional celibacy for Catholic priests. Once more selectivity ruled, which was all the more reprehensible in one case,[2] because it postdated by six years a very readable monograph on Moehler whose author gave due attention to the theological motivations of Moehler's animated defense of priestly celibacy.[3] This defense Moehler articulated at length on two occasions. First he did so in an article, "Some thoughts on the shortage of priests that has come about in our times," published in 1826. There he pointed out that all too often very unspiritual reasons, such as wealth and the routine practice of faith, prompted the growth of the number of priests. Conversely, "it was never the number of priests that secured for the Church its strength and vigor, and renewal. Always

[1] Should the slighting of the *Symbolik* in the collection of essays *Eglise est Une: Hommage à Moehler*, ed. P. Chaillet (Paris: Bloud & Gay, 1939), be taken for a suggestion that the Church can have unity without a clear profession of faith?

[2] J. Lynch, "Critique of the Law of Celibacy in the Catholic Church from the Period of Reform Councils," in W. Bassett and P. Huizing (eds.) (New York: Herder and Herder, 1972), pp. 57-75. Moehler's defense of obligatory celibacy is reported (p. 68) with undisguised criticism, whereas nothing critical is offered about those whom Moehler sharply criticized.

[3] I have in mind the publication in 1966 of Hervé Savon's *Johann Adam Moehler: The Father of Modern Theology* (tr. into English by C. McGrawth; Glen Rock, N.J.: The Paulist Press), a book originally published in French in 1963. Moehler's defense of celibacy is discussed on pp. 71-79, under the heading, "The Marriage of Priests."

relatively small was the number of those who carried the burden of the day."[4]

Historically this was evidenced, according to Moehler, in the rise of ever new reform groups within the clergy, both secular and religious. The rise of the new ones was needed because almost invariably the older institutions had grown lax. Cluny succeeded for a while in revitalizing the monastic orders, only to make room for the zeal of the mendicant orders that in turn soon were the target of reforming efforts. The often-low moral level of friars, coupled with their too large numbers, caused in part the success of the Reformation, which in turn was opposed by the Church through the rise of clerical orders, such as Jesuits, Theatines, Oratorians, and so forth. All this illustrated a force working within the Church that inspired select souls to join in an uphill struggle for the highest ideals of the priesthood.

This pattern of Church history appeared meaningful, Moehler warned, only if one grasped "the proper idea of the priesthood," and therefore it followed "from the nature of the priesthood that there can only be few priests." It was within that broader picture that Moehler touched on celibacy as an integral part of the priesthood: "For only those are really priests of God, who have experienced the breath of the divine Spirit, and received the holy kiss, who received the consecration of the spirit, the anointing of the heart; only such who do not open their mouths in the sanctuary, unless God himself unties their tongue. God has given his gifts only to such whom He himself consecrates later to his service." Logic therefore demanded from Moehler to ask the question, "How many can and do understand all this?"[5]

Without saying a word more on celibacy, Moehler concluded by noting that "although there are still many priests who externally appear to be such, truly interiorized priests are but few. And since

---

[4] I am quoting from the German original, "Einige Gedanken über die zu unserer Zeit erfolgte Verminderung der Priester, und damit in Verbindung stehende Punkte," *Theologische Quartalschrift* (1826), pp. 414–51. For quotation, see p. 436. The article was so unsparing of the clergy, secular and religious, and of bishops who admitted too many unworthy candidates to the priesthood, that Döllinger preferred not to include it in Moehler's collected works, referred to in note 10 below.

[5] Ibid., p. 436.

the holy and worthy appear most disfigured when constrained within an improper garb, a horrendous state of affairs is on hand through unworthy priests. This is why I take for a blessing that catastrophe," by which he meant the havoc played with the Church by the French Revolution and its Napoleonic sequel.[6] Therefore Moehler saw no other solution to the sharp drop in the number of the clergy than "the need for the spiritual rebirth of the entire clergy," which he felt was to come.[7]

Moehler should have noted here two points. There were many exemplary priests and bishops in France during the decades preceding the French Revolution, and during its Terror thousands of them chose martyrdom.[8] Also Thomas Aquinas rightly noted that although it is "better to have few good ministers than many bad ones," there will always be a sufficient number of them, because "God never so abandons His Church that apt ministers are not to be found sufficient for the needs of the people if the worthy be promoted and the unworthy set aside."[9] It was, however, dangerous to refer in the 1820s even to the great Scholastics. Moehler himself was not sympathetic to them. He preferred to immerse himself in the thought of the Church Fathers. He therefore could readily cope with references to the Fathers in a petition which lay professors and theology students of the University of Freiburg addressed to the government of Baden. They urged that the obligatory celibacy of priests be abolished, so that their cultural, moral, and spiritual level might be raised.

In his book-length analysis of the true merits of that petition,[10] Moehler stated more than once his conviction that only a

---

[6] Ibid. pp. 436-37.

[7] Ibid., p. 437.

[8] Salient facts are readily available in H. Daniel-Rops' book, *The Church in the Eighteenth Century* (Doubleday Image Books, 1964), pp. 332-67, where a prominent revolutionary from 1796 is cited: "Our revolution has failed in the sphere of religion" (p. 333). He also recalled A. Tocqueville, author of *L'Ancien regime et la Révolution française* (1859), who confessed that he had begun his study full of prejudices against the French clergy and ended it "full of respect" (p. 335).

[9] *Summa theologica*, Part III, Supplement, qu. 36, art. 4, ad 1am.

[10] "Beleuchtung der Denkschrift für die Aufhebung des den katholischen Geistlichen vorgeschriebenen Cölibats," in *Katholik* (1830), reprinted in *Gesammelte Schriften und Aufsätze*, ed. J. Döllinger (Regensburg: J. Mainz, 1839), pp. 177-266.

deeply spiritual understanding of the value of virginity and of the meaning of priesthood can justify the obligatory character of priestly celibacy. He saw the temporary continence imposed on the Jewish priesthood in the highest possible spiritual light: "The Tabernacle enclosed the tablets that had on them engraved the laws which Moses received on Sinai from God himself; the hearts of the priests pulsated in awe and trembling in awareness of that majestic, fear-inspiring legislation. In gratitude for all the mercies of the past and for the ones still to be obtained by the people of God, the Jewish priest brought his daily thanks offering." Moehler then could raise the question: "Was it possible for those priests, to think in such a context of their wives? In clear, pure thoughts were those mercies present during the day in the deeply moved soul of the pious priest, and holy, meaningful dreams occupied him during the night. Such a communing with God necessarily barred for a priest any consorting with his wife, who therefore remained far removed from him when he performed his duties in the Temple. The Law merely demanded what was plain common sense."[11]

No less uncompromisingly spiritual was Moehler's judgment on the Greek custom, or rather the Trullo legislation. According to him, "only a mind lost in sheer formalism could take the view that it was the Apostolic custom to let no one, except who is already married, be ordained. Henceforth Greek clerics married before they were ordained, although they married with the intention of becoming ordained." It should be noteworthy that Moehler here does not argue on the basis of historical evidence. He simply reconstructs the spirit or rather the spirituality of the Apostles in order to support his argument. He saw that spirit to be dishonored in the attitude initiated by Trullo: "A very low view of the priesthood is entertained by one who thinks of ordination only and primarily in that relation. Actually and in truth, the true priest is a priest born, because God destined him from eternity to be a priest, and therefore knows that he will be a priest; he prepares himself therefore for the priesthood and knows that he will be one. If however one couples his awareness of his eventually becoming a priest with

---

[11] Ibid., p. 210.

the intention of marrying before he becomes a priest, such a one in fact enters marriage as a priest. Whether the marriage takes place in this case before or after the ordination, comes pretty much to the same."[12] Moehler then asked anyone thinking clearly to consider whether the Greek policy, that practically forces marriage upon future priests, really corresponds to the practice of the early Church, still in close contact with the Church of Apostles.

The last item to be recalled about Moehler's profoundly spiritual and theological view of celibacy relates to his pointing out to the drafters of that petition that they obey a thwarted logic as they plead for the personal rights (today they would say, human rights) of priests to marry, asking indignantly: "How can the Church think to be justified in denying to so many men the right to marry, by forcing them into a lifelong state of celibacy?" Moehler replies by putting the same question in the following light: "Does the Church have the right to grant priestly ordination only to such whose soul is already anointed with the highest form of religious consecration, in whose souls the purest and most beautiful flowers of spiritual life are unfolding, and who live entirely and undividedly to the Lord, as the Apostle Paul puts it, that is, to use again the Apostle's words, who have received the gift of virginity?"[13] Moehler therefore could rightly urge that whatever the problem was (then or today) about the recruitment of priests, it could only be resolved by instilling more spiritual courage and magnanimity among Catholics. He had a special word for parents, who, more than anyone, had to be a source of inspiration, if their children were to opt for the priesthood, with no forethought to agitate, eventually, for optional celibacy.

Moehler would not have been the theologian he was, had he not pointed out that marriage as such does not generate Christian virtues. First, there have to be Christians, if their being married is going to display the highest and most difficult virtues. The mere physical union is not able to generate grace: "Nothing is farther from the Gospel than to think that Christian love is simply forth-

---

[12] Ibid., p. 233.
[13] Ibid., p. 237.

coming from marriage and the various ties involved in it."[14] If, however, grace turned marriage into a channel of grace, there could be no problem in looking at celibacy as a most logical state for the priesthood, the very instrument of grace.

It was grace, available to the married as well as to the single, that Moehler had in mind as the justification of his chief advice to the clergy itself. What he said of the clergy in the Germany of his time, fully applies to much of the clergy in the developed or affluent world today: "In truth, in Germany we must fear not the over-confidence but the pusillanimity of the priest. Between the two there stands in the middle the resolve to be oneself, and the least one can wish is that the priest be his true self." Moehler's final remark was aimed at the makers of that petition: by turning to the State "they would merely tie the clergy closer to the secular power and weaken the superiority of papal and priestly power."[15] Grace, or the supernatural, the papacy, and priestly celibacy once more loomed large as an undivided and indivisible triad.

Moehler's theologically and spiritually most elevated thinking about priestly celibacy stood out not only in his own contemporary context, but also exposes today the chinks in the armor of those stalwarts of the "new" theology who claim him for themselves. Of the various reasons that explain why Moehler could be so different in his own time, only one should be mentioned here. He himself spelled it out in 1835 to a friend: "Christ had been for me only a word, a notion . . . ; it was while studying the Fathers that for the first time I discovered so living and new concept of Christianity."[16] The very first patristic text Moehler dealt with in the course he gave as a young Privatdozent was Saint John Chrysostom's *Dialogue on the Priesthood*.

About the time Moehler was regaining his Christian soul from reading the Fathers, something akin happened to Newman. He referred to the writings of the Fathers as having been "simply and solely the one intellectual cause" of his conversion to Roman

[14] Ibid., p. 152.
[15] Ibid., p. 266.
[16] Savon, *Johann Adam Moehler*, p. 23.

Catholicism.[17] In the same context Newman also epitomized the supreme reason of his conversion. He found the ethos of the Catholic Church of his day remarkably similar to the ethos animating the Church of the Fathers, many of whom were both great theologians as well great saints. He had therefore no choice but to exclaim: "Be my soul with the saints!"[18] No wonder that Newman, another patron saint of the "new" theology, spoke no differently than Moehler about priestly celibacy.

Newman has been often referred to as the theologian of Vatican II.[19] Newman himself might wonder about the appropriateness of this halo accorded to him. As one who prophesied about a deluge of hostility in store for the Church, he would certainly wonder, or rub his eyes in disbelief, that Vatican II contains only five lines on what, according to the Council, is a permanent condition of the Church through all history. That condition is a permanent state of struggle against the powers of Evil. Such a struggle, since it is permanent, clearly has to be an always uphill struggle. The struggle involves the individual Christian on the most personal moral level.[20] Hardly anything more appropriate could have been stated about the basic predicament within which celibacy, or any other virtue for that matter, remains a struggle to be engaged at every new day dawning.

Yet not much more than a couple of lines have been said about that permanent condition (including its very personal component) by "progressive" theologians who dominated that Council

[17] J. H. Newman, *Anglican Difficulties*, with an introduction by S. L. Jaki (Fraser, MI: Real View Books, 1994), pp. 244–45 (Lecture XII, 2).

[18] Ibid., p. 259.

[19] Thus, in reminiscing about Vatican II, where he was a prominent figure, Cardinal Gracias of Bombay wrote: "Representatives of the Hierarchy from all over the world, theologians, philosophers, faithful from everywhere, and from all ranks, see in Newman a guide in their sincere search for the truth. "The Friends of Cardinal Newman," *The Examiner* 128 (May 21, 1977), p. 278.

[20] "A monumental struggle against the powers of darkness pervades the whole history of man. The battle was joined from the very origins of the world and will continue until the last day, as the Lord attested. Caught in this conflict man is obliged to wrestle constantly if he is to cling to what is good. Nor can he achieve his own integrity without valiant efforts and the help of God's grace." Pastoral Constitution on the Church in the Modern World" (#37), in *The Documents of Vatican II*, ed. W. M. Abbott (New York: Guild Press, 1966), p. 235.

as far as publicity-control was concerned. They certainly celebrated, in accord with the false optimism of the 1960s, the glorious material and cultural progress in store for humanity. They therefore did much to sublimate the awful reality of original sin and of its consequences, although Newman saw there the very starting point of a theology appropriate for modern man.[21]

Of course, Newman tried to help save that fallen man, including his modern kind, as he warned him that it is the Antichrist himself who uses most effectively material progress for his very purposes.[22] Newman, who refused to be an evolutionist,[23] would have been the last to suggest to fellow Catholics that they are caught up in a gigantic forward and upward moving stream of progressive evolution that would raise mankind one day, and still on this very earth, into a new, unimaginably superior noosphere. A Newman, who rightly deplored that it amounted "almost to a blasphemy to doubt"[24] the existence of people on other planets, would weep today on hearing an educated Catholic layman refer to his "cousins in other galaxies" as the source of his comfort and inspiration to cope with life on earth.[25] Yet, it is partly through taking cover with profuse references to Newman that champions of the new theology have sown the seeds of a strange spiritual flora and fauna wherein nothing old is tolerated and everything new is blithely endorsed. He would hardly be pleased with his being invoked as a justification of a theology replete with hollow phrases

---

[21] See my article, "A Gentleman [Newman] and Original Sin," *Downside Review* July 1996, pp. 192-215.

[22] Particularly telling are the four lectures Newman delivered in 1835 on the patristic idea of the Antichrist, reprinted in his *Discussions and Arguments On Various Subjects* (London: Longmans, Green and Co., 1897). See especially pp. 60-61.

[23] See my essay, "Newman and Evolution," *Downside Review* 108 (January 1991), pp. 16-34.

[24] *Grammar of Assent* (Doubleday Image Book, 1955), p. 299. See also pp. 166, 329 and 376 for further strictures of Newman on the logical fallacies involved in that belief.

[25] The case, which I know personally, is all the stranger, as the life of the Catholic in question was blessed with all the amenities that devolve to a successful Madison Avenue executive. Only when one morning his older son blew his head to pieces, did the father's eyes open to the crucifix which alone can provide meaning and strength in such circumstances.

and catchy words, all larded with quotations from him, quotations at times brazenly truncated, lest the true Newman should appear.[26] In that theological jungle there is clearly no place for the cultivation of Newman's views on celibacy.

Those views are all the more telling, because they appear spontaneously here and there in Newman's diaries and published works, and show thereby all the more forcefully how decisive was in his eyes the theological import of priestly celibacy. Yet Newman never wanted to be considered a theologian; he emphatically looked upon himself as a controversialist, although the topics he controverted almost always related to the very core of theology. In his eyes the chief task was to articulate the following assertion: God gave about himself and his aim with mankind a revelation over and above what man can learn about God by looking into himself or at the great nature around him. In other words, Newman's principal concern was the vindication of the supernatural dispensation.

This is why Newman never went to any length in articulating the cosmological argument, although he firmly held it.[27] He had reservations about the design argument, partly because of the form Paley gave it, and partly because it did not say anything about God's supernatural design for man. This does not mean that Newman lacked keen eyes and appreciation for the natural. Indeed, it was a very empirical fact, an existential experience available to any and all, that made the supernaturally revealing God loom obvious in Newman's eyes. He loved to describe that fact or experience as a proof that mankind became involved in "some terrible aboriginal calamity."[28] His views on Revelation, on grace, on sacraments, on Church were all conditioned by that huge reality of man's fallenness.

Telling glimpses of this are given in the introductory part of Section III of the *Development,* where he states why there has to be a growth of a truth initially revealed by God and why God had to

---

[26] For details, see my article, "Newman's Logic and the Logic of the Papacy," *Faith and Reason* 13 (1987), p. 261 and note 89 there.

[27] *Grammar of Assent*, pp. 275 and 383.

[28] *Apologia pro vita sua* (Doubleday Image Books, 1956), p. 320.

build into that revealed truth a factor whereby it is saved from gradual corruption. The growth, if it is truly one, has to be organic, which means the ever growing interconnectedness of theological doctrines: "These doctrines are members of one family, and suggestive, or correlative, or confirmatory, or illustrative of each other. One furnishes evidence to another, and all to each of them; if this is proved, that becomes probable." He then turns to the logical order between some dogmas: "The Incarnation is antecedent of the doctrine of Mediation, and the archetype both of the Sacramental principle and of the merits of Saints." A little later, but still in this context, Newman lists instances of one doctrine leading to another. Among them is the following chain: "The doctrine of the Sacraments leads to the doctrine of Justification; Justification to that of Original Sin; Original Sin to the merit of celibacy."[29]

A most momentous chain, which gives the fundamental perspective for a theology of priestly celibacy. The priest is a model, yes, a reminder of higher realities, and many other things in addition. But all these are secondary, or second-story facets of what basically constitutes a priest. The only empirical and therefore also logical starting point towards the rationale of the priesthood is original sin, the fallen human nature, that nowhere fell so deep as in relation to the proper use of sex. To mediate man's redemption from this disorderly, sinful state is the essential role of priesthood. Therefore, as Newman listed chapter headings to illustrate which dogma includes another dogma, he logically ended with the caption: "Celibacy is the characteristic mark of Monachism and the Priesthood."[30]

The foregoing details are a lead-up to Newman's grand conclusion about the organic growth of doctrine, in which there is nothing stated about priesthood and celibacy. Yet the fact that the conclusion immediately follows upon his remark that celibacy is characteristic of the priesthood, conveys something of Newman's profound conviction about celibacy as an indispensable, integral

[29] *An Essay on the Development of Christian Doctrine* (London: Basil Montagu Pickering, 1878), p. 94.
[30] Ibid.

part of priesthood, and indeed of the entire system of Christian dispensation and doctrine: "You must accept the whole or reject the whole; attenuation does but enfeeble, and amputation mutilate. It is trifling to receive all but something which is as integral as any other portion; and on the other hand, it is a solemn thing to accept any part, for, before you know where you are, you may be carried on by a stern logical necessity to accept the whole."[31]

To defend that whole, insofar as priestly celibacy was an integral part of it, was most dear to Newman. As one born and raised within a thoroughly Protestant ambience, and as one who knew full well its ingrained anti-Catholic prejudices, he, the consummate logician, learned to know fully the logical holes in them. In devoting an entire lectures series to those illogicalities, he had to deal with the ones that characterized Protestant views on the Catholic clergy in general and on their celibacy in particular. In general, he laid it down that nobody has proven that there are fewer improprieties within the Protestant clergy than among the Catholic. He meant all sorts of improprieties, such as love of money, thirst for power, arrogance, insensitivity and so forth. With respect to celibacy, he was not to stress much the fact that, certainly in the England of his time, the Catholic Church took great caution in selecting and educating future priests. Much less was he willing to hold high the example of the few very virtuous to offset the weight of the weaknesses of many others. He turned the tables on Protestants by stating: "I am very skeptical indeed that in matter of fact a married clergy *is* adorned, in any special and singular way, with the grace of purity; and this is just the thing which Protestants take for granted." Inevitable was then Newman's question: "What is the use of speaking against our discipline, till they have proved their own to be better?"[32]

Such a question, which sounds ominous in view of the present-day approval by most Protestant clergy of contraception,[33]

---

[31] Ibid.

[32] *The Present Position of Catholics in England* (London: Longmans, Green and Co., 1903), p. 134.

[33] With Karl Barth giving them the "dogmatic" lead in his *Church Dogmatics, Vol. III, The Doctrine of Creation*, Part Four (Edinburgh: T & T. Clark, 1961), pp. 273-75.

had, to use the modern theological parlance, much more phenomenological justification to it than do modern efforts to evaluate
priestly celibacy on a phenomenological basis. Newman's question is
therefore to be pondered most carefully by latter-day advocates of optional celibacy as long as they have a truly spiritual concern at heart
and want to be in Newman's camp. And if they do, they can derive
much help from pondering Newman's emphatic declaration: "Now I
deny that they [Protestants] succeed with their rule of matrimony [for
the clergy] better than we do with our rule of celibacy." Newman
was denying this on a ground which is as valid today to any reasonable reader of newspapers and magazines as it was in Newman's
time: "The public prints and the conversation of the world, by
means of many shocking instances, which of course are only speci-
mens of many others, heavier or lighter, which do *not* come before
the world, bring home to me the fact, that a Protestant rector or a dissenting preacher is not necessarily kept from the sins I am speaking of,
because he happens to be married." But something even worse was in
store for a married minister: "When he offends, whether in a grave
way or less seriously, still in all cases he has by matrimony but ex-
changed a bad sin for a worse, and has become an adulterer instead of
being a seducer." After this, almost anticlimactic was Newman's
observation that matrimony does only one thing for a married
minister: "His purity is at once less protected and less suspected."[34]

Newman today would, of course, probe into the theological
reasons why the media revels in the sexual scandals of Catholic
clergy, but shows far less interest in similar failures of Protestant
ministers.[35] After all, the media finds many allies in ministers of
main-line Churches, where the sixth and the ninth commandments
impose nothing more than indignation about what the media too
condemns, though not on moral grounds, such as the sexual abuse
of children and the sexual harrassment of women.[36] Quite differ-

There Barth rejects the inflexible doctrine of *Casti connubii* and endorses the
Lambeth Conference of 1930!

[34] *The Present Position of Catholics in England*, pp. 134–35.

[35] Thus, for instance, hardly anything is reported about the far larger number of
Protestant ministers charged with pedophilia.

[36] The situation in the American Armed Forces is a perfect illustration of modern man's truly fallen predicament. Although male soldiers will forever harrass

ent is the attitude of the media toward revivalist ministers who still preach the supernatural, whatever their addiction to biblical literalism. Newman would find the reason for this difference in the fact that the media, as part of a fallen world which refuses to recognize its fallenness, finds nothing so inconveniencing as being presented with the supernatural, and especially as it is witnessed by the celibacy of Catholic priesthood. Indeed for a fallenness which glories in taking its sexual failures, and even perversities, for natural virtues, nothing can appear more embarrassing than the mere sight of celibate priests.

About that media and world it is even more true what Newman wrote in reference to a married Protestant clergy: "The married state is no testimonial for moral correctness, no safeguard whether against scandalous offences, or (much less) against minor forms of the same general sin [of impurity]." What he said next could serve as a most needed warning to those new theologians who describe marital love as the rose-strewn high-road to the highest virtue: "Purity is not a virtue which comes merely as a matter of course to the married any more than to the single, though of course there is a great difference between man and man."[37]

Newman would not have been a theologian of celibacy, had he bogged down in matters of fact translatable into statistics. Of course, in this age, when Catholic theologians almost apologize for priestly celibacy by suggesting, directly or indirectly, optional celibacy as a panacea, it is not amiss to take for a much needed shock treatment Newman's blunt words: "I have as much right to my opinion as another to his, when I state my deliberate conviction

women soldiers and other women as well, who in turn will forever entice the male, they all are expected to display a high measure of self-discipline without reliance on God's grace, in a matter which poses great difficulties even with full reliance on it. Thus a legal system that bars God from the premises, while it lets them be flooded over with pornography and opens them to gays and lesbians, wants some of those living there to function as if they were in monasteries and nunneries. Of course, that legal system would not endorse Christ's warning about lustful looks that alone goes to the root of the matter. In sum, a society that does not believe in angels has no right to expect its soldiers, policemen, politicians and clergymen to boot, to behave like angels.

[37] *The Present Position of Catholics in England*, p. 135.

that there are, to say the least, as many offences against the marriage vow among Protestant ministers, as there are against the vow
of celibacy among Catholic priests."[38] And in an age when theologians love circumlocutions more than plain words and straight
logic, it should seem refreshing and instructive to hear a logician,
such as Newman, state the obvious: "But if matrimony does not
prevent cases of immorality among Protestant ministers, it is not
celibacy which causes them among Catholic priests." Objectors to
priestly celibacy achieve nothing until they come to terms with
Newman's terse appraisal of the case: "Till, then, you can prove that
celibacy causes what matrimony certainly does not prevent, you
do nothing at all."[39]

Newman could say something still far more profound, though
still very obvious. The root of the problem, within celibacy or marriage, was fallen human nature: "It is not what the Catholic
Church imposes, but what human nature prompts, which leads a
portion of her ecclesiastics into sin. Human nature will break out,
like some wild and raging element, under any system; it bursts out
under the Protestant system; it bursts out under the Catholic; passion will carry away the married minister as well as the unmarried
priest."[40] To describe human nature as infested with "some wild
and raging element" is hardly to the liking of new theologians,
who at times quote in support of their wild reasoning Newman's
words about "the wild living intellect of man."[41] Far from recom-
mending wild innovations, Newman deplored reckless instability
in reasoning and the capricious espousal of anything novel, seeing
as he did in all this the impact of original sin on man's mind. Some
new theological thinking about priestly celibacy, to be discussed
later in this chapter, fully deserves the *caveat* which he delivered as
if he had been a thundering Old Testament prophet: "It is the
world, the flesh, and the devil, not celibacy, which is the ruin of
those who fall."[42]

[38] Ibid.
[39] Ibid., p. 136.
[40] Ibid.
[41] *Apologia pro vita sua,* p. 322.
[42] *The Present Position of Catholics in England,* p. 136.

It is not possible to state more clearly and to demonstrate more strongly that the theology of priestly celibacy must start with a courageous statement on original sin and its effects. Apart from such a statement, that theology will have no foundations steeped in reality. At any rate, only a Newman unspoiled by ecumenical "good feeling" could have the courage to raise a question about "slothful priests," a question directed at Anglicans: "Why, where was there any religion whatever, established and endowed, in which bishops, canons, and wealthy rectors were not exposed to the temptation of pride and sensuality?"[43] Today one need only read the British newspapers to see the appropriateness of Newman's words as far the clergy of the Church of England is concerned. Although almost all of them are married, they are still sorely tempted and at times do fall with a crashing noise, which the media picks up with its contorted seismograph calibrated to suit an increasingly amoral public.

Newman indeed would be the last to say that he had not been tempted. In fact, being a deeply introspective soul and in love with his diary, he made it all too clear that he had been tempted again and again. But, most importantly, he also insisted that purity was a virtue, that is, a disposition acquired through hard practice, of doing the good readily. This has yet to gain wide currency in order to balance the endless references to Newman's early realization, when he was only 16, that God called him to a single life. He never considered this calling of his as a talisman, or a charisma, that disposed of temptations. In fact, when three years later he gained "the unshakable resolve to live and die single," he qualified it with the words: "with divine aid."[44] In 1824 he jotted down in his diary that he should "pray for purity, sobriety, chastity, temperance . . . pray against excess, uncleanness, worldly-mindedness, lying, insincerity."[45] In 1826, the year of his Anglican ordination, he noted that during the previous year he had been particularly saved from sins against purity.

[43] Ibid.
[44] Quoted in J. Tollhurst, "The Interchange of Love: John Henry Newman's Teaching on Celibacy," *The Irish Theological Quarterly* 59 (1933), p. 218.
[45] Ibid.

For Newman purity was an asset to be won and not to be taken for granted, a sacrifice, though one which "strengthened one's feeling of separation from the visible world."[46] Nor was the virtue of celibate purity to be less appreciated because it did not eliminate the feeling of being in need of that natural sympathy that marriage satisfies best.[47] Nor did it imply the bearing of blindfolds in the presence of truly Christian married life.[48] Still the virtue of celibate purity (especially when combined with Catholic priesthood) was something which Newman valued most intensely. Otherwise he would not have risked initiating and losing a lawsuit (which he indeed lost) against a notorious detractor of Catholic priesthood and its celibacy.[49] Nor could Newman fail to see that the honesty of Catholic priests with respect to their vow of celibacy was a tacit target of Kingsley's charge, that it was customary with Catholic priests to be less than honest, because it was impossible to be honest and celibate.[50]

Kingsley, an early champion of Darwin, did not have to term priestly celibacy rank duplicity at a time when applause greeted the same charge made by Darwin, in a roundabout way of course. Darwin saw nothing immoral in "the greatest intemperance" among the savages and the prevalence among them, "to an astonishing degree, of utter licentiousness and unnatural crime." No wonder that he deplored the raising of "the senseless law of [priestly] celibacy" to the rank of a virtue.[51] Soon to second Darwin came Francis Galton, the father of eugenics, who denounced the Church for having "brutalised the breed of our forefathers" by its resolve to "preach and exact celibacy" from those who by their "gentle nature" were fitted "to the deeds of charity, to meditation, to literature, or to art," and who, because "of the social condition

---

[46] *Apologia pro vita sua*, p. 130.

[47] *Autobiographical Writings*, pp. 137–38, quoted by Tollhurst, p. 221.

[48] Following John Bowden's death Newman wrote to his widow, saying that in seeing his late friend at home, he felt to be in the midst of the Holy Family. See Tollhurst, p. 220.

[49] An excellent account of the Achilli case is in M. Trevor's *Newman: The Pillar of the Cloud* (London: Macmillan, 1962), pp. 546–59.

[50] A view widely entertained then as now in Western society.

[51] Charles Darwin, *Descent of Man* (1871; 3rd ed.; London: Murray, 1876), p. 182.

of the time, . . . found no refuge elsewhere than in the bosom of the Church." Of this "policy, so brutal and suicidal" Galton was "hardly able to speak . . . without impatience."[52] The latter expression was a classic in the art of understatement for which the British have a special fondness.

Elsewhere, such as in the Germany of the *Kulturkampf*, hostility to priestly celibacy showed no restraint. It was during those decades that Matthias Josef Scheeben established himself as the foremost speculative theologian of the 19th century, spending almost all his priestly life as a professor of theology in the major seminary of the Archdiocese of Cologne. The most mature form of his theological thought is embodied in the second edition of his *The Mysteries of Christianity,* almost ready for print when Scheeben died in 1888 at the age of fifty-three. That work deserved being characterized as "the most original, the most profound, and the most brilliant work which recent theology has produced."[53]

That work does not contain a word on celibacy, but it contains pages on the nature of priesthood that make all too obvious the intrinsic connection between priesthood and celibacy. Above all, Scheeben's *Mysteries of Christianity* contains lengthy, profound as well as inspirational pages (he knew how to write to serious laymen interested in serious stuff) on Christ's redemptive priesthood and sacrifice, aimed at saving fallen man. There is for these times of ours, reverberating with feminist slogans in theology, much to consider in Scheeben's presenting the function of priesthood as a maternal function. About this maternal function Scheeben certainly raised the highest expectation in his reader by making a statement that sounds almost unbelievable. We are, he wrote, "still far from appreciating the mystery of the Church in all its greatness," even after considering that through the Eucharist "the Son of God dwelt bodily and essentially, with all the pleni-

[52] D. W. Forest, *Francis Galton: Hereditary Genius* (New York: Taplinger, 1974), p. 100.

[53] A remark of A. M. Weiss, O.P., quoted by C. Vollert, S.J., in his introduction to his translation of that second edition (St. Louis: B. Herder Book Co., 1947), pp. iv–v.

tude of his divinity, among His members in the bosom of the Church."[54]

Clearly, Scheeben meant to spell out something additional and most important at that. He saw it tied to the fact that as "a bride-groom [of the Church] Christ had a higher objective in view than merely to be yoked with all the members of the Church so that they might benefit their own persons by sharing in His dignity and honor." Christ also wanted the Church, his bride, to be a true mother in some of its members, "so that the heavenly rebirth of the human race might correspond to its natural generation, and the organization of the God-man's family might conform to the family of earthly man." Obviously, Scheeben means priestly ordi-nation, but the perspective into which he puts it is extraordinarily elevated: "To this end He [Christ] *weds* a part of the members of the Church in a *special* way, entrusts to their keeping the *mystical re-sources* belonging to the Church in common, and *overshadows* them beyond all others with the power of the Holy Spirit, so that they may *bear* Him children and bring them into closer fellowship with Himself"[55] The words given in emphasis should suggest that the priest as a man cannot therefore marry.

The same inference, again not spelled out, though forcefully intimated by Scheeben, follows from the parallel he draws between the function proper to Mary and that proper to the priest: "The miraculous conception of Christ and His birth from the womb of the Virgin is the model and also the basis of the further spiritual conception and birth of Christ in the Church through the priest-hood." Scheeben does not tire of giving further variations on this extraordinarily profound theme: "As Mary conceived the Son of God in her womb by the overshadowing of the Holy Spirit, drew Him down from heaven by her consent, and gave Him, the in-visible, to the world in visible form, so the priest conceives the Incarnate Son of God by the power of the same Spirit in order to establish Him in the bosom of the Church under the Eucharistic forms." And again: "Christ is born anew through the priesthood by a continuation, as it were, of His miraculous birth from Mary; and

[54] Scheeben, *The Mysteries of Christianity*, p. 545.
[55] Ibid., p. 546.

the priesthood itself is an imitation and extension of the mysterious maternity that Mary possessed with regard to the God-man." Now, if it is further true what Scheeben puts in a concise way, namely, that "the priesthood is for the Eucharistic Christ what Mary was for the Son of God about to become man,"[56] then a theology of priestly celibacy is on hand in a most concise, most profound, and most mystical way.

The Fathers, who during the fourth and fifth centuries rallied behind the celibacy of the clergy by tying it to the *virgin* mother of Christ and to her *virgin* Son, offered therefore a theological perspective that has some absoluteness to it. They would be the first to protest on seeing that absoluteness relativized in the context of pleas full of copious references to Vatican II and to its stated aim of remodeling the Church along the lines set by the great Church Fathers. They would have plenty of opportunity to raise their voice. They might not fret too much over the undue preoccupation with the individual, with the subjective experience, in the new theology. But, genuine theologians that they were, and therefore interested above all in what God said to man, rather than in what one man said to another about God, they would be incensed by two curious facets of much of the new theology, especially of its dicta on the theology of priestly celibacy: first, the endless references to an enriched, deepened reflection on already well known truths and principles, while offering nothing specifically deeper or richer; secondly, the persistent reluctance to spell out what is truly theological, after spending much time, energy, and space on what is essentially anthropological, psychological, and sociological.

Nothing illustrates this better than Rahner's famous Open Letter on the celibacy of the secular priest today. Prompted by an inquiry addressed to him by a priest, a former student of his, Rahner felt impelled to address his reply to priests in general, or rather to the younger generation of priests. And he wanted to be heard. Partly because of this, Rahner emphasized themes that set the tone of theological discourse in the 1960s. Not that he would have been willing to take seriously the sentimentalist component

[56] Ibid., p. 547.

of that discourse, or "the present vogue for getting emotional and melodramatic over the unhappiness, the distress, the torments, the frustration of many priests." He branded all that as "craven and senseless escapism." He called it "naiveté" to think that the abandonment of the celibacy law "would open the gates of paradise to the poor clergy whom nothing but an antiquated, unnatural ecclesiastical law holds back from happiness and the development of their 'personality'." He could "muster very little patience with this constant cry for 'happiness', this self-pity, the myopic idea that there is some 'happiness' or other in this world outside tranquilly accepting that here all symphonies remain unfinished."[57]

All this had to be said and said bluntly. Nor was it any less necessary to point out that in this life one can make only one choice with one's life and that no choice can be made without renouncing something at the same time. A fashionable abuse of the word choice was rightly denounced as Rahner noted that a choice was not a capricious casting around for ever-new opportunities, or tempting prey, which in the end vitiates the very enterprise: "One need not have lain in every bed . . . in order to reach the deliberate, manly decision that one will creep into no more."[58] The more subtle counterpart of this illusion was exposed by Rahner's warning about the married man who never stops boasting of his happily married life: "Sometimes I think he needs to convince himself."[59] Still, a merely cultural climate was the target of Rahner's remark, that if a young man of twenty-five can responsibly choose about a great number of important things, including his selection of a woman for a wife, he must be assumed to be capable of choosing celibacy responsibly. Again, in this culture of instant satisfaction, especially in the domain of sex, it was useful to point out that "at bottom human sexuality is not a fixed quantity but a task, a challenge, an opportunity, a tremen-

[57] K. Rahner, *Servants of the Lord* (New York: Herder & Herder, 1968), pp. 151-52.

[58] Ibid., p. 156.

[59] Ibid., 157.

dous riddle."[60] Beautiful as all this could be, it was not theology.

Theology was still not visible in the criticism which Rahner aimed at those who "at every theological street-corner sing the praise of individual ethics, . . . urge the logic of individual perception," but not when it comes to write the theology of their own celibacy: "But *here*, where a man's own celibacy is concerned, there seems to be an abrupt flight from one's own unique individuality, a hiding behind abstract theories as though one were only a random 'instance' of these, and it is suddenly assumed that what applies to other men must not apply to me as well."[61] Theology came in, of course, when Rahner insisted that whether celibate or married, one has to answer to God. Theology came in, of course, as Rahner warned repeatedly that celibacy, like any other virtue, has to be gained anew and anew,[62] and that what was true on the supernatural level was true also in the purely natural domain: "We never finish once and for all with the real problems of life, they are always being posed afresh in the most unexpected forms."[63]

Theology was fully present, of course, in Rahner's insistence that celibacy made sense only if it was chosen for the sake of a Kingdom that lasted through eternity. A priest, he said, had to ask himself: "Do I (not do others) believe stoutly, unshakably, in eternal life?"[64] It was theology to insist that faith demanded courage, that faith meant acceptance of the cross, of the scandal of Christ, that faith meant a constant immersion in prayer: "Keep praying your way into what Jesus says about discipleship, place yourself with your whole concrete life before the cross of Christ. Really and honestly face up to the cross and death of your Lord. . . . Then you will find yourself being drawn ever deeper into the mystery of that life which springs from the death of Christ. Your life is steeped in mystery. Celibacy is only part of it."[65]

---

[60] Ibid., p. 154.

[61] Ibid., pp. 160–61.

[62] Ibid, pp. 158, 161, 166, 168.

[63] Ibid., p. 149.

[64] Ibid., p. 167.

[65] Ibid.

All this is true theologically and deeply so, but hardly the most fundamental point in the entire theology of priestly celibacy. Of course, Rahner could plead that he did not want to write a theological treatise on priestly celibacy.[66] But most of the priests interested in reading Rahner's Open Letter would have hardly taken him to task on that score. They would have rather countered him by saying that what he said could just as well be applied to married people. Did not Vatican II say that all Christians—married, unmarried, or celibate—are equally called to a complete union with Christ? Is it not necessary for married people too to keep Jesus the crucified in focus? Why then should anyone who wants to be a priest have to choose a celibate life? Did they hear Rahner emphatically and in a sustained manner inform them about the only answer that can satisfactorily resolve that question?

The answer can only be found in an unequivocal emphasis on the ontological nature of priesthood. But this is the point which is not articulated in Rahner's famed Open Letter, so characteristic of the new theology, which resembles all too often pages of psychology, sociology, and phenomenology, with some biblical phrases thrown in for good measure. Yet a page or two could have been reserved for the ontological substance of priestly celibacy, with still a score of pages left for "timely" considerations. Scheeben showed that it could be done and superbly so. But what Scheeben offered could not be readily marketed by a champion of the new theology, in which the ontological essence of the Eucharist and priesthood are paid far less attention than the Eucharist's community-building force and the priest's service to the community.[67] Only that ontological nature of the priesthood can justify the validity of the Patristic and Scholastic view that the priest must take upon himself the sacrifice of celibacy because he "generates," the sacramental body of Christ, the absolutely, infinitely, purest bodily sacrifice.

Consideration of that purity makes sense, of course, only if the priest's theological eyes are fully open to the true source of human

---

[66] Ibid., p. 150.

[67] As shown by the articles "priest" and "celibacy" in *Sacramentum mundi,* whose five volumes were published under Rahner's guidance and editorship.

misery. For if celibate life, married life, and any and all aspects of human life—political, social, economic, artistic—can become cesspools, it is only because man has fallen in Adam. But those eyes were trained to be half shut, if not blindfolded, when the awesome and most experimental reality of original sin ceased to be a crucial topic in theology. This happened when theology was in the heyday of its "renewal," the sixties, a decade inebriated with the gravest of all heresies, namely, the expectation of Utopia on earth to be achieved by science and politics. Never perhaps in history was optimism more unrealistic.

Hence the theological crisis of priestly celibacy, which finds another telling illustration in the book on the subject by an another stalwart of the "new" theology. I mean E. Schillebeeckx's *Celibacy,* which he offers as "an effort" to find "a successful and meaningful expression" for priestly celibacy, because, according to him, such an expression has not yet been found. As a proof of this he offers a most peculiar argument. It has nothing to do with the intrinsic value of some arguments, but with their presumed invalidity: "With the destruction of traditional arguments, many people now feel that the reality of religious celibacy itself is slipping out from under their feet."[68]

What are those arguments, what destroyed them, and how were they proved invalid? One would look in vain for a clear answer in Schillebeeckx's book. Anyone reading that book with reasonably open eyes must come to the conclusion that Schillebeeckx spoke throughout that book not so much as a theologian but as a propagandist, and at times a very cheap one at that. For a theologian cannot take a change of climate in publicity, which he zealously fuels, for the refutation of arguments, especially if he sees the refutation so complete as to be equivalent to their destruction. In fact, the very word "destruction" gives away the often slipshod thinking which Schillebeeckx offers in lieu of theology.

This is shown already by the very first paragraph in the very first chapter of *Celibacy.* There Schillebeeckx makes Minucius Felix, a younger contemporary of Tertullian and author of the dialogue

[68] E. Schillebeeckx, *Celibacy* (New York: Sheed and Ward, 1968), p. 15.

*Octavius,* between a pagan and a Christian called Octavius, state: "We have no altars, no temples." From this Schillebeeckx rushes to the conclusion that bishops, priests and deacons of the early Church lived happily with their wives, siring children, since the celebration of the Eucharist was a domestic affair, performed in a family atmosphere.[69]

To tell the truth, Minucius Felix did not have to prove that Christians of his time did indeed have houses of worship in order to make his point: Christians worship an invisible God, utterly different from the pagans' tangible statues housed in splendid temples: "Now you think," Minucius Felix turns the tables on his opponent, "that if we have neither temples nor altars we are concealing the object of our worship?"[70] Moreover, Minucius Felix provides details about the character of the religious gatherings of his time that give the lie to Schilleebeckx' portrayal of the Eucharistic celebration as being then a family affair. Those details are part of his portraying the importance accorded by Christians to the virtues of modesty, chastity, and virginity:"With us modesty is paraded not in our appearance but in our hearts; it is our pleasure to abide by the bond of a single marriage; in our desires for begetting children, we know one woman or none at all. In our banquets . . . we temper gaiety with gravity, chaste in our conversation, even more chaste in our persons.Very many of us preserve . . . the perpetual virginity of our undefiled bodies . . . and, indeed, even modest intercourse causes not a few of us to blush."[71] Clearly, no basis here for the innuendos included in Schillebeeckx' encomiums of those Eucharistic celebrations as so many family affairs.

Even more revealing of Schillebeeckx's untrustworthiness as a theologian of priestly celibacy is his manhandling of the "one wife" phrase in Paul's letters to Timothy and to Titus. For him the phrase means that the bishop (the presbyter) and the deacon must cling to his wife. Then begins a piece of propaganda, and a very

---

[69] Ibid., pp. 19-20.

[70] *The Octavius of Marcus Minucius Felix,* translated and annotated by G. W. Clarke (New York: Newman Press, 1974), p. 111.

[71] Ibid., pp. 109-10. An ample literature is quoted there (pp. 213-14) concerning the existence of Christian houses of worship at that time.

cheap one that a few years earlier would not have been tolerated on the part of theology students, let alone on the part of candidates for professorship: "Catholic tradition has understood the text as a precept of the church leaders not to marry again after their first wife dies. Modern exegetes, including Catholics, translate it as follows: "cling undividedly to one wife, as one might say, 'homo unius libri,' a man who swears by one book."[72]

This is new "theological" handwaving and not a scholarly treatment of a very serious exegetical matter. Even the most elementary scholarship is, however, disregarded by Schillebeeckx as he passes over the fact that Paul in his first letter to Timothy also stipulates that widows "must be of one husband" (1 Tim 5:9) in order to deserve church support. According to Schillebeeckx' exegesis Saint Paul would have meant that such a widow should cling to her husband, a plainly self-defeating suggestion.

Schillebeeckx keeps up with a theologizing which is but a willful stacking of cards throughout the book. What has been said above (chapter 3) about the Paphnutius story should cast a dark shadow on Schillebeeckx's respect for scholarly research about that story, even as its evaluation stood in the mid-1960s. But Schillebeeckx simply distorts the plain words of Saint Synesius in saying that the saint "accepted his appointment [to be a bishop] only on condition that he might continue marital relations with his wife."[73] Rather, the saint said that if the bishop of Alexandria is of the view that he should accept the appointment, then he would accept it as God's will and live with his wife as if she were his sister. That such distortions of a plain text could be presented by a leader of the "new" theology speaks volumes about its true character.

Schillebeeckx's *Celibacy* rests on two theological arguments, one with a biblical hue, the other with a philosophical undertone. The former consists in the claim that celibacy is a charisma, independent of priesthood, and therefore cannot be demanded from everyone who wants to be a priest. The argument rests on Schillebeeckx's interpretation of the "eunuchs" in Jesus' reply to the apostles' puzzlement about his teaching on marriage: "Not all

[72] Schillebeeckx, *Celibacy*, p. 20.
[73] Ibid., p. 35.

can accept this teaching; but those to whom it has been given. For there are eunuchs who were born so from their mother's womb; and there are eunuchs who were made so by men; and there are eunuchs who have made themselves so for the sake of the kingdom of heaven. Let him accept it who can" (Mt 19:11-12). According to Schillebeeckx, those are "eunuchs" for the Kingdom of Heaven who were seized "by the existential inability to do otherwise." And he asks: "Has theology done too little justice to that biblical *experience* of existential inability to do otherwise?"[74] One should indeed thank theology for having given little attention to an effort that turns celibacy into a charisma and a rather strange one at that. As long as theology remains a science, that is, a consistent reasoning on the basis of some theological premises, it will refrain from turning a virtue, which is a disposition gained by hard struggle with the help of God's grace, into a charisma, lest it be obliged to take for charisma all the other virtues. Most importantly, it will not suggest that a charisma irresistibly puts one on the good path and keeps him there.

The other argument is even more self-defeating. On the one hand, Schillebeeckx claims that he "can only see the *abolition* of celibacy for priests as detrimental." He also opines that "perhaps our own age which thinks only of getting rid of things, is still not creative enough to fashion new forms of things in which the Christian relation between ministry and religious celibacy can *really* come to the fore." Futurology is different from eschatology, and even eschatology should be anchored in everyday patient endurance and hope, to hear Newman, still an Anglican.[75] On the other hand, Schillebeeckx expects the new understanding of celibacy to come forth from a "co-operation among theologians (laymen and priests), teachers, social psychologists, sociologists, psychiatrists etc., and also with Christians of other faiths. But this common search must take place in a *Christian* way: in faith, and this is always a being-committed to the biblical experience of religious celibacy

[74] Ibid., p. 71.
[75] The sermon, "Watching," is in Newman's *Parochial and Plain Sermons*, vol. IV (new ed.; London: Longmans, Green and Co., 1897), pp. 319-33.

as 'existential inability to do otherwise'."[76] On reading the foregoing list of experts on celibacy, one is tempted to think that Schillebeeckx came close to entrusting the cabbage garden to some old
goats with no appreciation of what faith, Christian faith, really is.

Apart from this, Schillebeeckx seems to restrict the nature and
role of faith. First, according to him, faith has to be biblical, as if
faith, Christian faith, would not be, in order to be logical, strictly
ecclesial, that is a response to the voice of those who even today
preach in Jesus' name with the authority bequeathed by him. Second, and no less strangely, the faith in question has to be tied to a
patently forced interpretation of "eunuchs for the sake of the
Kingdom" as an existential impossibility to do otherwise. Did
Schillebeeckx find in the entire history of the Church a single
such "eunuch" who never felt that he could not do otherwise and
opt for the married state? Precisely because those "eunuchs" were
exemplary, they kept in mind Paul's words about those who
thought they were standing upright (1 Cor 10:12).

The crucial failure of Schillebeeckx's search for a new theology of priestly celibacy lies with his failed ecclesiology. Should one
think that the Church's and especially the papacy's unrelenting uphill struggle, an often very successful struggle, over so many centuries, is not something supported by Jesus' promise of assistance? Is
it a proper ecclesiology to say that the people's *right* to priestly
ministry is "an ecclesiological fact that carries more weight than
the church's law of unmarried priesthood?"[77] Does not such an
antithesis (a very forced one, indeed, on even a cursory look) reveal
a lack of faith in a Church that rests ultimately not on the Bible
but on the authoritative teaching of the Apostles and their successors? Can anything else guarantee, in the ultimate analysis, that
only such and such writings, out of a large number of scripts, have
a divinely inspired character?

Faith in that authoritative voice is not a feeling, but an intellectually guided assent. Schillebeeckx offers a subjectivist distor-
tion of that faith as he speaks of it as a continued "awareness of the
apostolic experience of the early church" and anchors in it his idea

[76] Schillebeeckx, *Celibacy*, p. 141.
[77] Ibid., p. 140.

of celibacy as a charisma: "The kingdom of God contains within itself an inner objective quality which can be the origin of the inner conclusion that 'existentially I cannot marry'." But on such a basis one has no right to profess with him "no fear for the future, whatever actual changes may follow from it [for priestly celibacy]. . . . If this feeling is indeed present, then we can bank on the future, even if events may possibly turn out otherwise than we have been accustomed to traditionally."[78]

Let it, however, be assumed that Schillebeeckx did not reduce genuine faith to feeling, however strong. In that case it still makes little sense to base on a deepened or stronger faith one's view that optional celibacy would not be hurtful to the Church. Whether the Church can or cannot make celibacy optional is not something to be discussed here. The fact is that the Church has steadfastly resisted efforts, past and very recent, to make priestly celibacy optional. She did so in the unshaken conviction that a universally binding celibacy is less hurtful for the Church than an optional celibacy. Most importantly that conviction, precisely because it remained unshaken over centuries full of troubles that undermined sundry forms of human wisdom, must be rooted in the Apostles, our irreplaceable and indispensable tie to the absolute fullness which Jesus carried as a celibate. Only such a tie can sustain the conviction of the Church that in holding high the ideal of a celibate priesthood, she carries out an apostolic injunction to swim against the tide. After all, was it not faith that has always been supposed to help one carry the burden of priestly celibacy, as well as the burden of the indissolubility of marriage?

If the champions of the new theology really had a "deeper" insight, they should have seen and articulated the obvious, namely, that the recent crisis about celibacy was no different from any of the earlier crises. This new crisis was not generated by something intrinsically new in human nature as unfolded by the rise of 20th-century man, who may be more modern than men of earlier ages that already looked upon themselves as modern, by being much more modish than they were. The crisis is merely a new version of the weakness of man's old fallen self, a weakness fueled by sundry

[78] Ibid., p. 142.

forms of modernity. In all crises about priestly celibacy there stands out the crisis of faith. In a theologically almost primitive sense, the latest crisis too is a crisis of a faith undermined by weakened morals. No theological sophistication should ever obliterate this fact. Such a sophistication can, of course, distract from the age-old teaching of the Church that God always supplies the grace commensurate with the highest moral and spiritual standards.

Champions of that sophistication are ill-served by their art. It prevents them from reading the past accurately as well as from guessing the future correctly. Statistics about the implementation of priestly celibacy are no different from other statistics. They can easily become the superlative form of what begins with lies, continues with bigger lies and, if not with colossal lies, at least with artful distortions. At any rate, statistics can never serve as rule in faith and morals, or else the devil might be declared the winner. Faith, together with its theological interpretation, has its own compass which is firmly fixed in the direction of a star. Though seen but once, that star has never set.

# 7

# Altar and Witness

Faith is a word with many shades of meaning that form two main groups. The first designates what one believes; the second, one's act of believing. These two aspects of faith—one with emphasis on the objective content of a proposition to be believed, the other with emphasis on the subjective strength of believing—must go together if faith is to remain the support of everyday life. The same holds true also on the supernatural level if faith is to accord with Saint Paul's view of it as a "reasoned worship" (Rom 12:1). Not that he meant by the word "reasoned" (or *logike* in Greek) some logic-chopping or lengthy syllogisms. But by using precisely that word, which may be rendered also as "spiritual," he certainly did not give a blank check to those who, with or without sophistication, brandish the word "faith." Among the sophisticated, Karl Barth comes first to mind. It is still to be widely recognized the extent to which he severed St. Anselm's famed motto, "fides quaerens intellectum," from its Augustinian roots.[1] Had Augustine's phrase, "quantulumque ratio . . . ipsa antecedit fidem," which he coined in his great letter on the relation of faith and

---

[1] K. Barth, *Anselm: Fides quaerens intellectum: Anselm's Proof of the Existence of God in the Context of His Theological Scheme*, tr. Ian W. Robertson (London: SCM Press, 1960).

reason,[2] remained in Barth's and others' focus, much of the anti-intellectualism of the new theology might have been nipped in the bud and theological discussions of priestly celibacy would not have led to an overemphasis of celibacy as a charisma.

Those two aspects of faith certainly go together in its classic biblical definition: "Faith is confident assurance concerning what we hope for, and conviction about things we do not see" (Heb 11:1). Saint Paul gave a breathtaking hint of those things invisible: "eyes have not seen, ears have not heard what God has prepared for those who love him" (1 Cor 2:9). Among these things or realities that are unseen but the man of faith hopes for and is convinced about them, the supreme is Christ. By dwelling in the heart of the faithful, Christ enables them to grasp, through faith and charity, "fully . . . the breadth and length and height and depth of Christ's love" (Eph 3:18). Such is the ultimate result of the fact that Christ is the one "who inspires and perfects our faith" (Heb 12:2). All this is about something essentially invisible, including Christ ascended into Heaven.

It is this Christ, very real though invisible both in Himself and in his impact, whom the priest has to preach. He has to preach a Christ who was crucified and has risen, so that man may have a reasoned assurance that death, a chief result of Adam's fall, is not an irreversible end of life but a door opening to life eternal in union with the Triune God. Moreover, the priest not only has to preach that Christ, but, most importantly, also make Christ's sacrifice present on the altar as the fountainhead of eternal life. There on the altar, due to the officiating of the priest, one encounters the risen Christ, the foremost of all invisible realities. Equally invisible are the results of other specifically priestly functions too: the restoration of supernatural life through absolution to a sinner, the grace given through the sacrament of the sick—these results can only be seen by faith. They are not conditioned on the preferences of times, and therefore no new times can add or subtract to these functions of the priest. He himself must have particularly keen eyes for the realities of faith, or else he will have an identity crisis,

---

[2] "To a small extent reason itself precedes faith." In *S. Augustini epistulae* 123:3, in CSEL, vol. 34, p. 707.

which in turn will inevitably generate a crisis of his appreciation of his celibate state.

Almost any crisis of priestly celibacy had been a moral crisis before it became a crisis of faith, although the latter can greatly re-inforce the former. This feedback was very much at work in the crisis that emerged in the 1960s.[3] It was a time when a new no-tion of sainthood began to be celebrated, the saintliness of social involvement, the saintliness of promoting peace and of preventing war, the saintliness of caring for the environment, the saintliness of communing with Nature writ large, the saintliness of helping all denizens of earth to live a healthy, comfortable life, preferably in one of the newly "creative" ways. In this new mode of saintliness there remained no room for saints of old, unless they could be refashioned. The saint, and one of the greatest ever, who more than any other saint was put into the crucible of this quasi-secular re-canonization, was the Poverello, Francis of Assisi. He quickly loomed large, not without the assistance of some heedless friars, as the patron saint of lush green meadows, of crystal clear brooks and rivers, of brilliant blue skies, of invigorating sunrises and melan-choly sunsets. A good deal of this was faith in Nature and in Nature's man, but hardly ever in Nature's God and in God's pur-pose with man. Yet many theologians eagerly lined up as the band-wagon of environmentalism, with the goddess Gaia atop, was roll-ing by.

Process theology took on a new life when self-appointed renovators of theology churned out roundabout endorsements of "the lust of the eyes, the desire of the flesh, and the pride of life" (1 Jn 2:16)—so many embodiments of things tangible. Soon they be-came emboldened and declared with unmuffled fanfare that they knew better than the Vatican's declaration of 1967. There all sexual relations outside of marriage were spoken of as constituting plain defiance of God's absolute and immutable law. Members of a com-mittee commissioned by the Catholic Theological Society of America argued that there was nothing wrong with extramarital relationships if they were "creative" and "integrative." They claimed

[3] As rightly argued by D. von Hildebrand in his *Celibacy and the Crisis of Faith* (Chicago: Franciscan Herald Press, 1971).

to have reached a more profound grasp of Catholic moral principles by claiming that homosexual relationships were preferable to
sexual starvation, that masturbation was reprehensible only when it
caused "serious psychological maladjustment," and that, in general,
the sexual act was morally good in any form, provided it was "self-
liberating, other-enriching, honest, faithful, socially responsible,
life-serving and joyous."[4]

Parallel with such developments, references to things invisible
began to peter out. One wonders whether the invisible reality of
Christ was more powerfully intimated by communion in the hand
(first given as an option, and then imposed by "popular demand"),
than by receiving the host in a kneeling posture. The latter was
made quickly impossible with communion rails having been duly
dumped on the scrap-iron heap. It was no longer possible, even if a
priest still felt it right, to recall a remark of the Saint of Assisi as to
what he would do were he to meet Saint Lawrence and a priest at
the same time: "I would first kiss the hand of the priest and say:
Forgive me, Saint Lawrence, but the hands of the priest touch the
body of our Lord each day!"[5] But if such testimonies about the
grandeur of the priesthood were no longer the in-things to recall,

---

[4] The report of the committee, *Human Sexuality: New Directions in American
Catholic Thought,* ed. A. Kosnik (New York: Paulist Press, 1977) was characterized
by Reay Tannahill in her *Sex in History* (New York: Stein and Day, 1980) as "one
of the most surprising documents in the history of the Church" (p. 424). She let
herself be lulled into the mistaken belief that the reports of a committee of a
theological society, even if it is in America, is a document of the Catholic Church.
It did, however, document the Church of our days insofar as it failed to call
promptly to the carpet the mischief makers.

[5] Saint Francis could, of course, extol the dignity of the priesthood in distinctly
theological terms as well. The occasion was the long letter he addressed to the
General Chapter of the Order, gathered on Pentecost 1226. There, in turning to
the priests of the Order, he referred to the veneration due to the womb of the
Blessed Virgin Mary, to the hands of St John the Baptist baptizing Jesus, and to the
tomb in which Jesus laid, and drew the following lesson: "How worthy, virtuous,
and holy ought to be he, who touches with his fingers, receives in his mouth and
in his heart, and administers to others, Christ, no longer mortal, but eternally tri-
umphant and glorious!" Quoted from O. Englebert, *St. Francis of Assisi: A Biography* (1965; Ann Arbor, MI: Servant Books, 1979), p 263. Equally important, by
showing full respect towards priests of ill-repute, Francis rebuffed heretics who
claimed that the unworthiness of a priest voids his sacramental powers. See M. F.
Habig (ed.), *St. Fancis of Assisi. Writings and Early Biographies* (4th rev. ed.; Chicago:
Franciscan Herald Press, 1983), pp. 1605-06.

it was because faith itself, a faith centered on things invisible, began to drift out of focus. Worse, the remedies suggested to reverse this trend all too often glossed over that focus.

Increasingly less was said about the fact of temptations in an age when the "theological" glorification of nature cast doubt even on the possibility that nature can be tempting. Therefore less and less was said about that role of faith which is to notice and help resist temptations. Less and less was said about the fact that priestly celibacy is a never-ending task, that it is a never-ending duty of the priest to remain a man of faith, a man whose attention is centered on things invisible. Less and less support was given to priestly celibacy, obviously, because nothing so effectively removes the priest from the realm of things visible and tangible than does his celibate status. This fact, though often noted either approvingly or disapprovingly, the priest can never ponder enough. It indeed remains true of the priest more than of any other human being that "without faith it is impossible to please God" (Heb 11:6). Nor can the priest please others and even himself unless he stirs up his faith again and again. Faith above all or rather most fundamentally is meant by the grace which is in the priest through the imposition of the hands. It is his duty to stir up, again and again, the liveliness of that grace so that he may truly remain a man of faith.

Although all men of faith must be witnesses of it, this is particularly true of the priest. Witnessing is not, however, a public relations act into which "Christian witness" has all too often degenerated so that the media might be pleased. But precisely this parody of "Christian witness" invites a studied oversight of the evangelical counsels of poverty, obedience, and chastity. If "Christian witness" is truly to be such, it has to accept the contempt of the world, which turns into an outright hostility in the face of those evangelical counsels, especially the one on celibate chastity.

It is no accident that Christ, who sent his Apostles to be his witnesses, foretold them of a martyrdom in store for them. The Greco-Latin words "martyr" and "martyrium" took on this additional meaning of witness and witnessing, precisely because the Apostles and so many faithful were ready to witness with their death on behalf of Christ. This is why martyrdom has become the highest form of one's readiness to witness, that is, to sacrifice everything for Christ's sake. This is why the celebration of the Eucharist, which is the actualization in sacramental form of the supreme martyrdom, or Christ's witness of God's holiness and love, was soon done on altars constructed over the tombs of martyrs or on altars that included some of their remains. Saint Maximus of Turin registered around 400 an already long-standing rule: "Appropriately, therefore, and in fellowship, so to speak, it was decreed that the tomb of the martyr should be there where the death of the Lord is daily celebrated; ... so that they who died because He died should repose in the mystery of His sacrament. Not without merit, I say, and as it were in fellowship the slain martyr's tomb is assigned to the place where the slain members of the Lord are placed: so that the hallowed sanctity of one place should join to Christ those whom the cause of the one Passion had knit to Christ."[6]

This unity between martyrdom and Eucharist finds itself expressed time and again in the prayers over the gifts which the priest has to say just before he begins the eucharistic prayer or Canon. Thus on the feast of Saint Ignatius of Antioch (October 17) the priest prays: "Lord receive our offering as you accepted Saint Ignatius when he offered himself to you as the wheat of Christ, formed into pure bread by his death for Christ." The same prayer for the feast of Saints Cosmas and Damian (September 26) voices the belief that through the eucharistic commemoration of the death of those holy martyrs the Church offers to God "the sacrifice from which all martyrdom took its origin (de quo martyrium sumpsit omne principium)."[7] Those prayers also urge those (priests and faithful) who celebrate the Eucharist to ask for the grace of a martyr's readiness for self-sacrifice. The prayer over the gifts on the feast of Saint Paul of the Cross (October 19) has this to say: "May we who celebrate the mystery of the Lord's suffering and death,

---

[6] St. Maximus of Turin, Sermo 77, PL vol. 57, col. 690. Quoted from M. de la Taille, *The Mystery of Faith* (London: Sheed & Ward, 1950), vol. 2, p. 106.

[7] In the Pre-Vatican II Roman missal, this prayer was also used on Thursday in the third week of Lent, when the station church was that of Saints Cosmas and Damien.

put into effect the self-sacrificing love we proclaim in this eucharist." On the feast of Saints Cornelius and Cyprian (September 16) the prayer over the gifts states the same: "The Eucharist gave them courage to offer their lives for Christ. May it keep us faithful in all our trials."

This view of the Eucharist obtained its earliest and most dramatic witness in the martyrdom of Saint Ignatius of Antioch. On his way to Rome he sent a letter to the faithful in Rome: "I am writing to all the Churches, and enjoin all, that I am dying willingly for God's sake, if only you do not prevent it. I beg of you, don't do me an untimely kindness. Allow me to be eaten by the beasts, which are my way of reaching God. I am God's wheat, and I am to be ground by the teeth of wild beasts so that I may become the pure bread of Christ."[8]  The surname of Ignatius was Theophorus, around which a medieval legend spun a most appropriate interpretation: when the beast tore upon the martyrs' chest, the name of Christ appeared to be written on his heart. Forty years later the same connection between altar and priesthood found a memorable expression in the martyrdom of Saint Polycarp. When the men in charge started to light the fire, "a great flame blazed up and those of us to whom it was given to see beheld a miracle. . . For the flames, bellying out like a ship's sail in the wind, formed into the shape of a vault and thus surrounded the martyr's body as with a wall. And he was within it not as burning flesh but rather as bread being baked, or like gold and silver being purified in a smelting furnace. And from it we perceived such a delightful fragrance as though it were smoking incense or some other costly perfume."[9]

The final phase of the persecution did not fail to produce a similar testimony when Saint Quirinus, bishop of Siscia, a town on the southern border of Pannonia, suffered martyrdom in 308. Maximus, the local magistrate, on finding his various arguments roundly rebuffed and rebutted by the bishop, decided to use tor-

[8] Quoted from W. A. Jurgens, *The Faith of the Early Fathers* (Collegeville MN, 1970), pp. 21–22 (#53a).

[9] H. Musurillo, *The Acts of the Christian Martyrs* (Oxford: Clarendon Press, 1972), p. 15.

ture. As the bishop was being beaten he was told that, if he sacrificed to the gods, he would be made a priest of Jupiter. The bishop replied: "I am exercising my priesthood here and now by offering myself up to God." Then the bishop added something just as deep theologically by noting that the pastor's heroism was meant to inspire the faithful to act similarly: "I would willingly endure far worse treatment to encourage those over whom I have presided to follow me by a short road to eternal life."[10]

Those who held such a view of the enactment of Christ's eucharistic sacrifice by the priest and the faithful's participation in it could hardly see reason to complain of far lesser challenges to heroism, such as priestly celibacy and chaste marital living. It was rather those who had a lesser view of the Eucharist who began to find those lesser challenges appear ever greater. Almost a millennium and a half after the martyrdom of Saint Quirinus, another bishop suffered spiritual martyrdom at the hands of priests and laity, agonizing over the perfunctory manner in which Masses were said. He was Saint Alfonso, who suspended those priests rushing through the Mass in fifteen minutes; he also wrote a moving treatise on the true nature of the Mass to support his action. He began with the statement of Saint Cyprian that "the priest at the altar represents the person of Jesus Christ." Then Saint Alfonso exclaimed: "But whom do so many priests today represent? They represent only mountebanks earning their livelihoods by their antics. Most lamentable of all is it to see priests in religious orders, and some even of reformed orders, say Mass with such haste and such mutilation of the rite as would scandalize even the heathen. . . . Truly the sight of Mass celebrated in this way is enough to make one lose the faith."[11]

Clearly, if a priest leaves his flock in the dark about the true nature of what takes place in the Mass, a part of his flock will rejoice in having masses that last only fifteen minutes. These will not see any deeper by calling the Mass, according to the new custom, the Eucharistic celebration, which, with its new Canon II, need

[10] See *Butler's Lives of the Saints*, ed. H. Thurston and D. Attwater (New York: P. J. Kenedy and Sons, 1962), vol. 2, p. 473.

[11] Ibid., vol. 3, p. 246.

not last more than a quarter of an hour. Another part of the faithful will, however, feel crucified by the duty to attend the Eucharist turned into a "celebration." These and not the former group resemble the faithful whom the once famed Ignaz Döllinger had in mind when he came down firmly, time and again, on the side of priestly celibacy. The English-speaking world learned about this when, after Döllinger's death in 1888, the Rev. Alfred Plummer, the translator of several of his works into English, reported Döllinger's words to him: "You in England cannot understand how completely engrained it is into our people that a priest is a man who sacrifices himself for the sake of his parishioners. He has no children of his own, in order that all the children in the parish may be his children. . . . In almost all Catholic congregations, a priest who married would be ruined; all his influence would be gone. The people are not at all ready for so fundamental a change, and the circumstances of the clergy do not admit of it. It is a fatal resolution."[12]

Döllinger referred to the resolution whereby the Old Catholics, forerunners of many "New" Catholics, allowed in 1876 their clergy to marry. He urged, though in vain, a prominent delegate to the Synod of Bonn to vote against the resolution: "When the pastor cannot display to the people the personal sacrifice he owes to his parish, then he and the cause he must represent, are finished."[13] Once the Old Catholic clergy sided with the resolution, Döllinger took the view that they "became mere tradesmen and the cause of Old Catholicism was lost."[14] Plummer's report contained much of the same, in witness to the depth of Döllinger's conviction: "When a priest can no longer point to the personal sacrifice which he makes for the good of his people, then it is all over with him and the cause which he represents. He sinks to the level of men who make a trade of their work."[15]

[12] In Plummer's reminiscences of Döllinger in *The Expositor* 2 (1890), p. 470.

[13] See E. Michael, *Ignaz von Döllinger: Eine Charakteristik* (Innsbruck: Fel. Rauch, 1894), p. 295.

[14] Ibid., p. 297.

[15] Decades earlier Döllinger fulminated against the two Theiner brothers who in 1828 brought out what he called "a heavy artillery against priestly celibacy." "Is it not shocking," he wrote to a colleague, who later became bishop of Strasbourg,

By the time Döllinger died in 1890, hardly a priest within the Old Catholic Church opted for celibacy. It became true of the priests of the Old Catholic Church as well what Döllinger voiced to Plummer about Protestant ministers. Catholics know that the "small wants of the priest are supplied, and that he can devote all his time and thought to them. They know that it is quite otherwise with the married pastors of the Protestants. The pastor's income may be enough for himself, but it is not enough for his wife and children also. In order to maintain them he must take other work, literary or scholastic, only a portion of his time can be given to his people; and they know that when the interests of his family and those of his flock collide, his family must come first and his flock second. In short, he has a profession or trade, a *Gewerbe*, rather than vocation; he has to earn a livelihood."[16]

This is not to suggest that there were no Protestant ministers either in Döllinger's time or in our times who did not serve their congregation zealously and even at the cost of great sacrifices. The crucial point made by Döllinger rests with his theological understanding of the priesthood, which, for all his opposition to the dogma of papal infallibility, remained thoroughly Catholic. He knew that unlike ministers who celebrate at a table, priests officiate at an altar. Therefore their state of life must bear witness to the fact that the altar carries the self-sacrificing Christ himself.

Once it is considered that Christ sacrificed himself so that sins may be forgiven, another compelling reason for priestly celibacy emerges as well. The power of the keys to bind and loose, which Jesus gave the apostles, and the Spirit he breathed on them so that they forgive the sins of others, are at work when the priest listens to penitents so that he may absolve them from their sins. The sacrament of confession is not primarily a judicial tribunal, but a channel through which the perfect love shown towards the Father by the self-sacrificing Christ is imparted sacramentally to the penitent; for only perfect love sets off sins. The insistence of the Roman

---

"that priests themselves are rising against the Church? One should flay this Theiner in a stern review. See to it that a proper example be set in the *Katholik*." Ibid., p. 297.

[16] From Plummer's reminiscences, quoted above.

Catholic Church that its priests be celibate greatly contributed to the vigorous practice of confession among Catholics, a practice much less noticeable within Eastern Orthodoxy with its married clergy. The denial of the Eucharistic celebration as a sacrifice by the Reformers was a logical part of their denial of the power of priestly absolution, to say nothing of their rejection of celibacy for ministers.

Some of those who no longer see anything sacral in the priest-hood still often note on psychological grounds that a priest must be celibate if he is to hear confessions. Perhaps no one made that point more tellingly than the novelist Aurore Dupin, better re-membered as George Sand. The context was an Open Letter of hers, addressed in the pages of Le Temps,[17] the Parisian daily, à propos the marriage (and excommunication) of Père Hyacinthe, famous for his series of sermons delivered at Notre Dame. A cel-ebrated feminist of her time, George Sand was not bothered by the marriage itself. She had by then pleaded for free sexual intercourse among consenting adults, provided it was done in total love, and considered intercourse even in marriage a sin if such a love was no part of it. In the absence such a love, she wrote, one should "live a life of utter chastity."[18]

George Sand felt all the greater sympathy for the newly mar-ried Père Hyacinthe (who henceforth was known as Mr. Loyson), as earlier she had found him disingenuous as a priest who rejected hell, advocated optional celibacy, and yet supported the papacy. But once Père Hyacinthe broke with the Vatican over the dogma of in-fallibility and married, he became an ingenious and courageous figure in her eyes. Still, George Sand could not understand why the former Père Hyacinthe still wanted to be part of a "Catholic" Church (and function as a priest within it) different from Rome as well as from any of the churches initiated by Luther. At any rate, George Sand, with an almost maternal instinct, wished him well: "I

[17] Reprinted as ch. xvii in her Impressions et Souvenirs (3d ed.; Paris: Michel Lévy, 1873), pp. 272-78. References are to the English translation by H. K. Adams, Im-pressions and Reminiscences (Boston: W. F. Gill, 1877), pp. 213-20.

[18] See A. Maurois, Lélia: The Life of George Sand, tr. G. Hopkins (New York: Harper and Brothers, 1953), p. 325.

hope that it [the new "Catholic" Church] will have numerous ad-
herents; for, without either being Protestant or Catholic, I see, as
every one does, the fatal and disgraceful consequences of the celibacy of priests. Let them marry, then, and receive no confession!"[19]

One wonders what the former Père Hyacinthe must have felt
on reading this restriction on the priestly activities he envisaged
for himself and other priests who married. But George Sand was
not yet through. Her answer to the question, "Will Father
Hyacinthe hear confessions?" is noteworthy not only for its psychological insights, but even more so for its theological underpin-
nings. The theology, or rather religion, was based on the premise
that it should operate without any priestly mediation between the
individual and God: "I believe this mediator useless when he is not
harmful, and harmful when he is not destructive." Still George
Sand knew that most men, and especially women, will forever long
for the service of priests. But in doing so, they would and should
not choose the married kind for their confessors. Not that George
Sand did not envisage that those priests of a Church of the future,
as Father Hyacinthe imagined it, would "be at least as pure if not as
noble as Father Hyacinthe. Let such priests officiate at the wedding
of other priests and let them thereby set their regenerated consciences at peace."[20]

However pure and noble, those priests were not to be taken by
women for their confessors, because George Sand did not feel "the
secret of the confessional compatible with the existence of conjugal love." Even if she were a Catholic (and she was a fervent one in
her teens while in the Convent School of the English Ladies),
George Sand opined that she would not include within her confessions intimate details of her marital life: "Discretion is easier
than restraint; and moreover, I should say to my children: 'Never
have secrets that it is too hard to reveal, and you will never stand in
dread of the gossip of the vicar's wife'."[21]

But George Sand's ultimate vote was not for love, marital or
extramarital. Her public advice given to Père Hyacinthe could

---

[19] *Impressions and Reminiscences*, p. 218.
[20] Ibid., pp. 219-220.
[21] Ibid., pp. 218-19.

sound familiar to the readers of a novel of hers, *Mademoiselle la Quintinie*, where she depicted love as being so exclusive that it was never to be made a topic of conversation, however confidential, with a third party, be it a priest.[22] Only when her letters were published did it become public knowledge that the ultimate vote of that energetic feminist and lover was for something better than earthly love. After many years of experimentation with "total love," in and out of marriage, she came to a sobering conclusion: "If I had to start my life over again, I should choose to remain chaste."[23]

One may, of course, argue that George Sand considered it most improper for a woman to confess her sins, especially the ones relating to sex, to a priest, married or not, because she resented male superiority in any form. The one who classed men according to their readiness to surrender to her[24] unerringly recognized that in confessing one's sins one profoundly surrendered, a point which it took a truly believing great novelist, Mauriac, to plumb in its theological depths.[25] But in an animatedly feminist age such as ours, the insight of George Sand the feminist should appear to have a sophistication that does not lack depth.

Less sophisticated was Nietzsche, though still to the point, when he named as one of Luther's blunders the abolition of celibacy. Luther, Nietzsche wrote, who "gave back to the priest sexual intercourse," failed to understand that "three fourths of the reverence of which the people (and above all the women of the people) are capable, rests on the belief that an exceptional man in this respect, will also be an exceptional man in other respects." In fact Nietzsche saw in that reverence "the most subtle and insidious advocate" of "the popular belief in something superhuman in man, in a miracle, in the saving God in man." Consequently, "after

---

[22] See Maurois, *Lélia,* pp. 403-04.

[23] In a letter to a lover of Musset from 1867; ibid., p. 435. George Sand was then sixty-three.

[24] One of George Sand's potential targets was Heinrich Heine, of whom she remarked: "Il est tendre, affectueux, dévoué, romanesque en amour, faible même et capable de subir la domination illimitée d'une femme." See J. L. Sammons, *Heinrich Heine: A Modern Biography* (Princeton University Press, 1979), p. 201.

[25] See F. Mauriac's *Maundy Thursday,* tr. H. F. Kynaston-Snell (London: Burns Oates & Washbourne, 1932), pp. 36-37.

Luther had given a wife to the priest, he had to take from him auricular confession." The rest of Nietzsche's dictum attests the same
straight logic: "That was psychologically right; but thereby he
[Luther] practically did away with the Christian priest himself,
whose profound utility has ever consisted in his being a sacred ear,
a silent well, and a grave for secrets."[26]

To the witness of the dissident theologian, of the unbelieving
novelist, and of the rabidly anti-Christian philosopher, one may
add that of a famed diplomat, who, though a priest and later a
bishop, acted through much of his life as if he had no faith at all.
For Talleyrand's aphoristic remark, "You can only lean on something that resists,"[27] unwittingly conveys the profound pastoral
usefulness which celibacy provides for the exercise of the priesthood. Not that Talleyrand derived personal profit from his pithy
wisdom. Possibly the most skilled diplomat in his time in making
the most of the art of ruse, Talleyrand tried to exploit his part in
bringing about, in 1801, the Concordat between Rome and Na-
poleon for the purpose of having Rome validate his civil marriage.

In the extremely courteous terms of the letter which Cardinal
Consalvi wrote to him on June 30, 1802, one can feel Rome's age-
old steely resolve to stand firm and also its readiness to consider
any serious argument: "I really wished that your Excellency's request be fully granted and that the papal Brief contain the permission to marry [with the blessing of the Church], but how could
this be done when eighteen centuries of the Church's history do
not afford a single precedent? Your Excellency will observe in the
marginal notes made on the note sent by you that none of the examples are to the point: no consecrated bishop was ever dispensed
to marry. Your Excellency must clearly realize that the example of
eighteen centuries is such that the Holy See cannot, even in the
most pressing circumstances, depart from it. Your Excellency will
note that not only is there no instance to the contrary, but there

[26] F. Nietzsche, *Joyful Wisdom,* tr. T. Common (New York: F. Ungar, 1960), pp.
312-13. The passage is from Book V, "We Fearless Ones. The Peasant Revolt of the
Spirit."

[27] Quoted in I. F. Görres, *Is Celibacy Outdated?* (Westminster, MD: The Newman
Press, 1965), p. 86.

are several instances to the effect that the permission in question, requested repeatedly, was invariably refused by the Holy See." Consalvi then added that his delay in replying was caused "by the most careful researches to sift every evidence relating to the request."[28] Political pressure once more failed to be stronger than Rome's strength, although this time the matter could look insignificant compared with the request of Henry VIII.

About the awesome strength which celibacy gives the priest a priceless witness can be found in Rolf Hochhuth's reminiscences of a conversation he had on a Sunday with a very learned elderly Jesuit. The topic was, of course, Hochhuth's claim, made in *The Deputy*, that Pope Pius XII utterly failed as a spiritual leader when he did not condemn the Nazis explicitly for their extermination of the Jews. According to Hochhuth this was an act of utter selfishness, aimed at sparing his own flock from dire reprisals at the hands of Hitler. Whether Hochhuth reported that conversation with less tendentiousness than he dealt with the Pope, may very well be doubted. For Hochhuth cast the entire conversation in terms of his own insistence that this life down here is all we have. It wholly escaped him that, as Karl Jaspers pointed out, on that ground he had no right to take to task the Pope or anyone else for selfishness.[29]

The Pope's policy (which incidentally saved almost a million Jews[30]) cannot, of course, be justified if one lets oneself be lured into some aprioristic perspective about God. On this invariably blinding perspective rested Hochhuth's argument that if Jesus Christ was God, he could and should have prevented the beheading of John the Baptist. To defend such and similar tragedies with an eye on eternity, in which God's plans would balance matters, may readily force one, Hochhuth argued, to adopt an attitude of utter rigidity. This is precisely the principal impression Hochhuth

[28] F. Mathieu, *Le Concordat de 1801* (Paris: Perrin et Cie, 1903), p. 348. The author of this book was himself a Cardinal.

[29] Jaspers did so over Radio Basel. For the full text, see E. Bentley (ed), *The Storm over the Deputy* (New York: Grove Press, 1964), pp. 99-102.

[30] This fact was much in the news following the death, on February 10, 1997, of Father Robert A. Graham who had published in 11 volumes the supporting evidence gathered from the Vatican Archives.

gained from that conversation, during which he forced the good
Jesuit to suggest that he would readily die the next moment if God
demanded this sacrifice from him.

After recalling this conversation years later, Hochhuth specified the special insight he gained from it: "And on this Sunday I
became cognizant for the first time of what bottomless cunning
lurks in the Church's insistence on celibacy. That these priests are
obliged to live alone, that they do not have a single human being
to whom they can get thoroughly attached. They have no child, no
wife, and this gives them that unbelievable hardness which enables
them to reckon years not in the terms of a human life, but incom-
mensurably under the aspect of eternity."[31]

This insight was a rather forceful statement, essentially correct
in its logic, of a fact. The strength, be it called hardness, which celibacy gives to priests and through them to the Church, has often
been noted. The same cannot be said about what Hochhuth
claimed to be the explanation of celibacy. First, he wrongly implied that priests were forced to live a celibate life, as if anyone
who married at the age of twenty-five was forced to marry just
because he wanted to marry very much. Second, Hochhuth made
a wrong inference in saying that since priests do not have their
own life in a marital sense, "life itself, the life of other people, is not
of the same consequence to them as *life is for those to whom that is all
there is* (italics added)." One wonders whether Hochhuth ever
heard of St. Peter Claver, the heroic helper of castaway Negroes, of
Don Bosco, the protector of hapless boys, and of Father Damien,
who became a leper for the sake of lepers—to mention only a few
examples.

Undoubtedly there is a huge difference between two
perspectives, one closed, the other open to eternity. But Hochhuth's
inference that priests could not therefore show genuine compassion
rested on his forced definition of it. Hochhuth failed to note that
if this life *is all there is*, there was no room for compassion and
much less for a compassion consisting in one's sacrificing oneself
for others. Hochhuth's putting in the same category the Church's
thinking in terms of eternity and the Nazis' and Communists'

---

[31] *The Storm over the Deputy*, pp. 60-61.

thinking in terms of future generations for whose happiness the present generation may be treated inhumanly, may be left aside as another failure in logic. So much for his condemnation, "But it is always terribly inhuman to think this way,"[32] of thinking in terms of eternity, which he rightly took to be a logical characteristic of priestly celibacy.

Logic, for which the first step is of crucial importance, was missing when Hochhuth simply stated that it was this perspective of eternity that enabled the Church "from the beginning, to draw the strength to demand for 2,000 years such unheard-of sacrifices and victims [of priestly celibacy]."[33] Hochhuth failed to ask about the factor that made the Church capable of demanding such sacrifices. The possible and only logical answer—divine Revelation culminating in Christ's sacrifice and in his unfailing assistance of the Church—could not be considered by Hochhuth with any seriousness. After all, he emphatically recalled Bernard Shaw's phrase, "Beware of the man whose God is in Heaven," that serves as a motto for *The Deputy*.

Hochhuth's reflections on celibacy are recalled here at some length because they show in raw nakedness what makes the priest unacceptable to the world: it is the priest's commitment to the One who ascended into Heaven, a commitment made tangible by his celibacy. A priest deceives himself if he tries to explain his celibacy by removing out of focus, however slightly, the fact that God *is* in heaven. The same is true of all authors of theological essays and books on priestly celibacy who do the same, however indirectly. They mislead themselves as well as their readers by failing to recall that Saint Paul said not only of virgins but also of all Christians that if there is no God in Heaven, if there is no resurrection of the body, they are more miserable than everyone else. God in heaven and his merciful revelation make no sense, however, if there was no Fall and if one glosses over the Devil's role in that aboriginal calamity of man, to recall once more Newman's characterization of it.

[32] Ibid., p. 61.
[33] Ibid.

Priestly celibacy is not justified by its human usefulness. Saint Francis de Sales was half-joking when he referred to that usefulness in a conversation with an elderly lady who loved to bring up difficulties against the Catholic faith and raised, one day, the law of celibacy as something that scandalized her: "But, my dear," the bishop said, "you keep on coming to see me. Think of the time it takes to talk to you. How on earth could I manage to help you with all your difficulties if I had a wife and children!"[34] There will never be enough celibate priests to satisfy *that* type of pastoral need! Nor should one think that the shortage of priests capable of giving proper pastoral service would necessarily be alleviated if they were allowed to marry. News about the recurrent shortage of candidates to the Anglican and Lutheran ministries should speak louder than long arguments.[35] If priesthood amounts to a counseling service, able young men will choose the latter as a secular profession and not as an "ordained" hobby that pays far less and brings with it theological and ethical headaches even if one professes to be a liberal.

Priestly celibacy is not to be measured by the economy it affords to the Church in implementing her missionary projects, although it remains a telling point. What was true a hundred years ago, namely, that even an *unmarried* Protestant missionary costs seven times more than does a Catholic missionary priest,[36] should seem a foregone conclusion today when the cost of caring for a family is rapidly rising everywhere. The true *raison d'être* of priestly celibacy does not lie in economics, in psychology, and not even, say, in Gandhi's unconditional esteem of continence, let alone

[34] M. de la Bedoyere, *François de Sales* (New York: Harper and Brothers, 1960), p. 64.

[35] Quite recently the Church of England started a recruitement drive for young clergy who can bring "energy and enthusiasm" into the aging ministry. The drive was prompted by the fact that the number of male recruits to the theological colleges of the Church of England dropped from 64 in 1990 to 28 in 1995. See *The Daily Telegraph*, Oct. 23, 1996. Data relating to the 1960's concerning the shortage of pastors in the Lutheran Church in Germany were listed by Cardinal Höffner in his essay, "For the sake of the Kingdom of Heaven. Ten theses on Priestly Celibacy," in J. Coppens, (ed.), *Priesthood and Celibacy* (Milano: Ancora, 1972), p. 786.

[36] An admission by the Anglican bishop of Tokyo, E. Bickersteth. See *The Life and Letters of Edward Bickersteth* (2d ed.; London: S. Low, 1905), p. 214.

within his way of achieving it.[37] There is much more to priestly celibacy than in its playing a decisive role in the spiritual efficiency of the Catholic Church, a role often recognized by outsiders.[38]

To go to the very bottom of the *raison d'être* of priestly celibacy, one has to recall incidents in the lives of saints, of which one in the life of Blessed John of Salerno, a disciple of Saint Dominic himself, has a special instructiveness. What brought to light that incident in his life was the confession of a woman, who, being possessed by the devil, had just been exorcised by a priest, but in vain. The evil spirit shouted through her mouth: "Only he who was unburned in the fire can drive me out!" On being adjured to speak openly, the woman named John of Salerno, prior of the Dominican convent of the place, as the one the evil spirit referred to. She further disclosed that a girl once, feigning sickness, called John of Salerno to her bedside to make her confession, but actually to seduce him. She did not succeed in burning him to spiritual ashes in the cauldron of lust. The holy friar kept praying for her and in the long run the girl repented.[39] Such was the priest who alone made the devil tremble and take to flight.

Such priests alone will not be swayed for a moment by the new approach to sexual morality which casts all our understanding of it into the scientifically coated category of struggle for survival. There even the raping of adolescent girls by adult men is shrugged off as a mere example of the age-old competition among men for desirable women and, in the United States specifically, the byproduct of a "socially imposed monogamy." The competition among women for desirable men demands in turn that adolescent girls be barred from that competition, through the device of declaring their liaisons to be immoral. So goes the new wisdom of academia, productive of gems such as: "Sexual morality becomes fascinating from this perspective, since what is moral depends on

[37] Thus Gandhi insisted from time to time that a young girl share his bed or sleep next to his mat, and at times he requested the presence of two throughout the night, so that he might prove all the more convincingly to himself his complete freedom from carnal lust. See A. Koestler, *The Lotus and the Robot* (London: Hutchinson, 1966), p. 149.

[38] One of these was Gandhi himself.

[39] See *Butler's Lives of the Saints,* vol. 3, pp. 295-96.

whose interests are being served."[40] Why is it, one may ask, that celibate priests are particularly able to see through that skullduggery in morality?

Such priests alone will have noticed that sometime before this pseudo-sophistication had become a vogue, its motivations had been spelled out with no pretenses to intellectual refinement. "Promiscuity was socially accepted, even encouraged," wrote Karla Vermeulen, a senior at the Cornell School of Hotel Administration, in a guest editorial to *The New York Times,* when the rise of AIDS began to take the joy out of free sex. Her grief was visceral. It related to her perception that a never before experienced freedom for casual sex had suddenly vanished. With the pill on hand, whatever one could catch from one's partners "could be fixed with penicillin." But with the new plague on, even men were at a risk and, as a result, "they are as willing to make commitments as women traditionally have been, and monogamy is back in style."[41] Monogamy, to be sure, though only as a prophylactic, but not as a moral framework. A celibate priest may not be the last to see this for what it is, but he can certainly help clear the increasingly befogged vision of those entrusted to him, especially if they are young.[42]

The latter are increasingly enveloped by the rising tide of sexual seduction that spills all over the world, while presenting itself as the most noble of all natural fulfillments. In reality, that flood

[40] David Buss, professor at the University of Michigan and author of *The Evolution of Desire* (New York: Basic Books, 1994) as quoted in *The New York Times* (June 11, 1995, p. E6).

[41] "Growing up in the Shadow of AIDS," *The New York Times*, Sept. 30, 1990, Sec. IV, p. 21. One wonders why a young lady with such liberated views on sex chose hotel management as her profession.

[42] Here perhaps a personal experience may not be amiss. It relates to a young woman in her mid-twenties, who happened to find me in a church where I dropped in by chance on a rainy afternoon. She was visibly troubled. She felt that in the attic above the place where she worked, the devil was worshiped by a weird group of men and women. The conversation turned to prayer and to the reception of sacraments. She said she received communion every Sunday with her boyfriend, although they had lived together for the past six or so years. To my suggestion that she had been living in a state of serious sin and that instead of going to communion she should go to confession, she replied that an experience so delightful as being in bed with a boyfriend cannot be a sin. One wonders what kind of spiritual witness she heard preached during the Sunday masses.

carries in its dirty waves untold victims in soul and body; it sweeps along the wrecks of uncounted marriages; it does not leave untouched any facet of life. There has been immorality around ever since Adam took the apple from Eve. Long before the epidemic of AIDS, immorality wrought its havoc, such as when syphilis swept through Europe in the wake of the discovery of America. It is possible to write political history in terms of sexploits. It was, however, kept for our progressive times to present debauchery as something appropriate for those who are mature and healthy, and to evaluate the history of sexual practice in that morbid perspective.[43]

Most significantly, it was reserved for these tragically immature times of ours to see lust even in Christ, the most sacred person who ever appeared in human history. First it was merely the vagary of novelists. Clearly, if sexual satisfaction was man's means of penetrating the core of his existence, then even the resurrection of Jesus had to be seen as his awakening to sensual love. Not surprisingly, this U-turn in exegesis came in D. H. Lawrence's *The Man Who Died* (1932). Lawrence had already read into the entire cosmos the simultaneous love-and-repulsion experience, the leading idea of his notorious novels. Yet, the most revealing detail in *The Man who Died* is not so much that Lawrence makes Jesus feel cursed through the fact of his resurrection until the moment when he again meets Mary Magdalene, crouches to her, feels "the blaze of his manhood and his power rise up in his loins," and exclaims:"I am risen!" The truly telling point is that Jesus is made to achieve this supreme experience in the Temple of Osiris, where a tactful priestess enlightens him about true religion, pantheism, as culminating in sexual enjoyment.[44] In *The Last Temptation of Christ* (1951) Nikos Kazantzakis cast the life of Christ into a con-

---

[43] So did R. Tannahill in her voluminous *Sex in History* (New York: Stein and Day, 1982) that has the veneer of scholarship for one of its selling values, in addition to a flippant style and titillating details.

[44] D. H. Lawrence, *The Man who Died* (London: Martin Secker, 1931), p. 144. Then Jesus is also made to realize that his love, devoid of sexual climax, offered only "a corpse" to his disciples when he said to them:"This is my body—take and eat—my corpse" (p. 137). Equally telling is Lawrence's portrayal of the "risen" Christ as one who takes the crouching body of a woman as "the soft white rock of life" and mutters:"On this rock I built my life" (p. 144).

tinual personal struggle against the temptations of the flesh. Further, he makes Christ suffer the penalty for his repression of sex, by letting him be flooded over by sexual fantasies as he agonizes on the cross. Even the Austrian novelist, Leopold von Sacher-Masoch, refrained from going that far during the decadent *belle-époque* that saw the publication of his masochist narratives.

Needless to say, the Virgin Mary was not spared in the long run. In the French movie, "Hail Mary" (released by Goddard in Paris in 1985), she is a gasoline station attendant and Joseph a cabdriver, both driven by sex. The movie was promptly denounced for its "abuses and insults" to the Christian faith by John Paul II, who also led a prayer ceremony "to repair the outrage inflicted on the Holy Virgin." But this is not what gives theological instructiveness to the report in *Newsweek*. There the actress starring in "Hail Mary" is approvingly described as being "hardly bothered by the fuss. She's busy with her next movie, which, judging by the title, will do little to improve her standing with the Roman Catholic Church: it's called 'Blue as Hell'."[45]

Why only with the Roman Catholic Church? Why not also with the mainline Protestant Churches? The answer lies in the fact that many of their ministers have come to represent the "politically correct" or culturally acceptable religion in these progressively "mature" decades. Their practice of ordaining men inclined to homosexuality and women with lesbian proclivities (at times with actual practice) is a reflection on their newfangled image of Christ. For them it is blasphemous to see something sacrilegious in a Christ invested with sexual drives. They see docetism in taking Jesus for one who did not use his sex and was not tempted by it. For as some new theologians claim, Jesus' chief aim was not to denounce sexual transgressions but to neutralize sex into an activity no different from breathing or eating or blowing one's nose.

Much progress towards this "rectification" of the traditional view of Jesus as sexually inactive has been achieved, so goes the reasoning of T. F. Driver, associate professor at Union Theological Seminary, by the fact that "in Protestant theology any 'necessary'

---

[45] *Newsweek*, Sept. 16, 1985, p. 53.

link between sex and sin has been broken in modern time. This has been due to the biblical research fostered by Protestantism in the last two centuries. It is no longer held (outside Fundamentalism, and not always inside it) that Adam's sin was sexual desire."[46] Such a reasoning rests on confusing sin with its effect. One may argue that Adam's sin was not an illicit use of sex on his part, although hardly on biblical grounds. His coming to the fallen state where he "knows good and evil" and the biblical use of the verb "to know" to denote the sexual act, shall forever remain a powerful pointer of the sexual character of his erstwhile failure. Apart from this, Driver and his theological ilk should come clean about their view on the Incarnation and Redemption. Does it have anything to do with the age-old Christian understanding of those tenets or does it merely reflect a "tradition" amounting to the gossip of those who really do not feel the need to be redeemed? Most importantly, do they ever experience of their being fallen, or are they just beings whom an allegedly "failed" tradition prevents from being their "unfallen" selves?

Any answer to this question further supports the point made time and again in this book, that the theology of priestly celibacy cannot be articulated without proper attention to the fact, nature, and consequences of original sin. An almost total disappearance of awareness of original sin is revealed by the claim of the clergyman editor of the *Living Church,* that in his twenty-five years of Christian ministry he has not yet met "a single Christian who believes that Jesus was asexual or that the idea of his sexuality is blasphemous."[47] Yet no theological sophistication was needed for a plain Christian laywoman to write: "Through the devil we could visualize Christ as a tempted murderer, rapist, thief, or any other form of filth on which our mind so desires to dwell. If Mr Driver's theological opinions are samples of today's chic theological professors, I'll take the opinion of a poorly educated godly man whose

[46] See his article, "Sexuality and Jesus," *Union Seminary Quarterly Review* 20 (1964-65), pp. 235-46.
[47] See *Times,* April 9, 1965, p. 59.

spiritual belief has not been blighted by the ugliness of worldly filth."[48]

This was in 1965. One wonders what that devout Protestant lady would have written if told about what is now under investigation in the Episcopal Church: a group of its priests in Long Island, all married, allegedly held a "sexual baptism" in a child's swimming pool, took part in a homosexual orgy in front of the altar, and call each other by women's names in private.[49] There is nothing secret about the fact that homosexual and lesbian clubs can be found in all Protestant seminaries of liberal persuasion where the devil freely roams because he is never spoken of. Some Catholic seminaries in the United States also advanced in that direction, until the Vatican ordered, fifteen or so years ago, a Pontifical visitation of all seminaries "from sea to shining sea."

Bringing the devil into focus should reveal the relative unimportance of appraisals, favorable or unfavorable, of the percentage of priests who faithfully observe their celibacy. Late-nineteenth-century materialists, zealous champions of anticlericalism, and standard-bearers of all sorts of decadence were, of course, surprised when Ernest Renan published in 1881 his *Souvenirs de jeunesse*. There he evoked the years he had spent from the age of 12 until 25 under the direction of priests: "They primarily insisted on virtuous life, which was all the more their right because their comportment was irreproachable. Their sermons on this topic [chastity] made a deep impression on me, which helped me to remain chaste during all my youth. Their preaching had something solemn to it, which astonished me. Details of it became so deeply engraved in my mind that I do not recall them without a sort of terror."[50]

---

[48] Thus Mrs. George L. Potts in a letter to the Editor, *Newsweek*, April 23, 1965.

[49] According to the *Journal of the American Family Affiliation*, January 1997, p. 12, the case was reported in *The Washington Times* and *The Los Angeles Times*. Revealingly, no reference is made to *The New York Times*, which, so it seems, is much more interested in scandals of the Roman Catholic clergy.

[50] E. Renan, *Souvenirs d'enfance et de jeunesse* (4th ed; Paris: Calmann Lévy, 1883), pp. 12-13.

Renan spoofed the cliché view that if a priest leaves the priesthood it is because of a woman: "The perennial commonplace —Where is the woman?—by which lay people explain all such cases, is a fad that makes smile those who know matters as they truly are."[51] With such details in mind, never quoted in the literature, an extra credibility accrues to the celebrated passage in that same book of Renan: "The fact is that the usual remarks about the mores of priests is without any foundation. I have spent thirteen years of my life among priests, but I have not seen a shadow of scandals."[52]

If such remarks sound antiquated today, it is not so much because the mores of the Catholic clergy have gravely deteriorated in the affluent world. Priests are part of their culture, and contemporary culture has certainly progressed, especially during the last forty or so years, to a state worse than decadence. Of the countless evidences let only two be recalled, because they come from two dominating sectors of present-day culture, the sciences and the arts. Einstein was one of the greatest scientists. He was not particularly pleased that certain circles built his reputation into that of a secular Jewish saint. Even today those circles, so eager to muck up the sexual scandals of priests, leave largely untouched the incontrovertible evidence of lechery in Einstein's private life.[53] A. Pais, the major biographer of Einstein the scientist very much softpedaled matters in reporting merely that Einstein ruined both his wives.[54]

From the arts, a similar gloves-in-hand treatment of Picasso comes to mind.[55] Only a few dare spell out that this great master

[51] Ibid., p. 15.

[52] Ibid., p. 139. This is followed by a remark on confessions: "La confession peut avoir, dans certain pays, de graves inconvenients. Je n'en ai pas vue une trace dans ma jeunesse ecclésiastique. Le vieux livre où je faisais mes examens de conscience était l'innocence même."

[53] See R. Highfield and P. Carter, The Private Lives of Albert Einstein (London: Faber and Faber, 1993), a book full of unpublished material taken from the Einstein Archives.

[54] A. Pais, Subtle is the Lord . . .: The Science and the Life of Albert Einstein (Oxford: Clarendon Press, 1982), p. 302.

[55] The most recent case is the claim of John Richardson, author of a monumental A Life of Picasso, of which the second volume, covering the years 1907-1917, has just appeared (New York: Random House, 1996). In an interview with The In-

of painting was also a giant monster of immorality.[56] Usually some saving grace is seen for him, even in the face of his being characterized by one of his mistresses as one who "treated all women like goddesses and then as doormats." Feminists have yet to go on the warpath against Picasso, who "after 1910 paints his mistresses not as conventional figures, but perhaps as a guitar or an instrument that could be played,"[57] or rather merely used or abused, to put it more realistically. Picasso remains one of the great secular saints of a culture that smells of putrefaction.

The makers as well as the hapless victims of such a cultural disintegration are more upset by the presence of a virtuous priest than pleased by the sight of priests who join them by going the way of all flesh. For that culture the virtuous priest must have the clearsightedness and courage to designate it, as did John Henry Newman, with the scriptural phrase: *mundus in maligno positus est*, "the world is under the evil one" (1 John 5:19). The priest has to tell his flock that "he who sins belongs to the devil, because the devil is a sinner from the beginning," and that "it was to destroy the devil's works that the Son of God revealed himself" (3:8). The more virtuous a priest is, indeed the more chaste, the more apparent to him will be the agency of the devil. Saint John Vianney, whom the new theologians of priestly celibacy rarely if ever recall as the official patron saint of priests, often experienced the devil, precisely because he was a saint. Moral weakness, compromises with virtue, especially the virtue of chastity, are the best means of preventing confrontation with the devil—at least in this present life.

*dependent* (London), Richardson stated that in his relationships with women Picasso was "as much sinned against as sinning" (Oct. 19, 1996, p. 8). Tellingly, Richardson blamed Picasso's conservative, middle-class (read: traditional Christian) upbringing for his failures regarding women. Crowning such playing with truth was this title given the interview, "Picasso the seducer was more sinned against than sinning." Picasso, the great secular saint of sinning, had to come out on top.

[56] Thus Araina Stassinopoulos Huffington, *Picasso: Creator and Destroyer* (New York: Avon, 1989). See especially ch. 30, "The Loss of Innocence." It should be enough to take a quick look at almost any larger collection of Picasso's drawings, such as *Picasso: His Recent Drawings* (London: Pall Mall Press, 1969), to see the stunning extent to which Picasso celebrated sexual depravity, with touches of sodomy and bestiality thrown in for good measure.

[57] Richardson in the same report in *The Independent*.

The same letter of John from which one learns that the world is under the evil one contains many other instructions that are indispensable for grasping the dynamics that should animate a theological discussion of priestly celibacy. The latter is an existential engagement whereby one commits oneself to help as many as possible to belong to God, for the alternative is to belong to the devil. The devil, according to that letter of John, has many false prophets who have already appeared in the world and speak its language, which the world understands all too well (1 Jn 4:5). Those false prophets must be countered by the true ones, who can "distinguish the spirit of truth from the spirit of deception," because they have a true knowledge of God and obtain thereby a hearing from those who are of God (4:5-6). Such is the basic truth about which a priest must be a living witness to his congregation. Not a witness about social needs and environmental comfort, but about a destiny which is utterly supernatural in character.

This supernatural witness of the priest has for its chief target the most supernatural conceivable in the natural, or "Jesus Christ come in the flesh" (1 Jn 4:2). In proclaiming Christ, the priest's words must echo the jubilant certainty of John who referred to his having heard, seen with his eyes, touched with his hands "the word of life" (1:1). If there is a single passage in the entire Bible which breaks the moulds of a Hegelian religiosity, this is it. The priest has to be immensely more than a professor of religion who knows only the religion of professors, which hardly implies the act of kneeling in worship, unless it is the worshipping of one's mind unfolded à la Hegel. Hegel's "Wort," a mere "Idee," may have always floated in the metaphysical stratosphere, but it cannot become incarnate so as to be touched with human hands. The "word" celebrated by Hegel is an abstraction coupled with mystification, whereas the Word to be witnessed by the priest is incarnate because Jesus Christ wanted to bring us a redeeming love so that we may be saved through that love, which, as John pointedly remarked, is God himself (4:8).

That love cannot therefore be the one that parades as sentimentalism or emotionalism. It is a love that "laid down his life for us, and therefore we too must lay down our lives for our brothers"

(3:16). These words come to life in a priest, who will not preach mere altruism, but love of Christ and love for Christ's sake. What is wanted from the priest is not just any heroism but a heroism that serves what Christ's purpose was in revealing himself: to take away sins, which he was able to do because "in him there is nothing sinful" (3:5-6). This cannot help but bring up the measure of freedom from sin which a priest must aim at in spite of all his frailty. A frightening task not only because even the virtuous man falls seven times a day, though, unlike the wicked, he rises again and again (Prov 24:16), but also because the true sight of sin can hardly be endured by man. Saint John Vianney once asked God for the grace that he might see his own nothing ness. A vision was granted to him which he could not bear. Yet this was only the vision of man's nothingness, not of his sinfulness.

In a world where one sins only when one prevents fellow human beings from doing whatever they want, the priest must remain a witness about acts which are sinful because they touch on God, although apparently they relate only to oneself. Therefore the priest must also witness that such acts call for that expiation of infinite value that can be had only in Jesus Christ. The priest must bear witness against that sophisticated equivocating, wherein one bemoans the loss of the sense of sin in modern society, in order to limit sin to various forms of cruelty and injustice.[58] The priest must remind a society accustomed to the psychoanalytical sublimation of sin, that the only way to annihilate one's sins is to let them be forgiven by Jesus Christ. In a society for which only what legislation forbids is sin, but only because the law still punishes it, the priest must witness that sin is the true lawlessness (1 Jn 3:4).

Worse, the priest must specify sin and do so in the ever timely perspective of that First Epistle of John, where sin is listed as

---

[58] A classic case is *Whatever Became of Sin?* by the psychotherapist K. Menninger (New York: Hawthorn Books, 1973). He bemoans, in the concluding pages of his book, that only a small percentage of people burdened with guilt have shifted from priests, ministers and rabbis to professional psychiatrists. Clearly, in advising his fellow psychiatrists to learn "from our brother professionals, the clergy" (p. 220), Menninger reduces them to the level of his own profession. In lumping priests with ministers and rabbis, Menninger fails to point out that only priests do hear confessions and they alone know what he admits, namely, that "hearing confessions is not a pleasant process" (ibid).

"carnal allurements, enticement for the eye, the life of empty show," a list putting on the spot much of what the media brings into every home, where the impression is created that because it is everywhere, it is therefore acceptable. The priest has to tell his flock that, all appearances to the contrary, the world together with all its "seductions is passing away" (2:16-17). He has to preach to them that eternal life is the supreme goal, the greatest and only lasting treasure. He has to do that with the same contagious enthusiasm that transpires even now from John's declaration: "The testimony is this: God gave us eternal life and this life is in his Son" (5:11). His preaching must aim at the standard that animated John: "I have written this to you to make you realize that you possess eternal life" (5:13).

The priest has to remind his flock of the basic predicament of his and theirs: "Our relation to this world is just like His" (4:17), and only if they accept this can they look forward with confidence to Judgment day. He has to tell his flock that anything else is a lie, especially the illusion that one can know and love God without observing his commandments (2:4). He has to tell them that young men too can observe those commandments and thereby conquer the evil one (2:13). He has to tell those same young men that they can be strong (2:24), in clear allusion to their duty to master a weakness typical of maturing youth.

Such is a most ungrateful task in times when sexual licence is running rampant among the youth, prodded as they are by the ubiquitous glorification of sex. The priest must therefore show convincingly that his celibacy is a specially potent form of chastity. This strength he can acquire, because God's help is fully available to him. Of the countless statements of popes, saints, spiritual masters, theologians to that effect, let us here recall the words of Pius XI in his Encyclical on the priesthood. One of his concluding remarks referred to those priests who had entered the priesthood with less than fully spiritual motivations, or, as so many priests were suddenly saying in the 1960s, with less than fully mature insights. The countless varieties of such excuses were all met in advance by that great pope's always concise diction: "The grace of God, and especially that grace proper to the Sacrament of Holy

Orders, will not fail to lend aid, if he sincerely wishes to correct
whatever was originally amiss in his purpose and conduct. However it may have come about that he undertook the obligations of
the priesthood, the abiding grace of this divine sacrament will not
be wanting in power to enable him to fulfill them."[59]

Those who never tired in recent years of extolling the spiritual
splendors of the married state in order to bolster the cause of optional celibacy should pause. Those splendors or graces are given—
aren't they?—to enable one to cope with all the challenges of married life, which, in spite of its spiritual splendors, often runs
aground. Should then the failures of priests in regard to their celibacy be taken for a lack of divine help ready to assist them? Is there
not a subtle mistrust in God's grace as tied to the priesthood when
celibacy is pictured as a charisma which is not necessarily connected with the sacrament of ordination? Further, if priestly celibacy is to be abolished on account of the failures to observe it,
should not monogamous marriage too be abolished in view of its
obvious breaking down in countless instances? Should marriage
exist at all, if it occasions countless adulteries, endless disillusions,
the frequent beating up of wives and at times the murdering of
husbands?[60]

Such questions are queries concerning theological truths.
Their right resolution is of utmost importance. After all, that same
letter of John also states that Christians must be committed to
truth (3:19). Of course, truth, in that context too, is something
which is implemented, and done so above all in love—*veritatem
facientes in caritate*—which is selfless charity above all and not a sub-
tly self-centered sentiment. To give moral reality to truth calls for
such who are ready to confront those who "lead disorderly lives,"
while telling "those who are normal that it is they who deviate
from nature." The astonishing timeliness of this remark of Pascal
will appear even more so if its continuation is seen in the light of

[59] "Ad catholici sacerdotii fastigium" (1935). Quoted from the official English
translation, "The Catholic Priesthood" (Washington: National Catholic Welfare
Conference, 1935), p. 61.

[60] "There are a lot of battered women at Bedford Hills [prison] who killed their
husbands—women who, like me, had to act out of desperation," goes the caption
of a report in *The New York Times,* Jan. 8, 1997, p. B1.

priestly celibacy. Pascal likens such pretenders to normalcy to those who, while carried aboard a ship, claim that the harbor is moving away and turn language inside out to prove their point. To counter the ensuing cacophony, Pascal urges that "we need a fixed point to judge it." While it was plain commonsense to state that "the harbour is the judge of those aboard ship," he must have felt the gravity of his question: "but where are we going to find a harbour in morals?"[61]

The celibate priest ought to be that fixed harbor. Celibate priests have lived up to that role of theirs with particular effective ness. Could the Catholic Church, one may ask, display a unique resistance to the sexual aberrations of the times, were her priests married? The celibate priest certainly fits the bill as set forth by Pascal: "When everything is moving at once, nothing appears to be moving, as on board ship. When everyone is moving towards depravity, no one seems to be moving, but if someone stops he shows up the others who are rushing on, by acting as a fixed point."[62] By being that fixed point the priest serves as a reminder, a witness, within a mankind which finds it most repugnant to accept that it stands in need of being saved, because it is the victim of original sin.

The priest merely fools himself if he thinks that his resolve to function as a witness about a fixed point would ever be palatable to man. Nor can the priest perform that witness more effectively than by his celibacy, which more than anything else intrigues and irritates natural man. The latter, to hear Pascal again, will never accept that there is something profoundly wrong in the fact that "concupiscence has become natural for us and has become second nature," and therefore "there are two natures in us, one good, the other bad."[63] If there is anything to be understood by the priest, it is natural man's loathing of the mere idea, let alone the tragic reality, of original sin. This aversion cannot be broken down by mere arguments, however cogent. It must be confronted by a witness,

[61] *Pascal. Pensées,* tr. A. J. Krailsheimer (Penguin Books, 1966), p. 247 (#697).

[62] Ibid., p. 247 (#699).

[63] Ibid., p. 234 (#616).

which the celibacy of the priest makes most challenging in day to day existence.

Strong ties between priesthood and celibacy will have loose ends, and the promotion of optional celibacy will not reveal its fallacy, unless sustained attention is paid to some words of Pascal. He indeed may have had in mind priests and theologians perplexed by celibacy as he wrote: "Original sin is folly in the eyes of men, but it is put forward as such. You should therefore not reproach me for the unreasonable nature of this doctrine, because I put it forward as being unreasonable. But this folly is wiser than all men's wisdom, it is wiser than man. For without it, what are we to say man is? His whole state depends on this imperceptible point. How could he have become aware of it through his reason, seeing that it is contrary to reason and that his reason, far from discovering it by its own methods, draws away when presented with it?"[64]

Any issue of any major daily newspaper contains ample proof of a "rational resistance" to the reality of original sin, although it should seem to be precisely the Christian dogma which has the most empirical support on its behalf. The reverse side of that resistance is the espousal of concupiscence as something most reasonable, also set forward in any such issue. In order not to be swayed by this daily parody of reality, the celibate priest needs more than arguments. But he will always need them too. For truth, in order to be lived and therefore to be witnessed existentially, must first be conceptualized. No one can act as a fixed harbor in the midst of treacherous and filthy currents, unless he has clear ideas. In cultivating such ideas the priest is merely obeying a pattern set by the One in whose priesthood he shares.

For our Lord never tired of teaching, which, whatever else it may be, is reliance on concepts. The preservation of those truthful conceptualizations remains, to recall a most timely warning by Pascal, the great wealth of the Church. This wealth deserves to be protected even at the risk of strifes, just as nations have the right to go to war in order to protect their wealth. This is why it is morally wrong for states, so Pascal argued, to allow their wealth to be

[64] Ibid., #695 (p. 246).

pillaged under the pretext of safeguarding peace. "Likewise in the Church, when truth is injured by enemies of the faith, when attempts are made to uproot it from the hearts of the faithful, and make error reign in its stead, would it be serving or betraying the Church to remain at peace? And is it not obvious that just as it is crime to disturb the peace when truth reigns, it is also a crime to remain at peace when the truth is being destroyed?"[65]

In matters political it may be said with Scripture, Pascal continued, that there is a time for peace and a time for war (Eccles 3:8), although even there "it is the interests of truth which distinguish between them." It follows therefore that "there is not a time for truth and a time for error, and it is written, on the contrary: 'The truth of the Lord endureth forever' (Ps 97:2), and that is why Jesus Christ, who said he had come to bring peace (Jn 14:27), said also that he had come to bring war (Mt 10:34); but he did not say that He had come to bring both truth and falsehood. Truth is, therefore, the first rule and ultimate purpose of things."[66] No discourse on the theology of priestly celibacy can do with less than truth. Justice is truth put into practice. And since priestly celibacy makes sense only on theological grounds, theological truth about it is the condition of doing it full justice. In serving that justice, one also implements the dictum of Pascal: "The greatest of Christian truths is the love of truth."[67]

The occasion when the priest brings the strongest witness to this is his functioning at the altar, where he renders present the incarnate truth and love, that very Christ, who, to recall once more Saint Augustine's inimitable phrase, "is priest and sacrifice, and because a sacrifice he is also a priest."[68] Priests shall become confused about this witness of theirs if they feed themselves on books about celibacy which contain not a single paragraph on their consecrating the bread into the sacrificial Body of Christ, but are full

---

[65] Ibid., p. 346 (# 974).
[66] *Pascal. The Pensées*, tr. J. M. Cohen (Penguin Classics, 1961), p. 279 (#822). pp. 279–80.
[67] Ibid., p. 280 (#823).
[68] *Confessions*, Book X, ch. 43.

of sociological and psychological preachment about their service to that body of Christ which is the Church. As long as authors of such books will be hailed as full of apostolic zeal, as long as such books are sold in seminary bookstores as being full of seminal insights, the course of the future priest will be shunted into a railspur where sooner than later he comes up against a spiritual dead-end.[69] For celibate priesthood makes no sense if the priest thinks of himself mainly as a master of ceremonies, a presiding officer at banquets where the bread distributed is a mere memory of Christ. But the priest's celibacy will make full sense if he looks at the celebration of the Eucharist, the Mass, as a sacramental rendering of Jesus' sacrifice. Jesus had to be celibate in a superlative sense, because He was fullness itself, for only such fullness could achieve the redemption of man. This is the gist, the pivot, the fulcrum of anything offered as the theology of priestly celibacy or even as a modest contribution to it, such as this book.

---

[69] A tragic but most revealing example is the book mentioned in note 4 of the Introduction, a book in whose 144 pages there is not a single paragraph on what happens when a priest celebrates the Mass.

# Index of Names

Adrian I, pope, 102
Agnes, empress, 136, 143–44
Alexander II, pope, 128, 134
Alfonso, king, 136
Alfonso, saint, 190
Anastasius, bp. of Thessalonika, 99
Ancona, M. d', 64
Anno, archbp. of Cologne, 141–42
Anselm, saint, 43, 133, 183
Aristides of Athens, 38
Arius, 29, 41, 76, 90
Arquillière, H. X., 134
Athanasius, saint, 42, 96, 145
Auffray, A., 45
Augustine, saint, bp. of Hippo, 39–43,
    51–52, 59, 69, 81, 89–98, 138, 149,
    183–84, 215
Aurelius, archbp. of Carthage, 81

Balasurya, T., 21
Balsamon, 110
Barbet, P., 60
Baronius, card., 130–31
Barth, K., 150–51, 164–65, 183–84
Bedoyere, de la, M., 200
Benedict VIII, pope, 139
Benedict XIV, pope, 113
Biale, D., 85
Bickell, G., 73–75
Bickersteth, E., 200
Bilaniuk, P. B. T., 112–13
Biot, F., 149
Boehmer, H., 72
Boniface, pope, 81
Bosco, Don G., saint 45, 198
Bosco, Margarita, 45

Bousset, W., 28
Bowden, J. W., 139, 146, 169
Bruno of Toul, see Leo IX, pope
Bushnell, H., 148
Buss, D., 202

Capovilla, Mgr., 11
Carter, P., 207
Chaillet, P., 154
Chapman, J., 116
Cholij, R., 102, 106, 111, 114, 116
Chrysanthes, bp. of Spoleto, 99
Chrysostom, John, saint, 116–19
Cicero, 60
Clark, F., 55
Clarke, G. W., 177
Claver, Peter, saint, 198
Clement I, pope, saint, 62
Clement II, pope 129
Clement of Alexandria, 74
Cochini, C., 9, 74–75, 86, 112
Comte, A., 125
Consalvi, E. card., 196
Constantelos, D., 111–12
Constantine, emperor, 80
Coppens, J., 108
Cornelius, pope, saint, 189
Cosmas, saint (martyr), 188
Coulton, G. G., 144
Crouzel, H., 108
Cullmann, O., 22
Cyprian, saint, 38, 73, 78, 110, 153,
    189–90
Cyril of Alexandria, saint, 43, 55

Damasus, pope, saint, 84

# Index of Subjects

(continued from p. ii)

By the same author

*The Savior of Science*
(Wethersfield Institute Lectures, 1987)

*Miracles and Physics*

*God and the Cosmologists*
(Farmington Institute Lectures, Oxford, 1988)

*The Only Chaos and Other Essays*

*The Purpose of It All*
(Farmington Institute Lectures, Oxford, 1989)

*Catholic Essays*

*Cosmos in Transition: Studies in the History of Cosmology*

*Olbers Studies*

*Scientist and Catholic: Pierre Duhem*

*Reluctant Heroine: The Life and Work of Hélène Duhem*

*Universe and Creed*

*Genesis 1 through the Ages*

*Is There a Universe?*

*Patterns or Principles and Other Essays*

*Bible and Science*

★ ★ ★

Translations with introduction and notes:

*The Ash Wednesday Supper* (Giordano Bruno)

*Cosmological Letters on the Arrangement
of the World Edifice* (J.-H. Lambert)

*Universal Natural History and Theory of the Heavens* (I. Kant)

# Note on the Author

Stanley L. Jaki, a Hungarian-born Catholic priest of the Benedictine Order, is Distinguished University Professor at Seton Hall University, South Orange, New Jersey. With doctorates in theology and physics, he has for the past forty years specialized in the history and philosophy of science. The author of almost forty books and over a hundred articles, he served as Gifford Lecturer at the University of Edinburgh and as Fremantle Lecturer at Balliol College, Oxford. He has lectured at major universities in the United States, Europe, and Australia. He is honorary member of the Pontifical Academy of Sciences, *membre correspondant* of the Académie Nationale des Sciences, Belles-Lettres et Arts of Bordeaux, and the recipient of the Lecomte du Nouy Prize for 1970 and of the Templeton Prize for 1987.